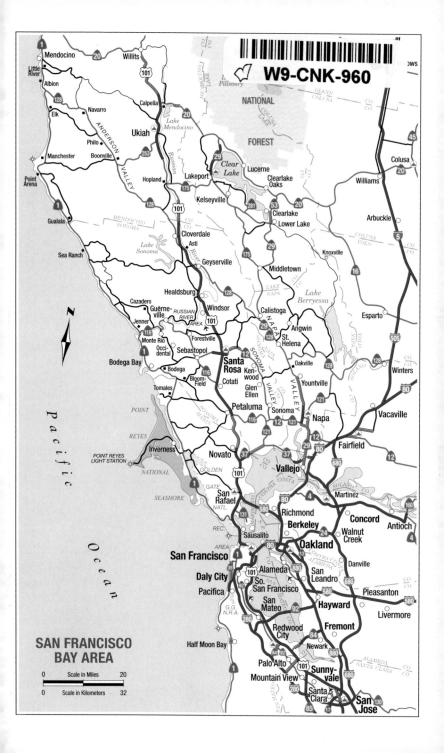

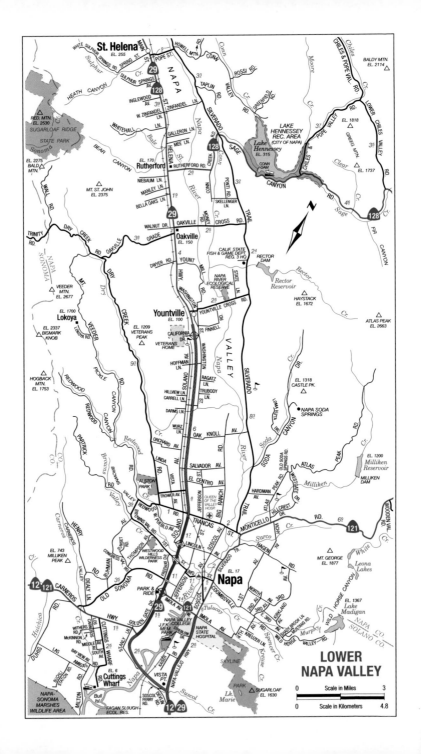

LOWER NAPA VALLEY

Scale in Miles
0 — 3

Scale in Kilometers
0 — 4.8

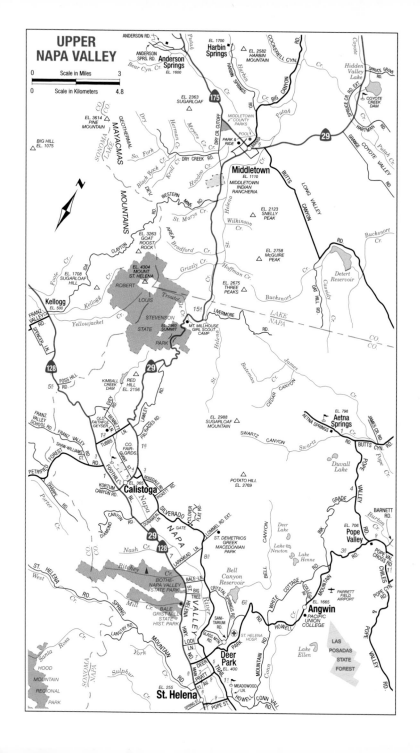

UPPER NAPA VALLEY

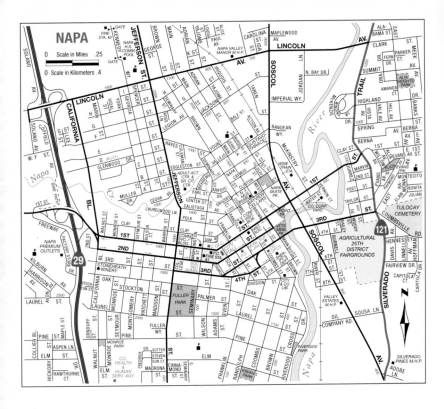

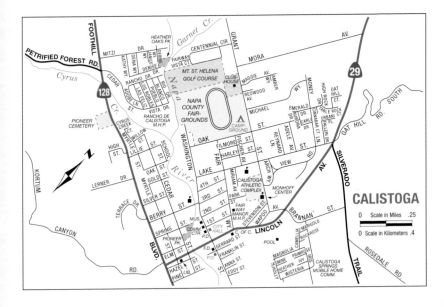

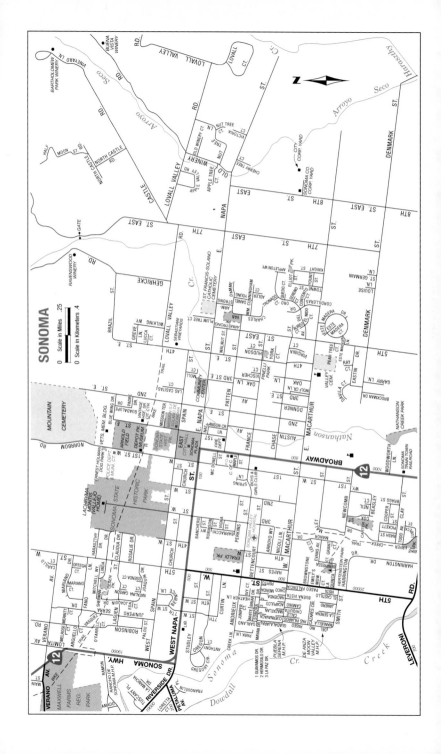

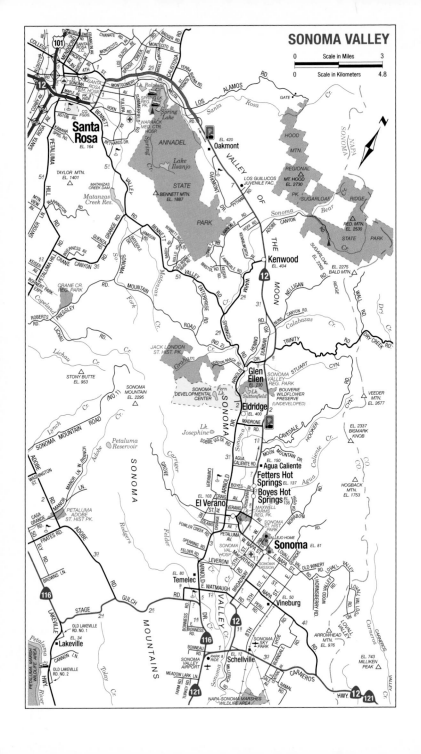

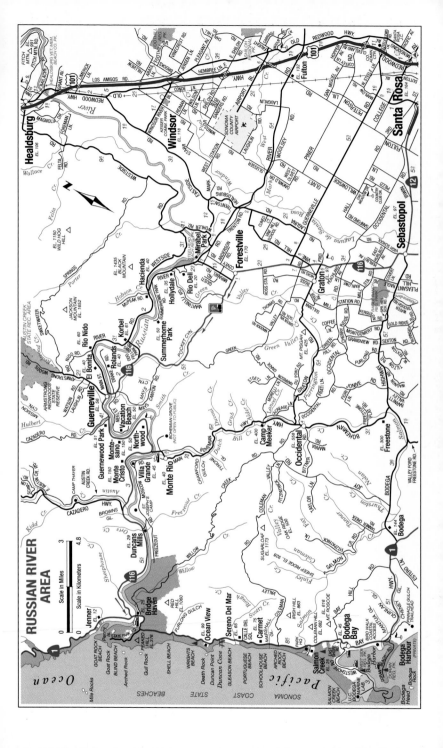

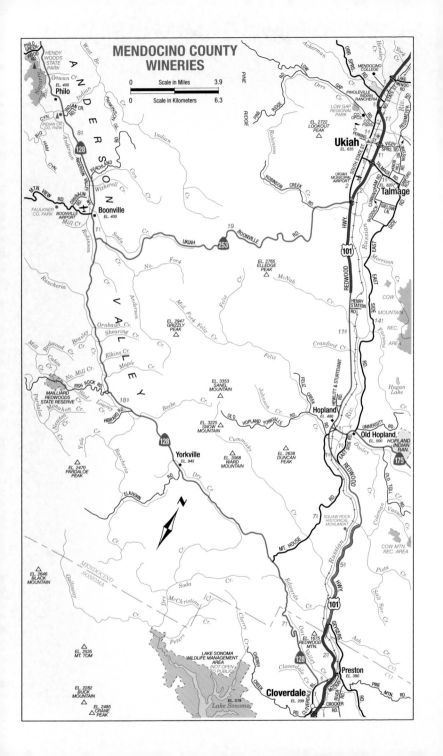

HIDDEN ®
Wine Country

HIDDEN®

Wine Country

Ray Riegert and Marty Olmstead

Ulysses Press®
BERKELEY, CALIFORNIA

Copyright © 2000 Ulysses Press. All rights reserved, including
the right to reproduce this book or portions thereof in any
form whatsoever, except for use by a reviewer in connection
with a review.

Published by: ULYSSES PRESS
P.O. Box 3440
Berkeley, CA 94703-3440
www.ulyssespress.com

ISSN 1527-747X
ISBN 1-56975-214-1

Printed in Canada by Transcontinental Printing

10 9 8 7 6 5 4 3 2 1

MANAGING EDITOR: Claire Chun
EDITOR: Lily Chou
EDITORIAL ASSOCIATES: Marin Van Young, Shola Ogunlana,
Lisa Kester, Jean Fujikawa
TYPESETTER: Claire Chun
CARTOGRAPHY: Pease Press
COVER DESIGN: Leslie Henriques, Sarah Levin
INDEXER: Sayre Van Young
COVER PHOTOGRAPHY:
FRONT: Robert Holmes (Mustard plants on the
Silverado Trail)
CIRCLE: Markham Johnson (Biking in the Wine
Country)
BACK: Robert Holmes (Sonoma City Hall)
ILLUSTRATOR: Doug McCarthy

Distributed in the United States by Publishers Group West, in
Canada by Raincoast Books, and in Great Britain and Europe by
World Leisure Marketing

All color maps copyright © 2000 AAA. All rights reserved. Used
with permission. www.aaa.com AAA

Hidden Wine Country was produced by Ulysses Press in associa-
tion with VIA Books. VIA Books is a division of the California
State Automobile Association (CSAA), 150 Van Ness Avenue, San
Francisco, CA 94102. VIA

HIDDEN is a federally registered trademark
of BookPack, Inc.

Ulysses Press 圣 is a federally registered
trademark of BookPack, Inc.

The publisher has made every effort to ensure the accuracy of
information contained in *Hidden Wine Country*, but can accept no
liability for any loss, injury or inconvenience sustained by any
traveler as a result of information or advice contained in this
guide.

To Beckett

Write to us!

If in your travels you discover a spot that captures the spirit of the Wine Country, or if you live in the region and have a favorite place to share, or if you just feel like expressing your views, write to us and we'll pass your note along to the author.

We can't guarantee that the author will add your personal find to the next edition, but if the writer does use the suggestion, we'll acknowledge you in the credits and send you a free copy of the new edition.

ULYSSES PRESS
3286 Adeline Street, Suite 1
Berkeley, CA 94703
E-mail: readermail@ulyssespress.com

✳

What's Hidden?

At different points throughout this book, you'll find special listings marked with a hidden symbol:

◀ *HIDDEN*

This means that you have come upon a place off the beaten tourist track, a spot that will carry you a step closer to the local people and natural environment of the Wine Country.

The goal of this guide is to lead you beyond the realm of everyday tourist facilities. While we include traditional sightseeing listings and popular attractions, we also offer alternative sights and adventure activities. Instead of filling this guide with reviews of standard hotels and chain restaurants, we concentrate on one-of-a-kind places and locally owned establishments.

Our authors seek out locales that are popular with residents but usually overlooked by visitors. Some are more hidden than others (and are marked accordingly), but all the listings in this book are intended to help you discover the true nature of the Wine Country and put you on the path of adventure.

Contents

1 WINE COUNTRY WANDERINGS   I

The Story of the Wine Country   6
Geology   6
History   6
Flora   8
Fauna   10
Where to Go   10
When to Go   12
Seasons   12
Calendar of Events   14
Before You Go   18
Visitors Centers   18
Packing   18
Lodging   18
Dining   19
Liquor and Smoking Laws   20
Phones   20
Traveling with Children   21
Women Traveling Alone   21
Gay & Lesbian Travelers   22
Senior Travelers   22
Disabled Travelers   23
Foreign Travelers   24
Outdoor Adventures   25
Camping   25
Fishing   25
Transportation   26

2 SOUTHERN NAPA VALLEY   29

Napa Area   32
Yountville to Rutherford   42
Outdoor Adventures   52

3 NORTHERN NAPA VALLEY   54

St. Helena   55
Calistoga   65
Outdoor Adventures   75

4 SONOMA VALLEY   **77**

Southern Sonoma Valley   78
Northern Sonoma Valley   89
Outdoor Adventures   95

5 NORTHERN SONOMA COUNTY   **97**

Santa Rosa   98
Healdsburg and Points North   108
Outdoor Adventures   114

6 RUSSIAN RIVER AREA   **116**

Sebastopol Area   118
Guerneville Area   124
Outdoor Adventures   132

7 MENDOCINO COUNTY   **134**

Hopland–Ukiah Inland Area   136
Anderson Valley   149
Outdoor Adventures   155

Index   159
Lodging Index   163
Dining Index   164
About the Authors and Illustrator   170

Maps

Wine Country and Beyond	3
Southern Napa Valley	31
Napa Area	33
Yountville to Rutherford	43
Northern Napa Valley	57
St. Helena	59
Calistoga	67
Sonoma Valley	79
Southern Sonoma Valley	81
Northern Sonoma Valley	91
Northern Sonoma County	99
Santa Rosa	101
Healdsburg and Points North	109
Russian River Area	119
Sebastopol Area	121
Guerneville Area	127
Mendocino County	137
Hopland–Ukiah Inland Area	139
Anderson Valley	151

OUTDOOR ADVENTURE SYMBOLS

The following symbols accompany national, state and regional park listings, as well as beach descriptions throughout the text.

▲	Camping		Waterskiing
	Hiking		Windsurfing
	Biking		Boating
	Horseback Riding		Boat Ramps
	Swimming		Fishing

ONE

Wine Country Wanderings

The greatest winemaking region on the entire continent, the California Wine Country is easily accessible in every sense of the word. Its demarcations are San Francisco Bay, the Pacific Ocean, the mountains on the east side of Napa and, roughly, the middle of Mendocino County. You could make that loop in the course of a day of driving, if there were any point to that. You could also spend months trying to get to know all the wines, wineries and welcoming residents and feel as if you had just barely scratched the surface.

Despite the exalted status of winemaking and all its attendant hype, this region is, at heart, farm country. The major crop may be grapes—hundreds of millions of dollars' worth by the time they are turned into wine—but for the most part, Sonoma, Napa and Mendocino counties are rural or at least semi-rural. Some world travelers are fond of saying that the heart of the California Wine Country reminds them of Provence or Tuscany; they share a Mediterranean climate, grapevines and olive trees, rolling hills and a certain hedonism, for sure. But those who come here first and truly sample the bounty of these counties, from the landscape to the lifestyle, may one day visit those European provinces and say, "Hmmm, reminds me of Sonoma."

Located roughly an hour's drive north of San Francisco, the counties of Sonoma and Napa benefit greatly from their proximity to the big city. They are considered part of the San Francisco Bay Area, which comprises the nine counties that actually abut the bay. Although parts of the Wine Country are equally close to Oakland or Sacramento, most visitors do head to the Wine Country as part of a trip to San Francisco. And thousands of recent immigrants to the area have arrived after living for decades in the city, in the East Bay or on the Peninsula. So to that rural sensibility, you can add a growing populace with a certain sophistication and a penchant for fine food, art, music and theater as well as the fervent hope that they can keep things the way they are. To wit, heavenly.

Hundreds of miles of two-lane country roads curve and climb through the gently sloping countryside. Travelers are almost always in view of one mountain or another, or close to a river or a farm or a winery. In winter, especially, it's possible to drive some of these roads without seeing more than a couple of other cars. Only a few cities—Napa, Sonoma, Santa Rosa, Sebastopol, Healdsburg and Ukiah—are really worthy of the term. The Wine Country is truly characterized by towns such as Calistoga, Guerneville and Yountville. Or by tiny settlements such as Rutherford, Geyserville and Boonville.

In short, you won't see any highrises. What you will see are scenic vistas: a mountain topped with forests, deer grazing by the roadside, jackrabbits hopping down vineyard rows, grape leaves changing colors in the sun, historic wineries, gently flowing rivers, Western falsefront buildings, soaring redwood trees, apple orchards, and at least one town plaza that is home to a free-ranging band of chickens.

There is so much to do and see in this part of the world that you could stay busy and quite content without ever visiting a single winery. There are many family-friendly activities, from riding a miniature train in Sonoma to horseback riding in Napa, canoeing in the Russian River, or hiking the hills of Mendocino. Bocce ball and *petanque*, the Italian and French variations of the steel-ball-hurling game of yore, are increasingly popular; several wineries have installed courts open to the public.

Community centers are incredibly ingenious at coming up with free and low-cost entertainment. The Luther Burbank Center attracts headliners from all over the world in fields as varied as the circus arts, jazz, rock and chamber music. In the summer, there seem to be festivals or fairs practically every weekend. In addition, many wineries offer mini-festivals (often at no charge) throughout the year, especially in spring and fall.

This piece of paradise has been attracting visitors and new residents since the beginning. When California wines were finally recognized as the world-class contenders that they are, the migration became more of a stampede. Although winemaking as well as feature filmmaking continue to lead as economic juggernauts, the telecommunications industry is about to take first place. When Silicon Valley began to run out of room, dot.com entrepreneurs looked north of the Golden Gate Bridge and saw the 101 Corridor (the highway between Petaluma and Santa Rosa) as the promised land. They have joined longtimers like Hewlett-Packard into making Telecom Valley a force to be reckoned with. The presence of these successful, non-polluting businesses has pumped even more money into Sonoma's economy.

Text continued on page 6.

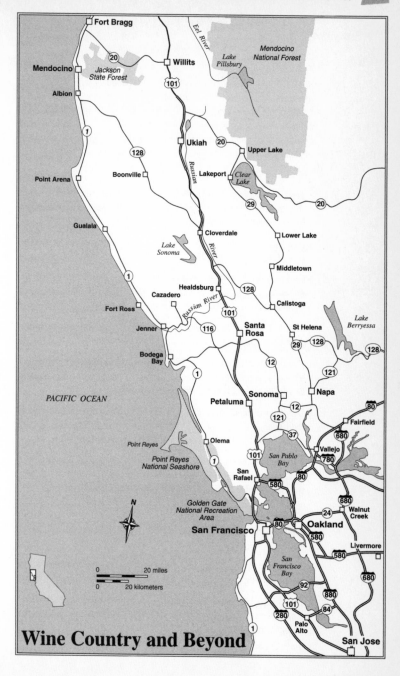

Wine Country and Beyond

Three-day Weekend

While it would take many visits to check out every winery and attraction in this part of the world, you can certainly experience the flavor of the Wine Country in a matter of days. All it takes is a little planning. This sample itinerary encompasses parts of Napa, Sonoma and Mendocino counties, and includes specific suggestions for winery visits, outdoor activities, shopping, restaurants and lodging.

Day 1
- Begin in Napa's Carneros district with a tour (reservation only) of the **Di Rosa Preserve** (page 34), a world-class collection of art from around the Bay Area. (Allow 2 hours)

- Head north on Route 29 and enjoy a Cal-Italian lunch at **Bistro Don Giovanni** (page 39).

- Turn into Yountville and browse the shops at **Vintage 1870** (page 44) before crossing Route 29 and taking the tour at **Domaine Chandon** (page 44).

- Visit the nearby **Napa Valley Museum** (page 44) for an introduction to the regional wine industry. (1 hour)

- Continue north on Route 29, stopping at the **Robert Mondavi Winery** (page 44) in Oakville or take a detour up the Oakville Grade to visit **Chateau Potelle** (page 36).

- Drive north to **Calistoga** (page 65) and book a spa session, a mud bath and/or a massage at Dr. Wilkinson's Hot Springs or another of the town's many facilities dedicated to relaxation.

- Enjoy a dinner of Cajun specialties at **Catahoula Restaurant and Saloon** (page 72). Spend the night at a spa hotel or one of the town's inns, such as the **Cottage Grove Inn** (page 69).

Day 2
- Start the day with a **balloon ride** at dawn, weather permitting. (2 hours)

- Head north along Route 128 through the **Alexander Valley** (page 110), stopping to taste at one of several roadside wineries. (1 hour)

- Drive into Healdsburg for lunch at **Bistro Ralph** (page 112) or stop into the **Oakville Grocery** (page 48) for picnic supplies to enjoy in the town's plaza.

- Take Route 101 north from Healdsburg to the outskirts of Cloverdale and turn west onto Route 28 to drive through the **Anderson Valley** (page 149). (1.5 hours)

- Stop at **Navarro Vineyards** (page 150) and/or **Pacific Echo** (page 150) to sample local vintages. (1 hour)

- Return to Route 101 and detour a few miles north to Hopland and have dinner at **The Crushed Grape** (page 143). Spend the night at either **Fetzer Vineyards Bed & Breakfast** (page 141) or the **Thatcher Inn** (page 141).

Day 3
- Head south on Route 101 to Healdsburg and take Westside Road south. Turn right at River Road and ride along the river to Guerneville; pick up Route 116 south. (1.5 hours)

- En route to **Sebastopol** (page 118) you will pass wineries that open in mid-morning, or save your energy for the antique stores in and around Sebastopol. (1.5 hours)

- Turn east on Route 12, a California Scenic Highway that leads to **Kenwood** (page 90). On the outskirts is **Château St. Jean Winery** (page 90). (1 hour)

- Enjoy a leisurely lunch at the **Kenwood Restaurant and Grill** (page 93).

- From Kenwood, take Warm Springs Road south to Glen Ellen to visit **Jack London State Historic Park** (page 89). (1 hour)

- Depart Glen Ellen via Route 12, bound for the town of **Sonoma** (page 81). Park at the Plaza, take a walking tour of the mission and the barracks, and browse the shops around the square. (2 hours)

- Have dinner at **Heirloom** (page 86) or **Deuce** (page 87), two of Sonoma's top restaurants where a reservation is necessary.

- Spend the night at one of the inns near the plaza.

In the Napa Valley, most arable land is restricted as an agricultural preserve, resulting in scant available land for development. Most of the traffic in this valley is produced by visitors, who add to the growing number of commuter cars.

Mendocino remains resolutely rural, mostly because of the rugged landscape and its distance from San Francisco; even the county seat, Ukiah, doesn't have a major hotel, let alone a commute-traffic problem.

As you travel about the Wine Country, you'll find few major highways. Route 101 runs north from San Francisco through the area, in fact all the way to the state line. Although it is four to six lanes wide, the highway runs right beside some wineries. And Route 29 is its Napa equivalent, four lanes from the bottom of the valley to Yountville, and then two lanes north to Calistoga. Virtually all of Napa's major wineries front this road, but there are exceptions.

The Story of the Wine Country

GEOLOGY

The natural elements that allowed for successful winemaking were in the makings for eons; once the geography, climate and soil evolved to the critical point, sure enough, someone came along and discovered that, all together, they made ideal conditions for growing grapes. Of course, things are still evolving, as continual shudders from the Rodgers Creek, San Andreas and lesser faults shake everybody up a bit. But they're nothing compared to the dramatic tectonic movements in the last 100 million years ago that transformed the area from an underwater landscape to the beginnings of what you see today. More recently—about three to four million years ago—a mammoth number of volcanic eruptions changed the landscape almost as dramatically, creating underground fissures of piping hot water that still spew forth today in the form of little hot springs and sizable gushers.

As a result of millions of years of earth movement, the Wine Country has natural phenomena such as the Russian River (more or less in the same place it's always been) as well as Mount St. Helena (the tallest peak in the region, towering over 4000 feet). Another result of volcanic activity is that several valleys—most notably, Napa, Sonoma, Dry Creek, Anderson, Alexander, Sanel and the Russian River—are protected by mountains from the cold winds and rain along the Pacific coast.

HISTORY

Some 5000 to 10,000 years ago, the Pomo Indians were the first to discover the Wine Country's hot springs, heading south once they had crossed the land bridge connecting Asia with North America. They settled in present-day Mendocino and Sonoma. The Wappo also settled in Sonoma as well as Napa, where they seem to have co-existed peacefully with the Nappa tribe around the Napa River. They gathered berries and acorns, fished the waters of nearby San Pablo Bay, and stalked the mountains for bear and deer.

Winemaking in California dates back to the 18th century when Spanish padres planted vineyards at the missions. The Franciscans in particular grew black grapes for sacramental wines, crushing them by foot in hide troughs, then fermenting the harvest in leather sacks.

Spanish vineyards spread north to Sonoma, where in 1823 a Spanish priest named Father Jose Altimira came north from Mexico to establish an outpost that would be called the Mission San Francisco de Solano. The town of Sonoma sprung up around that mission.

In Napa Valley, across the mountains east of Sonoma, George Yount, the area's original settler, cultivated grapes in 1843. During the next decade numerous Europeans, drawn initially by the Gold Rush, forsook prospecting for planting. A Prussian immigrant named Charles Krug became a pioneer in commercializing Napa wines. He also taught other early vintners like Jacob Beringer and Carl Wente, whose names even today adorn wine bottles.

The American Indians who had this place to themselves for thousands of years could never have conceived of what these new arrivals would do to their civilization, their population and their sacred places. While tribes still exist in small numbers, little visible evidence remains of their one-time culture. A museum here, an exhibit there and an Indian celebration from time to time is all a visitor is likely to see.

By the 1830s, the Mexican government decided to secularize their last mission and replace it with a presidio. General Mariano Guadalupe Vallejo was commissioned for this task, establishing the town of Sonoma in 1835. Vallejo installed his soldiers in newly minted barracks and laid out the plaza, the largest of its

HOME SWEET HOME

By the turn of the 20th century, Sonoma County was attracting new residents including horticulturist Luther Burbank, who settled in Santa Rosa. Novelist Jack London resided in the nearby town of Glen Ellen in 1904, living there until his death in 1916. Interested in ranching as well as writing, London exchanged farming lore with Burbank, who lived just up the road. Over in Napa, meanwhile, the state's first millionaire, Sam Brannan, established a hot springs resort with the odd name of Calistoga, and author Robert Louis Stevenson visited the valley, lodged in a cabin on Mount St. Helena, and called the local wines "bottled poetry."

kind in the state. In his push to settle the area, including Napa, he found a kindred soul in George Yount, the first white settler in Napa. Yount benefited greatly from the relationship, securing prized land grants and establishing the 11,814 Rancho Caymus in the central area of the Napa Valley.

Despite Vallejo's considerable power, in June of 1846 a band of roughhewn Americans arrested Vallejo and declared California the Bear Flag Republic (symbolized by a flag sporting a grizzly bear). The reign lasted some 25 days. By July, the United States, having captured Monterey and claimed California as its own, took control. Four years later, California became a state (and in 1911, the Bear Flag was adopted as the California state flag).

Thanks in part to the abundance of apple orchards in the Wine Country, California generates more honey than any other state.

In 1857, Agoston Haraszthy, a Hungarian count, founded the Buena Vista Winery in Sonoma. Commissioned by the California governor, he traveled through France, Italy and Germany a few years later, collecting cuttings from 300 grape varieties. Soon thereafter, the University of California perfected fermentation techniques and established a national center for viticulture and enology at its Davis campus.

California's wine business boomed. Four million gallons were produced in 1869, 28 million in 1900, and by 1911 the total rose to 58 million gallons. Then came Prohibition. From 1920 until 1933, an entire industry withered on the vine. Many wineries shut down; others converted their fields to orchards.

It took nearly 30 years for the industry to recover. Not until the 1960s, as wine became an increasingly popular national drink, did California's vineyards flourish once more. This long-awaited renaissance proved extraordinary. Within a five-year period, vineyard acreage doubled. Wineries mushroomed in the Napa and Sonoma valleys, along the Russian River, and elsewhere throughout the state. Family-run wineries blossomed, national companies like Coca-Cola and Nestlé moved into the vineyards, and French and Spanish winemakers, impressed with the quality of the wines, formed partnerships with local growers.

Winemaking is now a multibillion dollar business, with millions of people touring California's vineyards each year. And as for production, more than half a century after Prohibition, the state produced a whopping 489,554,000 gallons of wine in 1998, the last year for which statistics are available.

FLORA   They don't call it the Wine Country for nothing. As grapes fetched record-high prices at the end of the 1990s, the price of vineyard acreage skyrocketed, with an acre of premium Napa Valley real estate suitable for cabernet sauvignon going for around $50,000. And that's without the grapevines.

But there are plenty of other crops being raised here, though none as lucrative as grapes. In fact, different kinds of plants bloom and a variety of produce are harvested in Napa, Sonoma and/or Mendocino every month of the year; lettuces and other vegetables can be found fresh any time of year. From the mid-1800s, when the area began supplying produce to San Francisco, Sonoma and Napa have led the nation in growing gourmet produce. Starting with orchids and winter vegetables in January and February, then azaleas and rhododendrons in March through June, the year continues with strawberries, irises and daylilies, then roses, peaches, pears and figs and plums before the full summer season of blueberries, tomatoes, corn and several varieties of apples that ripen from July into December. Grapes are harvested in the fall, and the end of the year brings pumpkins, persimmons and walnuts to the tables and hearths all around the region. Some farmer's markets are open year-round, while others are summer affairs that run from May into October. Many farms welcome visitors to their properties, and some even allow visitors to pick their own berries.

As for what grows in the natural world, the list is almost endless. Another term for much of the Wine Country is the Redwood Empire, which is fading into disuse and never really included Napa anyway. The farther north you go, the more you will notice these giant trees. In these forests, shared with Douglas fir, wildflowers such as trillium, adder's tongue, redwood sorrel and huckleberry blossom as early as February.

Around this time, the vineyards and virtually every other disturbed field (meaning the soil has been turned over) turns bright yellow with mustard blooms that often appear as early as January and last through March. Most likely introduced to the area by immigrants planting a cover crop for fallow fields, it's here to stay, as are two other yellow-blossoming plants: Scotch broom, a shrub, and the acacia tree, which blooms as the mustard begins to fade. The native grasses that once flourished here have been overgrown by foxtail, wild oats and other grasses imported by European settlers.

Madrone, Ponderosa pine and several types of oak trees cover most hillsides in the heart of the Wine Country, sharing the landscape with occasional stands of non-native eucalyptus, a hearty hardwood whose aroma—a sort of menthol smell—often pervades wine that comes from vineyards planted nearby. Manzanita, with its distinctive reddish bark and white blossoms, is part of the chaparral ecosystem that crowns much of the wild land in this region.

The bright golden poppy, the state flower, as well as the purple lupine, can be seen on hillsides and along roadsides throughout the Wine Country. Another plant you will see constantly is the rose, in myriad shapes and colors, which is traditionally planted on the borders of vineyards.

FAUNA Residents will tell you that the animals they most commonly see, aside from sheep, cattle and horses, are deer, raccoons and opossums. If you hike far from a road, however, you are likely to run across coyotes, gray foxes and bobcats, and, less often, badgers, feral pigs, bats, tule elk and small gray foxes.

If you're careful, you probably won't run across a poisonous Western rattlesnake, but if you go far enough into the wilderness you may see black bears and mountain lions, which become a problem during periods of drought when they approach human habitats in search of water.

In streams and river beds reside a lively riparian population of river otters, skinks and pond turtles. Fishing in rivers at certain times of year may net you Chinook, coho or steelhead salmon. Fishing in lakes is likely to turn up small- and large-mouth bass or freshwater catfish.

Our feathered friends include hawks (six species) and owls (seven) as well as their prey. Some of the smaller birds winging their way around are woodpeckers, finches, flycatchers and warblers. Keep an eye out if you are near cliffs or high bluffs, prime cruising area for kestrels, peregrine falcons and the occasional golden eagle. The most rewarding birdwatching is around water, particularly San Pablo Bay, which borders the Carneros appellation. Habitats are being restored to encourage herons, egrets, various ducks and geese, ospreys and even enormous tundra swans.

▼ ▼ ▼ ▼ ▼ ▼ ▼ ▼ ▼ ▼

Where to Go

As you will discover, the real fun of exploring the Wine Country lies along the side roads and country lanes—it matters not whether you tour the region in the order of the following chapters. We have broken down the area into roughly equivalent sections, either in terms of geography or in terms of how much there is to see. You can sample the Wine Country by setting up headquarters in a single town or valley and stay within a few miles of home base, or you can easily reach all the other points on this map in a couple of hours. For your convenience, we have included a three-day itinerary at the end of this chapter.

The **Southern Napa Valley** chapter covers the lower end of the Napa Valley, including the city of Napa, Napa's portion of the Carneros appellation, and the towns of Yountville, Oakville and Rutherford. Founded on the banks of the Napa River, the city has a remarkable Victorian district, where a number of old homes have been pressed into service as bed and breakfasts. The downtown area is on the verge of a boom that's anticipated when the American Center for Wine, Food and the Arts opens in 2001. Major wineries such as Mondavi and Domaine Chandon, to name just two, can be found up the highway, but several intriguing wineries are tucked away in the hills.

In the **Northern Napa Valley**, shopping, restaurants and inns become a bit more chic and generally a bit more expensive. The charming town of St. Helena is chock-a-block with boutiques and home decor stores as well as the occasional café and bookstore. For a taste of the Wild West, you can head to the top of the valley to visit Calistoga, where bathing in hot water (or even mud baths) has been known to relieve an ache or two. Nearby is a state park where Robert Louis Stevenson honeymooned.

Scenic **Sonoma Valley** runs from the top of San Pablo Bay in a crescent that tops out at Santa Rosa. Here, you can not only sample fabulous wines but also learn the history of the Spanish missions and the founding of the Bear Republic. An eight-acre plaza planted with 200 types of trees and dozens of rose bushes beckons year-round with picnic tables. In summer, the Tuesday-night market is quite the after-work scene, with music as well as abundant local produce, breads and other artisanal products. Adventure author Jack London and, much later, the late, great food writer M.F.K. Fisher both chose the Sonoma Valley—in particular, the outskirts of the town of Glen Ellen—as their home. Here you can visit a museum devoted to London in a state park and find a winery that gives tours in a tractor-pulled tram. This village is the hub of this region, with excellent restaurants and shopping. Kenwood is known chiefly for its many wineries.

A recent count revealed that the Napa Valley now boasts some 242 wineries; Sonoma County, 172; and Mendocino County, 38.

When the valley ends at the county seat of Santa Rosa, **Northern Sonoma County** begins. By far the biggest city in the region, Santa Rosa is also the most trafficked. Some charming neighborhoods can be found near downtown, which unfortunately was divided when Route 101 was constructed, essentially chopping off Historic Railroad Square. Yet there are underpasses that access this popular enclave of shops, hotels, restaurants, cafés and nightclubs. About 15 miles north, Healdsburg has, like Sonoma, a downtown plaza flanked by oodles of stores and eateries, including a brew pub. It also has a regional museum and a boffo movie house where first-run and avant-garde films are the bill of fare. Healdsburg, with lush valleys in all directions, is the hub for winemaking, one of which, Dry Creek Valley, ends at Lake Sonoma, a busy recreational destination.

The **Russian River Area** is considered north and west of Healdsburg, though the river itself runs beside that town. Several delightful roads weave through this region, where wineries are clustered to exploit the fertile riverside soil. Sebastopol is a working town with plenty of shops and a handful of good restaurants. Most of the action in these parts happens in and around Guerneville, which somehow works as both a family and a gay summertime retreat, when visitors descend on the year-round residents.

The border of **Mendocino County** lies just beyond Cloverdale, north of Healdsburg. The inland valleys of this county, already famous for its dramatic coastline, are quietly becoming acknowledged for their excellent viticultural properties. Along with wine touring, a small museum that features exhibits on Indian life and a wonderful state park out in the Alexander Valley, a popular pastime involves hanging out at Lake Mendocino on the outskirts of Ukiah, the county seat that straddles Route 101.

When to Go

SEASONS

No wonder the great horticulturist and longtime Santa Rosa resident Luther Burbank called the area around Santa Rosa "the chosen spot of all the earth"—it is a plantlover's dream. The Wine Country is blessed with what most here consider an ideal climate; winter chill as well as summer heat are moderated by the proximity of major bodies of water. Still, winter does get cold with averaging lows of around 37° in December, January and February, with highs in the 50s. Almost all the rainfall in the area occurs in these months as well, although, technically, it could rain anytime. The average May rainfall, however, is far less than half an inch. Spring is fresh and breezy, with lows in the 40s and highs warming up to 80° or so. The average summer day tops out at 83°, but there are plenty of days where the temperature soars over 90°. Low humidity helps diminish the impact of all that heat and allows most nights to cool off even following hot days. Fall days can also be quite toasty, but all the truly warm weather ends by the beginning of November.

Many visitors here are surprised by the cool nights, even in summertime. That's because fog drifts up from San Pablo Bay, at the top of San Francisco Bay, making the Carneros region and, sometimes, the town of Napa especially prone to chilliness any time of year. The fog, mostly a summertime phenomenon, tends to drift in late afternoon and dissipate under the sun. Similarly, fog and ocean breezes blow in from the coast, keeping areas like the Russian River from overheating. Inland areas that receive no moderating maritime influence tend to get both hotter and colder than elsewhere.

As for the narrow valleys, the towns of Sonoma, St. Helena, Calistoga and Ukiah experience greater temperature extremes because both heat and cold are trapped between mountain ranges. Still, compared to other parts of the United States, this part of Northern California has an enviably moderate climate.

When in doubt, just think about those all-important grapes. They lie dormant in the winter, not minding one whit how much rain falls or how cold the ground gets. As things warm up in the spring, the vines sprout leaves and by the time summer arrives, even the casual observer can see grapes emerging in clusters. By September, the leaves turn red and gold as the grapes ripen to perfection, ushering in the harvest that hits its peak in October.

Tantalizing Those Taste Buds

If you like wine, or think you might, Northern California's Wine Country is one of the best places in the world to visit. Hundreds of wineries make infinite variations of dozens of types of wines. Whether you stop at two wineries or thirty, you can enhance each visit by knowing a little bit about how to taste wine.

Why is such a fuss made about tasting wine? At a basic level, thousands of people enjoy wine without knowing the first thing about swirling, sniffing or sipping. Let alone spitting. But the more you know about what different wines taste like, the more you'll get out of the experience.

In the tasting room, available wines are usually listed on a chalkboard behind the bar. These are listed in an order that starts with lighter wines and proceeds to heavier ones. You might begin by asking for suggestions, or choose one or two and simply ask for a taste. As a rule of thumb, few wineries in Sonoma charge for tasting; most in Napa generally charge a nominal fee such as $3.

Glass in hand, start by observing the color and intensity of the wine. Since you already know what it is, memorizing the appearance of the wine will help fix the image in your mind. If possible, hold the glass up to the light for a better look.

Next, take a few short sniffs—not a long snort—and see if the smell reminds you of anything. Then, swirl the wine gently. Unless you're good at this, you may want to set the bottom of the glass on top of the bar, hold the stem and rotate the glass quickly counterclockwise (if you're right-handed, this is the easier way). "Aerating" the wine releases additional aromas.

Now, at last, you get to taste. But alas, not to swallow—at least not yet. Sip a little wine onto your tongue and hold it there for a few seconds, letting your taste buds pick up all the flavors. It may taste of butter, olives, cherries or even violets—whatever it is, try to make all the associations you can. Is the wine heavy in your mouth, or does it feel more like water? These tactile sensations, along with how smooth or bitter the wine strikes you, all play a role.

The hard part is over. Enjoy a few sips of wine. Note how long the flavor stays in your mouth: does it evaporate or does it linger? A long finish is ideal. And if you're going to really get into this winetasting business, of course, you'll want to take some notes on all the above points. If you don't need notes but can rely solely on memory, either the wine is very good or very bad—or you have a future as a professional judge.

CALENDAR OF EVENTS

JANUARY   **Northern Sonoma County**   The beginning of a monthly series, **First Weekend in Alexander Valley** features special tastings and discounts at participating wineries throughout the year.
Russian River Area   Wine seminars and tastings and entertainment are the stuff of **Winter Vineland** on the third weekend.
Mendocino County   **Crab and Wine Days** showcase two of the county's major food products at restaurants, inns and wineries.

FEBRUARY   **Northern Napa Valley**   The blooming of wild mustard marks the start of the **Napa Valley Mustard Festival**, which runs through March and includes cooking demonstrations, food sampling, art exhibits, and winetasting.

MARCH   **Mendocino County**   Mendocino and Fort Bragg celebrate a **Whale Festival** with whale-watching cruises, art shows, and winetasting.

APRIL   **Southern Napa Valley and Sonoma Valley**   More than a dozen wineries in this, the southernmost appellation, band together to offer tastings, entertainment, and wine and food pairings at **April in Carneros**.
Northern Sonoma County   Get your **Passport to Dry Creek** for a weekend of food, wine and easy-to-swallow education.
Russian River Area   The entire town of Sebastopol turns out for the **Apple Blossom Festival**, staging exhibits, parades and pageants.

MAY   **Sonoma Valley**   The **Vintage Race Car Festival** features classic cars as well as classic Wine Country cuisine at Sebastiani Vineyards.
Northern Sonoma County   Countless blossoms are grown, cut and rearranged on floats during the annual **Luther Burbank Rose Festival** in Santa Rosa.
Mendocino County   The **Cloverdale Citrus Fair** is a country event featuring all the citrus grown in the exceptionally warm climate around Cloverdale.

JUNE   **Northern Napa Valley**   The **Napa Valley Wine Auction**, the largest charity event of its kind in the world, brings bidding excitement to the grounds of the Meadowood Resort in St. Helena.
Sonoma Valley   Formal or far-out, anything's fine as long as the colors are right at the **Red and White Ball**, a wine, food and music charity affair in Sonoma's Plaza. Also in the Plaza, even vegetarians will find plenty of food to enjoy at the legendary **Ox Roast**. Enjoy the Bard's dramas *al fresco* with a picnic dinner during the **Sonoma Valley Shakespeare Festival** at Gundlach Bundschu Winery.

Northern Sonoma County   The splendid, expansive lavender fields at Matanzas Creek are the focal point during the **Days of Wine & Lavender**.

Mendocino County   Farmers and winegrowers converge for a long weekend, celebrating the bounty of this northern county in a decidedly unstuffy atmosphere at the **Mendocino Wine Affair**.

Northern Napa Valley   The **Wine Country Film Festival** screens features and documentaries at local theaters as well as outdoors at a winery location; the second two weeks of the festival are held in Sonoma. The old-fashioned **Napa County Fair** at the Calistoga Fairgrounds offers down-home fun with fairs and equestrian events.

JULY

Throughout Sonoma County   The **Sonoma County Wine and Food Showcase** focuses on the region's fine foods and wines with winery dinners, barrel tastings and educational programs.

Sonoma Valley   Sonoma's **Fourth of July** parade is the town's favorite annual event, a day-long party that culminates in fireworks near the plaza. The Sonoma Plaza is ground zero for the summertime **Salute to the Arts**, a smorgasbord of artworks and fine food and wine. Foot races and world-famous pillow fights add a country vibe to the blow-out **Kenwood Fourth of July Celebration**.

Past movies that premiered at the Wine Country Film Festival include Eat Drink Man Woman, Tin Cup and Shall We Dance?

Northern Sonoma County   The **Sonoma County Fair** brings ten days of food, fun, flowers, wine competitions, livestock auctions and horseracing to the fairgrounds in Santa Rosa.

Throughout Napa Valley   The **Music in the Vineyards** series of chamber concerts plays at various vineyards throughout the month.

AUGUST

Sonoma Valley   The second half of the **Wine Country Film Festival** (the first half is in Napa in late July) showcases shorts, features and documentaries in theaters as well as outdoors at Jack London State Historic Park.

Russian River Area   Held at the height of the picking season, the **Gravenstein Apple Festival** in Sebastopol is a family-oriented weekend with an animal petting zoo, arts and crafts, and cooking demonstrations. The annual **Sebastopol Shakespeare Festival** features the works of the Bard in a fun, summertime setting.

Northern Napa Valley   The **Calistoga Beer and Sausage Festival** cooks up a feast of microbrews, cider, homebrews, sausages and sauces at the fairgrounds.

SEPTEMBER

Sonoma Valley   The Valley of the Moon Vintage Festival is a weekend of parades, arts and crafts, winetasting and gourmet food at the Sonoma Plaza and the Sonoma Mission and Sonoma Barracks. The laid-back **Sonoma Valley Harvest Wine Auction** takes place over Labor Day weekend with barbecues, wine auctions, winery dinners and a barrel of fun.

Northern Sonoma County   More than 100 varieties of the late-summer fruit are available for tasting at the **Kendall-Jackson Heirloom Tomato Festival**, which also features gourmet foods, food and wine seminars, and entertainment.

Russian River Area   The two-day **Russian River Jazz Festival** occurs over a musical weekend at Johnson's Beach in Guerneville.

Mendocino County   The **Mendocino County Fair and Apple Show** in Boonville is a three-day event featuring rodeo, sheepdog trials, rides for kids, and country-and-western dancing.

OCTOBER   **Throughout Napa Valley**   Artists throughout the valley hold **Open Studios** during two weekends of free, self-guided tours.

Southern Napa Valley   Ghosts and goblins and an assortment of family fun are the focus each fall at **Halloween at Vintage 1870** in Yountville.

Northern Napa Valley   The CIA **Greystone Golf Classic** stars vintners and other celebrities along with wines, dinners and culinary education.

Northern Sonoma County   The full bounty of the county is showcased at the **Sonoma County Harvest Fair**, where great weight is given to the wine competitions.

Mendocino County   The **Hopland Fall Passport Weekend** is an entrée into some of the top wineries in and around Hopland, with special tastings and discounts on purchases.

NOVEMBER   **Southern Napa Valley**   The big holiday tree is lit this month, along with most of downtown Yountville, and special events and entertainment are provided at Vintage 1870 as the **Festival of Lights** runs from late November through New Year's Eve.

Northern Napa Valley and Sonoma Valley   Holiday in Carneros is a full weekend of open houses, holiday festivities and food and winetastings at more than a dozen wineries in this appellation.

DECEMBER   **Southern Napa Valley**   The Napa County Landmarks society arranges a **Holiday Candlelight Tour** through various historic neighborhoods.

Northern Sonoma County   A New Year's Eve with lots of music and entertainment but absolutely no alcohol has become a tradition at Santa Rosa's **First Night**.

Making the Most
of a Winery Visit

With hundreds of wineries, the temptation to pack too many into your itinerary is hard to resist. But it's a bad idea—those one-ounce pours can add up. The general rule is three, maybe four, in a day of tasting. One way to keep consumption to a minimum is to use the spit bucket, either for spitting or for pouring out the rest of a glass after a taste. Save those swallows for the wines you really love. Another tip is to avoid drinking anything at those wineries that offer other attractions, such as a historic building or an interesting tour.

When there are four wineries I want to see in the course of one day, I like to start early because the odds of over-consuming are less in the morning. If you make two judicious stops in the morning, break for lunch and maybe get some exercise, you can still visit one winery after lunch and another at the tail end of the day.

Winery hours are usually from 10 a.m. or 11 a.m. until 4 p.m. or 5 p.m. Expect to pay a fee anytime you taste reserve wines; as a general rule, the larger Napa wineries charge for tasting while those in Sonoma and Mendocino do not, but there are plenty of exceptions.

Large wineries schedule tours and tasting all day and permit you to drop by unannounced. Though impersonal, they're convenient to visit and provide a wider variety of wines. Small wineries, where the operation is family run and tours are personalized, create the most memorable experiences. Often the winemaker or a member of the family will show you around or at least pour you a sample, providing a glimpse into their lives as well as their livelihoods. Since the family members will be leaving their normal duties to help you, they usually insist on advance reservations.

▼▼▼▼▼▼▼▼▼▼
Before You Go

**VISITORS
CENTERS**

Several agencies provide free information to travelers. The **California Office of Tourism** will help guide you to areas throughout the Wine Country. ~ 801 K Street, Suite 1600, Sacramento, CA 95812; 800-862-2543; www.gocalif.com.

For information on Sonoma and Mendocino counties, contact the **Redwood Empire Association**. ~ 2801 Leavenworth Street, San Francisco, CA 94133; 415-394-5991, 888-678-8507; www. redwoodempire.com.

Also consult local chambers of commerce and information centers, which are mentioned in the various area chapters.

PACKING

There are two important guidelines when deciding what to take on a trip to Northern California. The first is as true for Wine Country and Northern California as anywhere else in the world—pack light. Dress styles here are informal, which is a good thing because laundromats and dry cleaners are few and far between. The second rule is to dress in layers, since temperatures can vary greatly during the course of a day—a warm morning or afternoon can unpredictably become a brisk evening.

In general, you'll be safe almost anywhere in a pair of pressed jeans and a clean shirt. In Sonoma, you'll get extra points if you wear cowboy boots; in Napa, if you wear linen. The resorts are not necessarily formal, but a tie at night for gentlemen and a dress or nice pants for women will cover the bases. Wearing modest shorts at wineries is perfectly acceptable.

Other essentials to pack or buy along the way include sunscreen and sunglasses, perhaps an umbrella, and a camera with which to capture your travel experiences. And don't, for heaven's sake, forget your copy of *Hidden Wine Country!*

LODGING

The image of a country inn dominates many people's idea of Wine Country accommodations. But that's not quite half the story. For one thing, many inns are located in small towns. For another, there are a number of small hotels in the cities, although large hotels are the exception—you won't find any Hyatts or Ritz-Carltons, that's for sure. If you are careful, however, you can find inexpensive motels and even affordable B&Bs in addition to those perfect, luxurious inns.

The busiest times are summer and fall. Do not arrive for a weekend without reservations unless you like to live on the edge. The number of visitors drops sharply from late November to early March, a time when many accommodations either advertise discounts or will at least consider knocking a few dollars off the price of a room, especially mid-week.

To help you decide on a place to stay, I've described the accommodations according to price (prices listed are for the high season; rates may decrease in low season). *Budget* hotels are generally less than $60 per night for two people; the rooms are clean and comfortable. The *moderately* priced hotels run $60 to $120 and provide larger rooms, plusher furniture, and more attractive surroundings. At *deluxe*-priced accommodations you can expect to spend between $120 and $175 for a bed and breakfast or a double in a hotel or resort; you'll check into a spacious, well-appointed room with all modern facilities and you'll usually see a restaurant, lounge and a cluster of shops. If you want to spend your time (and money) in the very finest accommodations, try *ultra-deluxe* facilities, which will include all the amenities at a price above $175.

Contact **Bed & Breakfast California** to give you a hand in finding a cozy place to stay. ~ P.O. Box 282910, San Francisco, CA 94128; 800-872-4500, fax 408-867-0907; www.bbintl.com, e-mail info@bbintl.com.

Zinfandel wines are only made in California, not in Europe. The origin of this grape was a mystery until modern DNA testing traced it to an obscure vineyard in northern Italy.

For those traveling with a large group, or those wanting to enjoy the Wine Country from a residential perspective, **Wine Country Rentals** offers elegant homes in the Napa and Sonoma valleys. ~ P.O. Box 543, Calistoga, CA 94515; 707-942-2186, fax 707-942-4681; www.winecountryrentals.com, e-mail info@winecountryrentals.com.

DINING

Because of wonderful grapes and first-rate produce, Sonoma and Napa restaurants excel in offering the widest array of local wines, paired with fresh-from-the-farm vegetables and regional seafood and poultry.

Whether it's an inexpensive taco or a four-course splurge, the quality is highly consistent. In addition to renowned restaurants, you'll find everyday kinds of places frequented by the locals as well as wallet-friendly diners and ethnic places.

Within a particular chapter, the restaurant entries describe the establishment as budget, moderate, deluxe or ultra-deluxe in price. Dinner entrées at *budget* restaurants usually cost $9 or less. The ambience is informal café-style and the crowd is often a local one. Many if not most ethnic restaurants can be found in this category. *Moderately* priced restaurants range between $9 and $18 at dinner and offer pleasant surroundings, a more varied menu and a slower pace. *Deluxe* dining establishments tab their entrées above $18, featuring sophisticated cuisines, plush decor, and more personalized service. *Ultra-deluxe* dining rooms, where $25 will only get you started, are gourmet gathering places where you should expect exceptional food and outstanding service. Restaurants that offer prix-fixe menus (where you get a number of courses, sometimes accompanied with different wines) for a single price, tend to be extremely pricey, but are often the best value.

Lunch in the Wine Country can be a simple hamburger or something involving salmon or foie gras. The midday meal is virtually without exception priced lower than dinner. Opting for lunch instead of dinner is not only a money-saver, but also increases your chances of getting a table at the restaurants most in demand.

Breakfast menus vary less in price from restaurant to restaurant. Even deluxe-priced kitchens usually offer light breakfasts that cost a fraction of their other meals.

LIQUOR & SMOKING LAWS

The legal age for purchase and consumption of alcoholic beverages, including wine, is 21; proof of age is required. You can buy alcoholic beverages at liquor, grocery and many drug stores daily from 6 a.m. to 2 a.m. Some restaurants, nightclubs and bars have licenses to sell beer and wine only, but most have licenses to sell liquor from 6 a.m. to 2 a.m. Remember when driving: the highest blood-alcohol level allowed under law is .08, which allows for about two drinks over two hours.

Smoking is illegal in California restaurants, bars, stores and office buildings, including wineries and other public gathering spaces. You won't find any special rooms set aside for smokers, either, though you might see signs outside indicating designated smoking areas.

PHONES

The area code for Sonoma, Napa and Mendocino counties is 707. It is not necessary to dial "1-7-0-7" before calling among these counties, or anywhere within the 707 area code, though longer calls qualify as toll calls. Toll-free numbers, such as those to hotels and inns, may begin with 800, 888 or 877; you need to dial "1" before dialing the number.

In case of emergency, call 9-1-1.

MARRIAGE LICENSES

Weddings have become big business in the Wine Country. From big resorts to intimate inns to even hot-air balloon companies, it seems everyone has a way to get you hitched. They can take care of everything (except the license), from food to flowers to food and drink. A good source is the local convention and visitors bureau. Another source is a book called *Here Comes the Bride* by Lynn Broadwell (Berkeley: Hopscotch Press), which details dozens of appropriate wedding places, planners and services. If you're thinking of getting married in the Wine Country, you need a California marriage license. To obtain a license in Sonoma (707-565-3800) or Mendocino (707-463-4370), call the appropriate county clerk for details.

Visiting the Wine Country with kids can be a real adventure, and if properly planned, a truly enjoyable one. A number of wineries welcome children but you could also enjoy a busy and interesting vacation in this area without ever setting foot in a tasting room. After all, thousands of families live in the Wine Country and make use of its public parks and other attractions throughout the year. To ensure that your trip will feature the joy, rather than the strain, of parenthood, remember a few important guidelines.

TRAVELING WITH CHILDREN

Children under age 5 or under 40 pounds must be in approved child restraints while riding in cars/vans. The back seat is the safest.

Use a travel agent to help with arrangements; they can reserve spacious bulkhead seats. Also plan to bring everything you need on board—diapers, food, toys and extra clothes for kids and parents alike. If your visit to the Wine Country involves a long journey, plan to relax and do very little during the first few days.

Always allow extra travel time. Book reservations well in advance and make sure the lodging has the extra crib, cot or bed you require. It's smart to ask for a room at the end of the hall or away from the highway to cut down on noise. Also keep in mind that many bed-and-breakfast inns do not encourage or may not allow children as guests.

Most towns have stores that carry diapers, food and other essentials; in cities and larger towns, 7-11 stores are often open all night (check the Yellow Pages for addresses). Chain grocery stores such as Safeway and Albertson's are open late, sometimes 24 hours a day.

Hotels often provide access to babysitters or you can check the Yellow Pages for state licensed and bonded babysitting agencies.

A first-aid kit is always a good idea. Also, check with your pediatrician for special medicines and dosages for colds and diarrhea.

Finding activities to interest children in Northern California could not be easier. Especially helpful in deciding on the day's outing are *Places to Go with Children in Northern California* (Chronicle Books) and the Friday and Sunday entertainment sections of the *Santa Rosa Press Democrat*, the only major daily published in the region.

Traveling solo grants an independence and freedom different from that of traveling with a partner, but single travelers are more vulnerable to crime and should take additional precautions.

WOMEN TRAVELING ALONE

While the crime rate in Napa and Sonoma is very small indeed, don't let that give you a false sense of security or override common sense. It's unwise to hitchhike and probably best to avoid inexpensive accommodations on the outskirts of town; the money saved does not outweigh the risk. Bed and breakfasts and youth hostels are generally your safest bet for lodging, and they also foster an environment ideal for bonding with fellow travelers.

Keep all valuables well-hidden and hold onto cameras and purses. Avoid late-night treks or strolls through questionable sections of town, but if you find yourself in this situation, continue walking with a confident air until you reach a safe haven. A fierce scowl never hurts.

These hints should by no means deter you from seeking out adventure. Wherever you go, stay alert, use common sense and trust your instincts.

If you are hassled or threatened in some way, never be afraid to scream for assistance. It's a good idea to carry change for a phone call and a number to call in a case of emergency. Northern California boasts nearly 900 women's organizations, including rape crisis centers, health organizations, battered women's shelters, National Organization of Women (NOW) chapters, business networking clubs, and artists' and writers' groups. You can find a complete listing of these groups at www.euronet.nl~fullmoon/womlist/countries/usa/california.html.

Emergency services, including rape crisis and battered women's hotlines, can be found in local phone books or by calling directory assistance.

For more hints, get a copy of *Safety and Security for Women Who Travel* (Travelers Tales, 1998).

GAY & LESBIAN TRAVELERS

In the Wine Country, the most gay-friendly area is around Guerneville, where many resorts cater expressly to gays and lesbians. **Legacy of Sonoma County** is a traveler-friendly phone line that provides information and referrals about lodging, dining and nightlife in the area. ~ 707-526-0442.

The local gay and lesbian newspaper is *We the People*, which comes out once a month and is available throughout the area. The free bimonthly *Mom . . . Guess What!* serves all of Northern California with political scoops, travel tips, restaurant reviews and more. ~ 916-441-6397, fax 916-441-6422; www.mgwnews.com.

SENIOR TRAVELERS

The Wine Country is an ideal spot for older vacationers and has a growing number of retirement communities. The mild climate makes traveling in the off-season possible, helping to cut down on expenses.

The **American Association of Retired Persons**, or AARP, offers members travel discounts and provides escorted tours. ~ 601 E Street NW, Washington, DC 20049; 800-424-3410; www.aarp.org, e-mail member@aarp.org.

For those 55 or over, **Elderhostel** offers educational programs in California. ~ 75 Federal Street, Boston, MA 02110; 877-426-8056, fax 617-426-0701; www.elderhostel.org.

Be extra careful about health matters. Bring any medications you use, along with the prescriptions. Consider carrying a medical record with you—including your current medical status and medical history, as well as your doctor's name, phone number and address. Also be sure to confirm that your insurance covers you away from home.

California stands at the forefront of social reform for persons with disabilities. During the past decade, the state has responded to the needs of the blind, wheelchair-bound, and others with a series of progressive legislative measures.

DISABLED TRAVELERS

There are also agencies in Northern California assisting travelers with disabilities. For tips and information about the greater San Francisco Bay Area, contact the **Center for Independent Living**, a self-help group that has led the way in reforming access laws in California. ~ 2539 Telegraph Avenue, Berkeley, CA 94704; 510-841-4776, fax 510-841-6168; www.cilberkeley.org.

There are many organizations offering general information. Among these are:

The **Society for the Advancement of Travel for the Handicapped**. ~ 347 5th Avenue, #610, New York, NY 10016; 212-447-7284, fax 212-725-8253; www.sath.org, e-mail sathtravel@aol.com.

The **Travel Disabilities Information Service**. ~ Corman Building, 12th Street and Tabor Road, Philadelphia, PA 19141; 215-456-9600; www.mossresourcenet.org.

Mobility International USA. ~ P.O. Box 10767, Eugene, OR 97440; 541-343-1284, fax 541-343-6812; www.miusa.org, e-mail info@miusa.org.

CRUISIN' THROUGH THE COUNTRY

If you're in San Francisco and are planning to tour the Wine Country, the most unique—and likely the most luxurious—way to do so is by boat. Catch the **California Wine Country Cruises** at San Francisco's China Basin for three- or four-night excursions up the Sacramento River to Sonoma, Napa Valley, and Old Town Sacramento. In addition to soaking up views of the Bay and riverfront towns from the decks of these 100-passenger ships, you'll get to enjoy gourmet meals served in the dining room; and an on-board wine expert will impart knowledge about winemaking. So rest up in your comfortable stateroom before heading out to visit those wineries and historic sites. ~ 2401 4th Avenue, Suite 700, Seattle, WA 98121; 800-426-7702, fax 206-441-4757; www.cruisewest.com, e-mail info@cruisewest.com.

Flying Wheels Travel. ~ P.O. Box 382, Owatonna, MN 55060; 800-535-6790, fax 507-451-1685; e-mail thq@LL.net.

Travelin' Talk, a network of people and organizations, also provides assistance. ~ P.O. Box 1796, Wheat Ridge, CO 80034; 303-232-2979; www.travelintalk.net, e-mail info@travelintalk.net.

Access-Able Travel Service has worldwide information online. ~ 303-232-2979; www.access-able.com

Or consult the comprehensive guidebook, *Access to the World—A Travel Guide for the Handicapped*, by Louise Weiss (Holt, Rinehart & Winston).

Be sure to check in advance when making room reservations. Many hotels and motels feature facilities for those in wheelchairs.

FOREIGN TRAVELERS   **Passports and Visas**   Most foreign visitors are required to obtain a passport and tourist visa to enter the United States. Contact your nearest United States Embassy or Consulate well in advance to obtain a visa and to check on any other entry requirements.

Customs Requirements   Foreign travelers are allowed to bring in the following: 200 cigarettes (1 carton), 50 cigars or 2 kilograms (4.4 pounds) of smoking tobacco; one liter of alcohol for personal use only (you must be 21 years of age to bring in alcohol); and US$100 worth of duty-free gifts that can include an additional 100 cigars. You may bring in any amount of currency, but must fill out a form if you bring in over US$10,000. Carry any prescription drugs in clearly marked containers. You may have to produce a written prescription or doctor's statement for the customs officers. Meat or meat products, seeds, plants, fruits and narcotics are not allowed to be brought into the United States. Contact the **United States Customs Service** for further information. ~ 1300 Pennsylvania Avenue NW, Washington, DC 20229; 202-927-6724; www.customs.treas.gov.

Driving   If you plan to rent a car, an international driver's license should be obtained prior to arrival. Some rental car companies require both a foreign license and an international driver's license, along with a major credit card and require that the lessee be at least 25 years of age. Seat belts are mandatory for the

WINE COUNTRY ADVENTURES

For backpackers and daytrippers, state parks in the Wine Country offer a chance to escape the crowds while exploring forests, meadows and mountain ridges. **Backroads** organizes five- to six-day hiking and biking jaunts; most meals and lodging are included. ~ 801 Cedar Street, Berkeley; 510-527-1555, 800-462-2848; www.backroads.com, e-mail goactive@ backroads.com.

driver and all passengers. Children under the age of 5 or 40 pounds should be in the back seat in approved child-safety restraints.

Currency   American money is based on the dollar. Bills in the United States come in seven denominations: $1, $2, $5, $10, $20, $50 and $100. Every dollar is divided into 100 cents. Coins are the penny (1 cent), nickel (5 cents), dime (10 cents), quarter (25 cents), half-dollar (50 cents) and dollar. You may not use foreign currency to purchase goods and services in the United States. Consider buying traveler's checks in dollar amounts. You may also use credit cards affiliated with an American company such as Interbank, Barclay Card, VISA and American Express.

Electricity and Electronics   Electric outlets use currents of 110 volts, 60 cycles. For appliances made for other electrical systems, you need a transformer or other adapter. Travelers who use laptop computers for telecommunication should be aware that modem configurations for U.S. telephone systems may be different from their European counterparts. Similarly, the U.S. format for videotapes is different from that in Europe; some souvenir videos are available in European format on request.

Weights and Measurements   The United States uses the English system of weights and measures. American units and their metric equivalents are as follows: 1 inch = 2.5 centimeters; 1 foot (12 inches) = 0.3 meter; 1 yard (3 feet) = 0.9 meter; 1 mile (5280 feet) = 1.6 kilometers; 1 ounce = 28 grams; 1 pound (16 ounces) = 0.45 kilogram; 1 quart (liquid) = 0.9 liter.

Outdoor Adventures

CAMPING

The state oversees more than 260 camping facilities. Amenities at each campground vary; for a complete listing of all state-run campgrounds, send $2 for the *Guide to California State Parks* to the **California Department of Parks and Recreation**. ~ P.O. Box 942896, Sacramento, CA 94296; 916-653-6995. Reservations for campgrounds may be made by calling 800-444-7275.

In addition to state and Wine Country campgrounds, Northern California offers numerous municipal, county and private facilities. See the "Parks" sections in each chapter for the locations of these campgrounds.

FISHING

Anglers in the Wine Country can drop a line in northern Sonoma County at Lake Sonoma or the Russian River north of Healdsburg. Lake Mendocino near Ukiah is also a favored spot. See "Fishing" in "Outdoor Adventures" for more information.

For current information on the fishing season and state license fees, contact the **Department of Fish and Game**. ~ 3211 S Street, Sacramento, CA 95816; 916-227-2244, fax 916-227-2261; www.dfg.ca.gov. There is also a regional office in Napa Valley. ~ 7329 Silverado Trail, Napa, CA 94599; 707-944-5500.

▼ ▼ ▼ ▼ ▼ ▼ ▼ ▼ ▼ ▼ ▼
Transportation

CAR

The quick, painless and impersonal way to the Napa Valley is along **Route 80**. From San Francisco, the freeway buzzes northeast to Vallejo, where it connects with **Route 37** and then **Route 29**, the main road through Napa Valley.

An alternative course leads north from San Francisco along **Route 101**, the major north–south artery in Sonoma County; parts of it are two-lane while other parts are four-lane. From this freeway you can pick up Route 37, which skirts San Pablo Bay en route to its junction with Route 29. **Route 116** runs in a southeast–northwest axis from Route 101 in Rohnert Park all the way to Guerneville and other areas of the Russian River.

For the most scenic drive, turn off Route 37 onto **Route 121**. This rural road, which also connects with Route 29, provides a preview of the Wine Country. The curving hills along the way are covered with vineyards, ranches and sheep farms. **Route 12** segues from Route 121 and leads through the town of Sonoma and all the way north to Santa Rosa.

AIR

Two airports are close enough to the Wine Country to require less than a two-hour drive.

The **San Francisco International Airport**, better known as SFO, sits 15 miles south of downtown San Francisco off Routes 101 and 280. A major destination from all points of the globe, the airport is always bustling.

Most domestic airlines fly into SFO, including Alaska Airlines, American Airlines, Continental Airlines, Delta Airlines, Hawaiian Airlines, Southwest Airlines, Trans World Airlines, United Airlines and USAir.

International carriers are also prominent here. Aeroflot, Air Canada, British Airways, Canadian Airlines International, China Airlines, Japan Airlines, Lufthansa German Airlines, Mexicana Airlines, Philippine Airlines, Qantas Airways, Singapore Airlines and TACA International Airlines have regular flights into San Francisco's airport.

To avoid the crowds and parking hassles at SFO, consider landing in Oakland, just across the Bay. Domestic carriers that service **Oakland International Airport** include Alaska Airlines, America West Airlines, American Airlines, Continental Airlines, Delta Airlines, Southwest Airlines and United Airlines. International carriers here are Corsair, Martinair Airlines and Mexicana Airlines.

SFO Rides is a free service that will help you plan your way to and from SFO via buses, shuttles, taxis, limousines and more. ~ 800-736-2008, fax 650-794-6508.

Evans Airport Service provides regularly scheduled shuttle transportation to the Napa Valley from both San Francisco and

Oakland airports. You can also arrange chartered limousine service to other parts of the Wine Country. ~ 707-255-1559.

The **Sonoma Airporter** runs regular shuttles to and from SFO. Reservations are suggested and pickup can be arranged. ~ 524 West Napa Street, Sonoma; 707-938-4246.

Most major agencies have outlets at both the San Francisco and Oakland airports. These include **Avis Rent A Car** (800-331-1212), **Budget Rent A Car** (800-527-0700), **Dollar Rent A Car** (800-800-4000), **Hertz Rent A Car** (800-654-3131) and **National Car Rental** (800-227-7368).

CAR RENTALS

Several other companies, listed in the Yellow Pages, offer free pickup at and delivery to both airports.

Greyhound Bus Lines has frequent service to the Napa Valley, Santa Rosa, Healdsburg, Guerneville, Geyserville and points farther north. ~ 800-231-2222.

BUS

Golden Gate Transit provides bus service from San Francisco to some Sonoma County towns. Allow around two hours to reach Santa Rosa and another half-hour to reach Healdsburg. These buses serve commuters; on weekends, you must disembark in Petaluma and transfer onto Sonoma County Transit buses to reach other towns. ~ 415-455-2000, 707-541-2000.

NAPA VALLEY Napa Valley Transit operates between Calistoga and Vallejo, with links to the local valley transportation as well as the Vallejo Ferry and bus lines. Bike racks are available on all buses, which run daily except Sunday from 5:30 a.m. (6:30 on Saturday) until 7:30 p.m. Fares are based on distance traveled, with regular adult fares starting at $1. ~ 707-255-7631, 800-696-6443; TDD 707-226-9722.

PUBLIC TRANSIT

The VINE (**Valley Intracity Neighborhood Express**) provides bus service along five routes within the city of Napa. ~ 707-255-7631, 800-696-6443; TDD 707-226-9722.

SONOMA COUNTY Sonoma County Transit buses connect all the cities in the county on a daily basis. Fares are usually less than $2; some stops are within walking distance of wineries. ~ 355 West Robles Avenue, Santa Rosa; 707-585-7516, 800-345-7433.

Santa Rosa CityBus serves 13 routes within the city every day, with slightly shorter hours on Saturday and Sunday. Exact change of $1 is required; children under 5 ride free. Transfers are free. ~ 707-543-3333, TTY 707-543-3926.

Healdsburg Municipal Transit operates a single bus route daily from 9 a.m. to 4 p.m., for a regular fare of $1. ~ 707-431-3324.

MENDOCINO COUNTY From Santa Rosa you can pick up coastal connections on **Mendocino Transit Authority**, which travels

Route 1 from Bodega Bay to Point Arena. There's only one bus a day in either direction. ~ 707-923-5038.

Mendocino Stage, a local line, serves Point Arena, Mendocino, Fort Bragg and Ukiah. ~ 707-964-0167.

Dial-A-Ride is a share-ride service that provides door-to-door transportation on a limited basis within Ukiah and its immediate surrounds. In-town fare is $3 for adults and $1.50 for seniors/disabled within the city limits, but the price rises drastically for trips beyond those limits. ~ 707-462-3881.

TAXIS   **NAPA VALLEY**   The **Napa Valley Cab** company ("The Red One") is available for intra-valley service around the clock and offers flat-rate service to the airports. ~ 707-257-6444, 800-640-8885.

SONOMA COUNTY   The **Bear Flag Taxi** company serves the Sonoma Valley. ~ 707-996-6733.

The Santa Rosa–based **George's Taxi** (707-546-3322) and **Yellow Cab** (707-544-4444) serve Rohnert Park, Cotati, Sebastopol and Windsor. There's a 20-percent discount for service from any bar and to and from any airport shuttle. **A-C Taxi** (707-525-4888) serves all of Sonoma County.

RUSSIAN RIVER AREA   **George's Taxi** (707-546-3322) and **Yellow Cab** (707-544-4444) serve the Russian River area. There's a 20-percent discount for service from any bar and to and from any airport shuttle.

MENDOCINO COUNTY   Limited taxi service in Ukiah and on the Mendocino coast is available through the **Mendocino Transit Authority.** ~ 707-462-3881.

TWO

Southern Napa Valley

The very name "Napa," to many people, is synonymous with the best wine produced in the entire country. The lush valley is now prime real estate, but in its early years, Napa lagged behind neighboring Sonoma. The first white explorers arrived in 1823 in search of a site to build Mexico's northernmost mission; they chose nearby Sonoma, instead. As a result, southern Napa Valley lacks the historical significance of its neighbor in many ways but has plenty to offer on its own merits.

One of the original 27 California counties, Napa is bounded by Lake County on the north, Sonoma on the west, Yolo and Solano on the east, and San Pablo Bay, the northwestern part of San Francisco Bay, on the south. At the top of the valley is Mount St. Helena, source of the mineral-rich soil in much of the region; through the 40-mile agricultural preserve runs the Napa River, another fount of nutrients for the picturesque vineyards that carpet the valley floor and spread up onto the slopes of the Mayacamas Mountains.

A pioneer named George C. Yount planted grapes around present-day Yountville, using vines obtained from General Mariano Vallejo's Sonoma estate. (Yount dubbed the settlement Sebastopol, but it was later renamed in his honor. Good thing, since there is a city named Sebastopol in neighboring Sonoma County.) From this land-grant vineyard, Yount made his first wine in 1841 out of Mission grapes introduced to northern California by the Franciscan fathers in the 1820s.

While most of the first wineries opened in the neighborhood of St. Helena as early as the 1860s, others were eventually established throughout the valley. Microclimates were observed, setting the stage for the establishment of prestigious appellations such as Stags' Leap (east of Yountville) and the Rutherford Bench (between Yountville and St. Helena) as well as the Carneros, the southernmost appellation.

In the early 1970s, vintners became increasingly aware of the potential of planting vineyards in the Carneros district that borders the bay on the south. Cool temperatures and steady maritime breezes—sometimes actual winds—are considered excellent conditions for grapes such as pinot noir and chardonnay, both of which are used in the making of California sparkling wine. Some newcomers, such as Domaine Chandon (which belongs to Taittinger, the French champagne house) and Artesa (which belongs to the Spanish winemaking family, Codorniu), established stunning facilities and make outstanding wines, both still and sparkling. Meanwhile, existing wineries in Napa began planting vineyards there and/or purchasing grapes from growers in the appellation.

On the rim of the Carneros lies the county seat, the city of Napa. Founded by Nathan Coombs (who had been a member of the Bear Flag Party that declared independence from Mexico in 1845 in the heart of Sonoma), the city lagged Sonoma in development; its first building wasn't constructed until 1848.

If you were parachuted into downtown Napa, you wouldn't recognize it as Wine Country since it looks like many Bay Area towns. You won't see a lot of wine shops or ritzy resorts but you will see a plethora of Victorian buildings, several of which have been converted into bed-and-breakfast inns.

It comes as a surprise to some visitors that Napa is a river town. The Napa River was crucial to the burgeoning wine industry as a conduit to San Francisco Bay, where wines could be distributed out of the big cities. In Napa are some unusual cultural destinations, including an opera house and an indoor-outdoor gallery devoted to regional art as well as a hillside winery with an art collection that rivals small European museums. In addition, Napa is home to the only tourist train in the entire Wine Country.

The city of Napa is the workhorse of the valley—county offices are located here along with the last batch of relatively inexpensive housing. This is where everyone goes to shop at home and garden centers, discount clothing outlets, and national chain stores. It's as if the valley residents realized they had to sacrifice some place in order to preserve the agricultural splendor elsewhere, and Napa was it.

Surrounding the town, however, are highly regarded vineyards as well as a major-league resort. Napa is a good choice to establish headquarters if you're interested in visiting wineries in both the Napa and Sonoma valleys. Downtown is enjoying something of a renaissance, and the riverfront is finally being recognized as the fabulous resource that it is. As you will discover, there is much more to do here than sample wine. There are hot-air balloon rides, parks for hiking, the river for fishing, and walking tours through the Victorian district, now on the National Register of Historic Places.

Yountville, Rutherford and Oakville do have residents, but their raison d'être is the production of wine. Vineyards and wineries, including such world-famous names as Mondavi, dominate the landscape as well as the local consciousness. But all three have wonderful places to eat and spend the night. It's just that there is no downtown in any of these towns.

On weekends from early summer to late fall, the entire valley throngs with tourists. So try to visit during the week, and plan to explore not only the main highway, which often suffers from bumper-to-bumper traffic, but also the Silverado on the east side of the valley and the numerous east–west roads that connect the two. An ideal itinerary will carry you up the valley on Route 29, then back down along the parallel roadway.

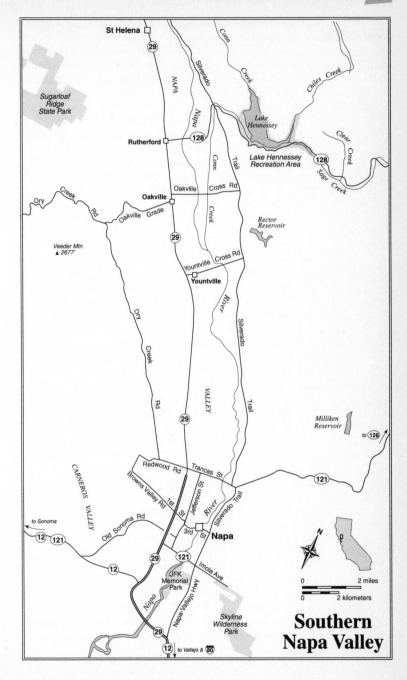

Southern
Napa Valley

▼▼▼▼▼▼▼▼▼▼
Napa Area

From the north shore of San Pablo Bay, the southern portion of the Napa Valley runs up to the town of Oakville. The city of Napa anchors the region, but for visitors the county seat pales in importance when compared to the world-famous vineyards that surround it on every side. Skimming the bay is the Carneros district, where pinot noir and chardonnay are the king and queen.

North of the city are the small towns of Yountville, Rutherford and Oakville, where some of the most prized grapes are grown in climactic conditions considered ideal for cabernet sauvignon and certain other varietals. The area is mostly rural; Napa has the most shops and restaurants but the least charm, though that may change as the valley continues its meteoric rise as a top tourist destination.

SIGHTS

Some people in the city of Napa resent the fact that the town is often treated as a stepsister to the more glamorous upper Valley and as a distant, poor relation to the more tourist-savvy Sonoma just 18 miles away. But this river town has its own charms, including an impressive collection of Victorians. Moreover, the county seat is expecting a humongous boost when the American Center for Food, Wine and the Arts opens just east of downtown, an event expected in 2001.

The Carneros appellation extends into both Napa and Sonoma counties along the rim of San Pablo Bay and straddles Route 29, bordered by Browns Valley Road and Imola Avenue on the north; only a small portion of the city of Napa lies within the designation. Known for its cool and windy climate, it is considered ideal for growing pinot noir and chardonnay grapes.

The varietals that flourish here are also the grapes used to make champagne, so it's not surprising that a number of wineries are known for their sparkling wines. (Unless otherwise noted, all wineries offer regular or self-guided tours and are open daily except for Thanksgiving, Christmas and New Year's Day.)

Approaching the town of Napa from the south, turn east from Route 29 to Route 37 and continue to Kelly Road. Tucked inside a business office complex is one of the valley's most unusual attractions. If you'd like to sample something light and refreshing besides wine, make a stop at the **Hakusan Sake Gardens**. The self-guided tour reveals how rice is converted into sake. Afterwards, relax in the tasting room that overlooks a rock garden and try both hot and cold sakes, all of which are for sale. Tasting fee. ~ Turn south onto Route 29 from Route 121 and head towards the town of Vallejo. Turn left at Kelly Road and look for signs to this unusual facility; 1 Executive Way, Napa; 707-258-

HIDDEN ►

6160, 800-564-6261, fax 707-258-9371; www.hakusan.com, e-mail sake@hakusan.com.

From the sake factory, return to Route 29 and go north until the turnoff for Route 121. Travel a few miles towards Sonoma to find one of the most impressive assemblages of art in northern California. Keep an eye out for cut-out cows dotting the hillside

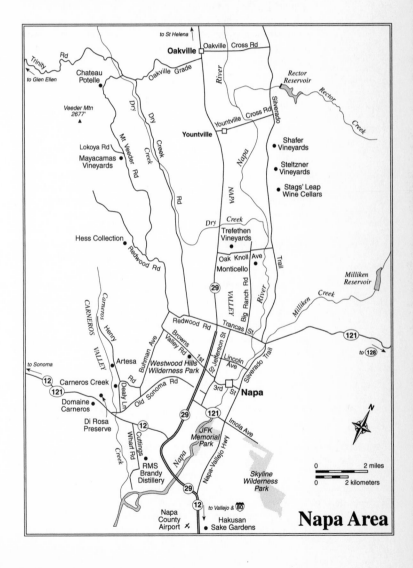

Napa Area

and you'll know you've arrived at the **Di Rosa Preserve**. This unusual rural setting befits the one-man vision, perhaps the world's largest collection of Bay Area art. Rene di Rosa, a former journalist who has been collecting for decades, has amassed more than 1700 paintings, sculptures, drawings, photographs and videos. He has installed these pieces in a series of buildings and, where appropriate, in the great outdoors on the grounds of a former winery, including on the shores of a 35-acre lake. From the whimsical to the deeply moving, the artwork is more than enough to fill the two-hour guided tours (9:25 a.m. and 12:55 p.m. weekdays; 9:25 a.m. and 10:25 a.m. Saturdays), available by reservation only. Closed Sunday and Monday. Admission. ~ 5200 Carneros Highway, Napa; 707-226-5991.

Almost across the road from the art preserve, **Domaine Carneros** is housed in a building that could pass as a French chateau. That's because it's the New World offshoot of Taittinger, the famous champagne house. In this imposing setting, you can sample sparklers in the tasting room or on the patio. In addition to regularly scheduled winery tours, Domaine Carneros offers vineyards tours each Friday morning, weather permitting. Tasting fee. ~ 1240 Duhig Road, Napa; 707-257-0101, fax 707-253-3020; www. domainecarneros.com, e-mail sparklingwine@napa.net.

Some of Napa's prettiest and least-traveled roads can be found in this section of the Carneros district, where several wineries are tucked away. One is **Carneros Creek**, which was established in 1972 as the first winery built in the area in some 40 years. It is known for its pinot noir though about 15 percent of its production is in chardonnay. Samples are available in the pleasant tasting room; picnic tables sit in the shade of an arbor. Tours by appointment. Tasting fee. ~ 1285 Dealy Lane, Napa; 707-253-9463, fax 707-253-9465; www.carneroscreek.com, e-mail wineinfo@ carneroscreek.com.

Up the road, **Artesa** (pronounced ar-TESS-uh) opened on a hilltop in 1991. A stunning 127,000-square-foot winery that is

TOURING TIPS

Most Napa Valley wineries charge for tasting their wines, often a nominal fee or one that includes a souvenir glass. The large wineries are open every day except for major holidays, while the smaller ones usually operate on a limited schedule. A handful require reservations, a stipulation noted in the following descriptions where applicable. Bear in mind that wine cellars are typically cool, around 65° year-round, so carry a wrap if you plan to take extensive tours of the properties.

dug into the top of the hill, Artesa boasts one of the most dramatic approaches in the Wine Country, with a sweeping staircase rimmed by waterfalls, fountains, reflecting pools and sculptures. The nearly wraparound view from the top includes hillside vineyards and north San Pablo Bay. Originally known as Codorniu Napa, the winery switched its focus to still wines in 1997. Today the winemaker, formerly of Chateau St. Jean, makes chardonnay and pinot noir as well as other varietals. Tasting fee. ~ 1345 Henry Road, Napa; 707-224-1668, fax 707-224-1672; www. artesawinery.com.

From Artesa, return to Route 121 and head east. Before you reach Route 29, you will be turning left for another unique attraction. Guests may tour the RMS **Brandy Distillery**, which specializes in alambic brandy; 4000 barrels of brandy are harbored in the Barrel House. Unfortunately no tasting is allowed. The tour culminates in a "sensory evaluation," where guests can sniff the differences in the six separate distilled grape varietals used in the final brandy. ~ 1250 Cuttings Wharf Road, Napa; 707-253-9055, fax 707-253-0116; www.rmsbrandy.com.

To reach the city of Napa, continue east on Route 121, then turn north on Route 29; take the 1st Street exit, which will lead you to 2nd Street, heading one-way downtown. If there is no street parking, you can easily find public lots.

The **Napa Valley Conference and Visitors Bureau** is a good place to get started on a tour of the entire valley. They will supply you with maps and brochures for the area. ~ 1310 Napa Town Center, Napa; 707-226-7459, fax 707-255-2066; www. napavalley.com, e-mail info@napavalley.org.

If someone in your traveling party wants to be a fireperson when she grows up, the whole family might like a brief stop at the **Napa Firefighters Museum**, just a couple of blocks away from the visitors bureau. Engines, ladder trucks, hose carts and other equipment as well as uniforms and old photos would look better in a real firehouse, but it's a nice enough display. Closed Monday and Tuesday. ~ 1201 Main Street, Napa; 707-259-0609.

North of Napa, the serious Wine Country begins, with wineries seemingly every 100 yards. One worth a slight detour is **Monticello**,   ◀ HIDDEN
where a pretty if small-scale version of Jefferson's Virginia home serves as company headquarters. Best bets for tasting are merlot, cabernet and chardonnay and, if available, a late-harvest semillon. Tours are offered daily at 10:30 a.m., 12:30 p.m. and 2:30 p.m. from May through October. Tasting fee. ~ 4242 Big Ranch Road, Napa; 707-253-2802, 800-743-6668, fax 707-253-1019; e-mail wine@monticellovineyards.com.

Just off Route 29 is the site of the valley's second-oldest winery. **Trefethen Vineyards** now occupies the 1886 Eschol winery property. The last gravity-flow winery in the valley, Trefethen presses its grapes on the top floor, ages them on the second and bottles them on the ground floor. Ones to try include the estate-grown cabernet sauvignon and chardonnay as well as the less-expensive versions of these two varietals. ~ 1160 Oak Knoll Avenue, Napa; 707-255-7700, fax 707-255-0793; e-mail winery@trefethen.com.

Not terribly far from Route 29, on the west side of the valley, you can find one of the valley's most outstanding attractions. Located on the site of the former Christian Brothers' Mont LaSalle winery, the **Hess Collection** is where fine wine meets fine art. The self-guided tour is unique: It is the only winery in the valley that includes two floors displaying some 130 museum-quality artworks by contemporary European and American artists. The Hess Collection also refers to the cabernets and chardonnays that are just being released and are available for sampling in the ground-floor tasting room. Tasting fee. ~ 4411 Redwood Road, Napa; 707-255-1144, fax 707-253-1682; www.hesscollection.com.

HIDDEN ► From Hess, return to Redwood and take Mount Veeder Road north to another out-of-the-way winery. **Mayacamas Vineyards** provides an entirely different setting from the wineries on the valley floor. Located deep in the mountains west of Napa Valley, it sits astride an extinct volcano. The blocks of vineyard appear hewn from surrounding rock walls. Indeed, the fields of chardonnay and cabernet sauvignon rest on terraces along the mountainside. Like the encircling hills, the winery is made of stone, built in 1889. Tours of this special place are by appointment; it lies about ten miles off Route 29 along winding mountain roads. Closed weekends. ~ 1155 Lokoya Road, Napa; 707-224-4030, fax 707-224-3979; www.mayacamas.net, e-mail mayacama@napanet.net.

HIDDEN ► Back on Mount Veeder Road and nestled on the slopes of Mount Veeder away from the hubbub (about ten miles from Route 29 via the Oakville Grade), **Chateau Potelle** is the dream-come-true of a French couple. The winery and its acreage, located at an altitude ranging from 1600 to 2000 feet, produces

---

ALL ABOARD

An unusual option for touring the Wine Country is to climb aboard the **Napa Valley Wine Train**, which runs daily between the city of Napa and the vineyards slightly north of St. Helena. Travelers may choose the lunch, brunch or dinner trip, each of which takes three hours and smoothly chugs past some of the most scenic parts of the valley. The 1915 Pullman cars have been beautifully restored; the dining car is straight out of a romance novel. ~ 1275 McKinstry Street, Napa; 707-253-2111, 800-427-4124, fax 707-253-9264; www.winetrain.com.

about 20,000 cases of estate-grown zinfandel, cabernet and char-donnay, plus other varietals grown elsewhere. You can buy goat cheese and a baguette here and enjoy your purchases on the tasting room deck. No tours. Closed Tuesday and Wednesday. ~ 3875 Mount Veeder Road, Napa; 707-255-9440, fax 707-255-9444; e-mail info@chateaupotelle.com.

Return to Route 29 and the Silverado Trail to continue your tour. On the east side of the valley, several top wineries are clustered in the prized Stags' Leap district, known for its top-notch cabernet sauvignons. The wine that put California on the world map came from **Stags' Leap Wine Cellars**, which wowed oenophiles by beating out even the French Bordeaux entries in the now-famous Bicentennial tasting in Paris. A nice touch here: the winery offers free non-alcoholic beverages for the designated driver. Tasting fee. ~ 5766 Silverado Trail, Napa; 707-944-2020.

The nearby **Steltzner Winery** is revered for its cabernet sauvignon; several vintages are usually available for tasting. For something different, you might sample the claret or a South African varietal known as pinotage. Tasting fee. ~ 5998 Silverado Trail, Napa; 707-252-7272.

You will find a handful of small inns in downtown Napa though accommodations in this area tend towards chain lodging and small motels on the outskirts of town.

LODGING

Even in a town heavy on Victorians, **La Belle Epoque** is a standout. A colorful Queen Anne–style number built in 1893 by noted architect Luther M. Turton, it houses four spacious rooms and two suites named for wine varietals. Antiques such as an Eastlake queen bed, silk oriental carpets, and a Belgian armoire distinguish the accommodations, several of which have canopied beds and/or stained-glass windows. The breakfasts are so elaborate that a menu for tomorrow's meal is displayed each afternoon. Tastings are held in the wine cellar each evening. The inn, which is near downtown shops and restaurants, also has two suites in a Victorian across the street. ~ 1386 Calistoga Avenue, Napa; 707-257-2161, 800-238-8070; www.labelleepoque.com, e-mail innkeeper@labelleepoque.com. DELUXE TO ULTRA-DELUXE.

Reasonably priced bed and breakfasts are nearly nonexistent in the Wine Country, with one exception—**Churchill Manor**. Located on an acre of landscaped, flower-filled grounds just south of downtown Napa, the manor, built in 1889, is now a ten-room inn. The rooms are furnished with European antiques, and exquisite redwood columns front the main staircase. The innkeepers serve a full breakfast in the tile-floored sunroom, and on nice mornings you can take it out on the veranda, which surrounds three sides of the home. In the evenings, complimentary wine and cheese are offered. There are also tandem bikes to ride and a sitting room with games and puzzles to enjoy. ~ 485 Brown Street, Napa; 707-253-7733, fax 707-253-8836. MODERATE TO ULTRA-DELUXE.

The **Old World Inn** is at its most glorious in spring and summer, when wisteria and jasmine and then roses and other shrubs are at their peak of flowering. The unusual decor features a lot of stenciling, especially phrases sketched on the walls. Rooms are in bright colors such as mint green or blue and yellow; the 11th room is in a detached cottage on the far side of the outdoor hot tub. Two-night minimum April through November with a Saturday stay. ~ 1301 Jefferson Street, Napa; 707-257-0112. DELUXE TO ULTRA-DELUXE.

As usual, the cheapest lodging has the least desirable address, but in the Napa Valley, that's all relative. Look around Soscol Avenue or near Route 29 for the best deals. An example of the latter is the 34-room **Chablis Lodge**. The rooms are larger than usual, with a wet bar, coffeemaker and small refrigerator; some have kitchenettes. In summer, you'll be glad to see the small pool. Be sure to ask for accommodations on the far side of the highway. Continental breakfast is included. A two-night minimum stay is required on weekends. ~ 3360 Solano Avenue, Napa; 707-257-1944, 800-443-3490, fax 707-226-6862. DELUXE.

There is no Cabernet Sauvignon Lodge—think what that might cost—but on the north side of town, the **Chateau Hotel** might be considered the equivalent of a screwtop. Accommodations here are ordinary, quite clean and wonderfully situated for exploring the entire valley. All of the two-story motel's 115 rooms have refrigerators. Continental breakfast is included. A two-night minimum stay is required on weekends. ~ 4195 Solano Avenue, Napa; 707-253-9300, fax 707-253-0907; www.napavalleychateauhotel.com. MODERATE.

DINING

The truly chic restaurants are clustered around Yountville and St. Helena, but Napa offers some bargains and your best chance at ethnic food. There are a few coffee shops downtown that can provide you with a substantial snack.

HIDDEN ►

If you wonder where the locals are, you can find a lot of them at the **Foothill Café**, a modest establishment off the tourist path on the unfashionable side of town. Hearty soups and salads, elegant entrées like lamb shank, duck breast and ahi tuna, and knockout desserts make this a delightful alternative to the fancier, pricier up-valley restaurants. Closed Monday and Tuesday. ~ 2766 Old Sonoma Road, Napa; 707-252-6178, fax 707-258-9415. MODERATE TO DELUXE.

HIDDEN ►

Downtown Napa isn't the easiest place in the valley to reach, but there's a restaurant that makes the trip well worth the effort. **Celadon**, accessible via path or footbridge, is tucked into the

Author Picks

CHAPTER FAVORITES

I love the **Di Rosa Preserve**—especially the outdoor sculptures that inject a refreshing dose of whimsy into an area that can take itself a bit too seriously. *page 34*

My favorite place to stay in this neighborhood is the **Vintage Inn Napa Valley**, where all the rooms have cross-ventilation and the pool and hot tub are a blessing at the end of a strenuous day of winetasting. *page 48*

I wouldn't call the cooking at the **Foothill Café** "downhome," but its unpretentious yet fine cuisine is a refreshing change from its up-valley competitors. *page 38*

A feeling of inspiration strikes me whenever I visit **Artesa**, with a setting even more dramatic than the stunning architecture because the hilltop offers panoramic views of the Carneros district. *page 34*

Exchange Building. Seafood is tops on Greg Cole's menu of "global comfort food," as are many Thai- and Indonesian-influenced dishes, a number available in small servings ideal for mixing and matching. A great selection of wines by the glass rounds out the attractions in this high-ceilinged spot; grab a creekside table in good weather. Closed Sunday. ~ 1040 Main Street, Napa; 707-254-9690. MODERATE.

On the east side of town, hunt for the **Old Adobe Bar and Grille**. Housed in an 1840 adobe with original thick walls and exposed beams, this restaurant adds fish, pasta, steaks and prime rib to its Mexican standards. Murals of Mexican village life (and a full bar) add to the ambience. ~ 376 Soscol Avenue, Napa; 707-255-4310. MODERATE.

Napa's culinary scene got a shot in the arm in early 2000 with the opening of **Saketini Asian Diner and Lounge**, located in a shopping center on the north side of town. One long yellow wall and simple furnishings, including several counter seats, play second string to the food, a blend of things Chinese, Japanese, Thai and Hawaiian. Tiger shrimp satay, sushi, seared tuna, hibachi-style salmon with ponsu sauce and spicy baby-back pork ribs show off the talents of the Hawaiian-born chef, who came to Saketini from the upscale Brix up the road. ~ 3900 Bel Air Plaza, Napa; 707-255-7423, fax 707-255-6014. BUDGET TO MODERATE.   ◄ HIDDEN

Blessed with one of the loveliest settings in the Wine Country, **Bistro Don Giovanni** evokes Tuscany for some. The fare is decidedly Mediterranean—delectables like focaccia, grilled meats, housemade pastas and grilled portobello mushrooms with sautéed greens and onion rings. In warm weather, linger on the shaded porch; when it turns cool, warm yourself in front of the large, open fireplace. ~ 4110 St. Helena Highway, Napa; 707-224-3300, fax 707-224-3395. MODERATE.

SHOPPING The majority of Napa's retailers can be found on the perimeter in a variety of large shopping centers. Specialty shops tend to be found downtown.

Copperfield's Books is the local branch of a regional chain that has shops in Sonoma and one up in Calistoga. It's an invaluable source for local authors and guidebooks and carries a very good selection of magazines. ~ 1303 1st Street, Napa; 707-252-8002.

Though not well known outside of foodie circles, **Shackford's** has been catering to cooking fanatics for a quarter of a century. Inside this plain-looking store is an array of equipment and gadgets, from Cuisinarts to cookbooks to cake-decorating supplies to talking snack dispensers. Most shoppers are astounded to discover things they never knew they needed. Closed Sunday. ~ 1350 Main Street, Napa; 707-226-2132.

Napa's Premium Outlets is home to major retailers like Ann Taylor, Calvin Klein and Timberland, among many others. (Take the 1st Street exit off Route 29.) ~ 629 Factory Stores Drive, Napa; 707-226-9876.

HIDDEN ► Across the river from downtown, the JV **Warehouse** is where wallet-watching wine lovers know to look for ongoing bargains. The stock, discounted because bought in bulk, changes over time, but there are always deals. Sometimes a particular bottle is only a couple of dollars cheaper than at the grocery store, but it's worth the effort if you're buying half a case or more. ~ 426 1st Street, Napa; 707-253-2624.

NIGHTLIFE The **Ring's Lounge**, an upscale lounge at the Embassy Suites Napa Valley, is a pleasant spot for quiet conversation as well as live piano performances on Friday and Saturday. ~ 1075 California Boulevard, Napa; 707-253-9540.

Downtown Joe's features rock, pop and blues bands nightly except Monday, Tuesday and Thursday. ~ 902 Main Street, Napa; 707-258-2337.

Jazz and other bands crank it up on Tuesdays and Thursdays at the **Saketini Asian Diner and Lounge**. ~ 3900 Bel Air Plaza, Napa; 707-255-7423.

Marlowe's is the best place to find live rock and blues, as well as Latin favorites, on a regular basis in the Napa Valley. Cover. ~ 1637 West Imola Avenue, Napa; 707-224-2700.

Since 1933, the **Napa Valley Symphony** has been entertaining with classics as well as a handful of modern pieces. From

The Carneros District

The grape-growing appellation that spans a swath along the north rim of San Pablo Bay is unusual for several reasons, chief among them being that it straddles two counties. The bulk of the Carneros lies in Napa but also includes a chunk of the southern Sonoma Valley. While there are no historic buildings along the lines of the town of Sonoma's mission and barracks, the area shares the history of the surrounding region. Here, the wine industry grew up, matured, struggled through the last phylloxera infestation, rebounded and finally achieved recognition in the 1980s. Its prominence in wine circles has continued to grow since it was named an American Viticultural Appellation (AVA) in 1983.

Carneros shares San Francisco's marine climate, with milder winters and summers than the valleys, giving the appellation a longer growing season suited to certain grapes. Because of the slow maturation in this climate, Carneros grapes reach maturity at lower sugar levels and higher acids, resulting in a great depth of flavor extract.

The moderate climate and fertile lands of the Sonoma Valley attracted early settlers who traveled through the area that today is served by Routes 12 and 121 (the latter known in this neighborhood as the Carneros Highway). As early as 1850, while hay was still free to those who would cut it, workers traveled by barge to Carneros (from the Spanish word for the sheep, or rams, once common here) to load hay and grain for transport to San Francisco. Farmers followed, raising sheep and cattle and cultivating grapes, pear, plums, apples and apricots.

While most of these vines were destroyed by phylloxera, the Stanly Ranch survived and helped start Napa's reputation for growing quality grapes. In 1942, Louis M. Martini, a longtime buyer of Stanly grapes, bought some 200 acres of the old ranch and replanted them with pinot noir and chardonnay. But by the close of World War II, little wine was being produced in Carneros. The current crop of wineries started up in 1972, when Francis Mahoney established Carneros Creek, the area's first new winery in nearly four decades. Today, the appellation's vineyards are harvested not only by Carneros winemakers but also by wineries from other parts of Sonoma and Napa.

Most of the roads in this part of the Wine Country (once you get off Routes 12, 121 and 29) tend to be small and less-traveled than their counterparts. It would be easy to visit most of the 16 or so wineries here in a weekend.

mid-October through April, the group presents multiple perform-ances of five programs. Call for locations and programs. ~ 707-226-8742.

Among its unusual offerings, the **Jarvis Conservatory** presents occasional programs of *zarzuella*, the seldom-performed Spanish opera form, in addition to regularly scheduled "open opera" the first Saturday of each month (in summer, it's also held on the third Saturday), when it's first come, first sing. ~ 1711 Main Street, Napa; 707-255-5445.

PARKS

JOHN F. KENNEDY MEMORIAL PARK 🏃 ⛴ 🚤 With hiking trails along the Napa River, this is one of the valley's best parks. You'll also find softball fields and playgrounds in this 340-acre parcel. Non-motorized boating is allowed. ~ 2291 Streblow Drive, Napa; 707-257-9529.

SKYLINE WILDERNESS PARK 🏃 🚲 🐎 🚣 With 35 miles of trails good for hiking, mountain biking and horseback riding, this 850-acre park is a bit of wilderness just two miles from down-town Napa. From its oak-studded hills, you can see San Fran-cisco on clear days. A small lake, once used as the water supply for Napa State Hospital, is favored for bass, crappie and bluegill fishing. Facilities include restrooms, showers and barbecue pits. Day-use fee, $4. ~ 2201 West Imola Avenue, Napa; 707-252-0481.

▲ There are 30 RV sites, $18 to $20 per night; a handful of tent sites are $12 per night.

WESTWOOD HILLS WILDERNESS PARK 🏃 On the west side of Route 29, this 111-acre park is home to the modest Carolyn Parr Nature Museum (707-255-6465) and plenty of hiking trails. Closed Monday through Friday except by appointment. ~ Browns Valley Road at Laurel Street, Napa; 707-257-9529.

▼▼▼▼▼▼▼▼▼▼▼▼▼▼▼▼▼
Yountville to Rutherford

Yountville thrives in a postcard setting, flanked by vineyards with the Maya-camas Mountains off to the west. (If you really want to get an overview, take one of the hot-air balloon flights offered here.) Formerly known as Sebastopol (now the name of a Sonoma city), it got its current name around 1860, after North Carolinian George C. Yount settled here on the 11,000-acre land grant known as Rancho Caymus. Lately the town has been on a building spree, with several inns built in the past few years along with some of the valley's best-known dining palaces. It's home to only about 3500 people, meaning there's a restaurant for roughly every 400 citizens.

A couple of miles north along Route 29 is Oakville, estab-lished in the 1870s as soon as the train line was extended that far from Napa. There is no real town center here; its raison d'être is the presence of notable wineries such as Robert Mondavi and Opus One.

Rutherford, due north, got its start as a railroad station that, in the 1880s, was named for Thomas L. Rutherford, who had married a granddaughter of George Yount. The town is even smaller than Oakville but boasts, among other things, Beaulieu Vineyard, which recently celebrated its 100th anniversary.

Yountville seems like a small country town until you see its wee neighbors to the north. At first, it appears that Oakville and Rutherford exist mostly to serve as the address for some of the country's top wineries. But in all three towns you'll find excellent restaurants and, in Yountville, great inns as well as an im-

SIGHTS

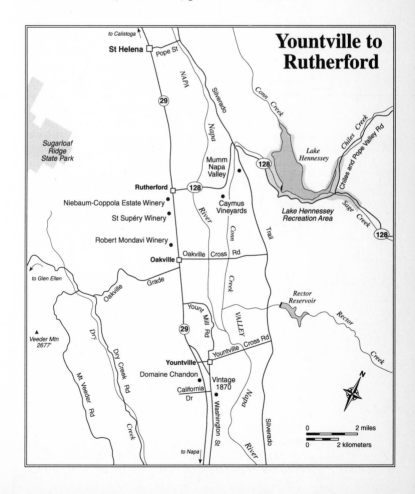

Yountville to Rutherford

portant museum. Washington Street is the main artery of the latter, running parallel to Route 29 one block to the east.

HIDDEN ►   **The Napa Valley Museum,** which opened in 1998 not far from
one of the country's best-known wineries (Domaine Chandon),
is not your mother's museum. Far from stuffy, it's a vibrant center for the arts. But its most stunning attribute is the high-tech
permanent exhibit, "California Wine: The Science of an Art." The
museum celebrates the history, culture and lifeblood of the area,
with changing exhibits of arts and crafts and a lively schedule of
classes, many aimed at children. Closed Tuesday. Admission. ~ 55
Presidents Circle, Yountville; 707-944-0500, fax 707-945-0500;
www.napavalleymuseum.org.

Domaine Chandon, owned by France's fabled champagne
producer, Moët & Chandon, sits on a knoll west of town. Producing some of California's foremost sparkling wines, this winery provides a close look into the production and bottling of the
bubbly. It's housed in a modernistic building with barrel-vaulted
ceilings and contains a small wine museum as well as a gourmet
restaurant. The regularly scheduled tours are free. Tasting fee. ~
1 California Drive, Yountville; 707-944-2280, fax 707-944-1123;
www.dchandon.com, e-mail dchandon@napanet.net.

Vintage 1870, the highest-profile structure in all of Yountville,
began life as the Groezinger Winery. A multistory red-brick building, it's now home to more than a dozen boutiques and specialty
shops. ~ 6525 Washington Street, Yountville; 707-944-2451.

They charge an arm and a leg (okay, $25) for tastings at **Opus
One,** but then, you can be pretty confident you'll enjoy the experience. At least if you love red wine. The futuristic edifice is
worth a peek at any rate; its enormous semicircular barrel cellar
is modeled after the one at the Chateau Mouton Rothschild winery
in France. ~ 7900 Route 29, Oakville; 707-963-1979, fax 707-
944-1753; www.opusonewinery.com.

Among the largest in the Napa Valley, **Robert Mondavi Winery**
is a Spanish mission–style building offering two informative
tours by reservation. Choose between the basic production tour
with tasting or a three-hour-long look at the entire process from
vineyard to laboratory to winery (the latter is only offered a few
days a week). The chardonnay and fumé blanc are excellent and
you can also sample reserve wines by the glass. In addition to visiting the art gallery, you may want to attend summer jazz concerts held on Saturday nights in the courtyard. Tasting fee. ~
7801 St. Helena Highway, Oakville; 707-963-9611; www.robert
mondavi.com, e-mail info@robertmondavi.com.

Continuing along Route 29 you'll drive through the tiny
town of **Rutherford,** passing a patchwork of planted fields. In a
valley virtually spilling over with wineries, how does a new one
get noticed? In the case of **St. Supéry Winery,** it's by constructing

a first-rate gallery with numerous exhibits on Napa Valley wine-making. Three-dimensional displays include a replica of an actual grapevine growing out of deep soil, smell-a-vision (a contraption that enables you to smell four of the aromatic components of wine), and topographical maps that show why the valley is good for grapes. An outdoor tasting area and a restored Victorian add spice to the winery tour. Tasting fee. ~ 8440 St. Helena Highway, Rutherford; 707-963-4507, 800-942-0809, fax 707-963-4526; www.stsupery.com, e-mail divinecab@stsupery.com.

One of the prettiest wineries in Rutherford is the **Niebaum–Coppola Estate Winery**, where movie great Francis Ford Coppola and his wife Eleanor have been making wine since 1975. In 1995 they purchased the adjacent Inglenook Château and vineyard, unifying the original 1879 estate of winemaker Gustave Niebaum. The ivy-draped château houses the Centennial Museum, where the history of winemaking at the estate is chronicled. Specialties of the winery include rubicon, chardonnay, cabernet franc, merlot and zinfandel. Tasting fee. ~ 1991 St. Helena Highway, Rutherford; 707-963-9099; www.niebaum-coppola.com, e-mail service@niebaum-coppola.com.

> Five of Francis Ford Coppola's Oscars along with artifacts from his films are displayed in the Centennial Museum at the Niebaum–Coppola Estate Winery.

To reach the wineries along the Silverado Trail, take the Rutherford Cross Road, which leads east to meet the trail.

A winery with an old French name, **Mumm Napa Valley** is a good place to see *methode champenoise* production via daily tours. Located on an oak-shaded hillside, the pitched-roof winery looks like a redwood barn. In the tasting room you can sample flutes of sparkling wine. Tasting fee. ~ 8445 Silverado Trail, Rutherford; 707-942-3434, 800-686-6272, fax 707-942-3470; www.mumm.com, e-mail concierge@sparkling.com.

LODGING

The **Yountville Inn** is one of the newer lodges in town but not the prettiest, at least from the outside. However, the 51 rooms distributed among seven buildings alongside Hopper Creek are attractive, with a fieldstone fireplace, French doors, a small patio or deck, woodbeamed ceiling and refrigerator. Continental breakfast is included. ~ 6462 Washington Street, Yountville; 707-944-5600, 800-972-2293; www.yountville.com. DELUXE TO ULTRA-DELUXE.

Practically next door to Vintage 1870, the diminutive **Napa Valley Railway Inn** consists of restored boxcars and cabooses. The result is an assortment of appealing, if a bit too rectangular, guest accommodations, which are roomier than you might think. ~ 6503 Washington Street, Yountville; 707-944-2000. MODERATE TO DELUXE.

Five distinctive rooms comprise **Petit Logis**, a single-story inn in the heart of town. Five rooms sport lovely murals and high

The Silverado Trail

The Silverado Trail, an old stagecoach road, parallels Route 29 on the east and links with it via a succession of cross-valley roads as it runs 29 miles from Napa to Calistoga. Fully paved, this route is a favorite among cyclists as well as leisurely drivers. In addition to glimpses of Napa Valley as it was in the 1960s, it's an excellent place to search out small wineries. All along this rural stretch are family-owned vineyards, set on the valley floor or tucked into nearby hills. To reach it, you can follow Trancas Street east from Route 29 through Napa and turn left onto the Silverado Trail. Or better yet, head north from Napa on Route 29 to Oak Knoll Avenue and turn right, which will take you past **Monticello** (page 35), a winery in a replica of Thomas Jefferson's mansion, before crossing the Napa River and intersecting the trail. Here's a sampling of the wineries you'll find along the route:

SHAFER VINEYARDS   About two miles north of the Oak Knoll intersection on the Silverado Trail, Shafer Vineyards lies at the base of a rocky outcropping surrounded by fields of chardonnay, merlot, and cabernet sauvignon grapes. Removed from the road, it's a placid spot with views of the fields and the valley. Tours of the winery (which include tastings) and wine cave are by appointment only. Closed weekends. ~ 6154 Silverado Trail, Napa; 707-944-2877, fax 707-944-9454; www.shafervineyards. com; e-mail shafer@shafervineyards.com.

CAYMUS VINEYARDS   Nine miles north of Shafer Vineyards, after skirting the town of Yountville, the Silverado Trail brings you to this unpretentious winery run by Chuck Wagner and his father Charlie, whose parents were Napa winemakers in the early 1900s. The best part of a wine-tasting here is when Charlie pours a glass of their premium cabernet sauvignon or Conumdrum (a proprietary blended white wine) and begins spinning stories about Napa Valley way back when. Tastings by appointment only. ~ 8700 Conn Creek Road, Rutherford; 707-967-3010, fax 707-963-5958.

ceilings. Breakfast is included in the room rate; guests have a choice of two nearby restaurants. ~ 6527 Yount Street, Yountville; 707-944-2332; www.petitlogis.com. MODERATE.

For a dash of history with your evening glass of port, consider the **Maison Fleurie**. A lodging place since 1873, this stone building is currently a fashionable bed and breakfast. There are seven rooms in the old ivy-covered structure and six others in two adjacent buildings, each room crowded with antiques. Quilts and

STERLING VINEYARDS   In a few more miles you'll pass the turnoff to the village of St. Helena. Another seven miles will bring you to Sterling Vineyards near the outskirts of Calistoga. Set atop a knoll near the head of Napa Valley, this Greek monastery–style winery is reached via an aerial tramway (fee). The gondolas carry visitors to a multitiered, brilliant white building that commands sentinel views of the surrounding valley. Once atop this lofty retreat, a self-guided tour leads through various wine-making facilities to an elegant tasting room. It also takes in the spectacular stained-glass windows and 18th-century church bells that add an exotic element to this unusual winery. ~ 1111 Dunaweal Lane; 800-726-6136, fax 707-942-3467; www.sterlingvineyards.com, e-mail info@svclub.com.

MOUNT ST. HELENA   If you continue north after arriving in Calistoga, the Silverado Trail trades the warm, level terrain of the valley for the cool, rugged landscape of the mountains. It climbs and winds through thick coniferous forests and past bald rockfaces. In touring Napa, you've undoubtedly noticed the stately mountain that stands sentinel at the north end of the valley. Mount St. Helena, named by 19th-century Russian explorers for their empress, rises 4343 feet, dominating the skyline.

ROBERT LOUIS STEVENSON STATE PARK   Perched on the side of Mount St. Helena is Robert Louis Stevenson State Park. The Scottish writer and his wife honeymooned in these parts, camping in the hills and enjoying the recuperative air. Here he wrote sections of *The Silverado Squatter* and studied settings later used in *Treasure Island*. Today the Memorial Trail leads through this undeveloped park one mile to an old mine and a monument commemorating the spot where Stevenson spent his honeymoon. Then a fire road continues four more miles to the top of Mount St. Helena. From this impressive aerie the entire Napa Valley lies before you, with views stretching from the Sierra Nevada to San Francisco. ~ Route 29, about eight miles north of Calistoga; 707-942-4575, fax 707-942-9560; www.cal-parks.ca.gov/districts/silverado/rlssp215.htm.

teddy bears adorn the beds, while chandeliers and brass lamps illuminate the historic setting; all have private baths and many have fireplaces and spa tubs. As a contemporary touch, there is a swimming pool, a jacuzzi and mountain bikes available for guest use. Breakfast is buffet style, and afternoon wine and tea are served daily. ~ 6529 Yount Street, Yountville; 707-944-2056, 800-788-0369, fax 707-944-9342; www.foursisters.com, e-mail info@foursisters.com. DELUXE TO ULTRA-DELUXE.

The **Vintage Inn Napa Valley** is ideally located for exploring the Wine Country. Rose gardens and trickling fountains surround smart-looking, two-story villas with brick facades and wood shingles on the roof. Eighty rooms are like mini-suites, adorned with fireplaces and shuttered windows, marble wet bars and baths—all in all, some of the most desirable rooms in the valley. The complimentary breakfast buffet is quite extensive. An Olympic-sized pool and tennis courts are also found here, and Yountville's exclusive shops and eateries are but a short stroll away. ~ 6541 Washington Street, Yountville; 707-944-1112, 800-351-1133, fax 707-944-1617; www.vintageinn.com. ULTRA-DELUXE.

Perched on a hillside studded with olive trees, **Auberge du Soleil** is a curious blend of French Mediterranean–style cottages named after French winegrowing regions and decorated in breezy California/Southwest style. Bare Mexican tile floors, louvered doors, fireplaces and private terraces are a refreshing change from the cluttered feel of older hotels in the valley. Thirteen low-rise cottages stagger down the hill, all but two of them containing four rooms. There's also a pool to relax in. ~ 180 Rutherford Hill Road, Rutherford; 707-963-1211, 800-348-5406, fax 707-963-8764; www.aubergedusoleil.com, e-mail info@aubergedusoleil.com. ULTRA-DELUXE.

Crafted from white oak, the Spanish Colonial **Rancho Caymus Inn** is a romantic retreat with stained-glass windows, a colonnade, a courtyard and gardens. There is a total of 26 rooms; in the split-level rooms you'll find queen-size carved wooden beds, private balconies, and charming adobe beehive fireplaces. ~ 1140 Rutherford Road, Rutherford; 707-963-1777, 800-845-1777, fax 707-963-5387; www.ranchocaymus.com. ULTRA-DELUXE.

DINING

The reputations of some of the restaurants in this neighborhood are in inverse proportion to the size of the towns. The gamut ranges from haute cuisine to hot dogs, priced accordingly.

Domaine Chandon, while losing a little luster from its crown over the past five years, is still a dependable choice for outstanding Wine Country cooking. This is a grown-up restaurant, where entrées arrive as complete dinners such as herb-crusted

DINING AL FRESCO

Oakville Grocery is a prime place to stock up for a picnic. This falsefront country store sells wines and cheeses, fresh fruits, specialty sandwiches, and baked goods, as well as a host of gourmet and artisanal items. ~ 7856 St. Helena Highway, Oakville; 707-944-8802, 800-973-6324; www.oakville-grocery.com, e-mail ogccorp@aol.com. BUDGET TO MODERATE.

rabbit with wild mushroom–romano bean ragout and potato "risotto," grilled lamb sirloin with saffron couscous, English peas, cipollini onions and white-bean chili sauce, and caramelized scallops with saffron pearl pasta. Prices are steep, but in keeping with country-club surroundings, sophisticated food and ultra-smooth service. No dinner Monday and Tuesday. ~ 1 California Drive, Yountville; 707-944-2892, fax 707-944-1123; www.chandon. com. DELUXE TO ULTRA-DELUXE.

The only thing generic about **The Diner** is its name. This un-   ◄ *HIDDEN* assuming Yountville eatery, popular with local residents, prepares a mix of Mexican and Californian dishes. Dinner ranges from burgers and salad to burritos and quesadillas; add specialties like fresh seafood dishes. Breakfast and lunch vary from Mexican dishes to include cornmeal pancakes, housemade sausage, and omelets. Such a bargain. Closed Monday. ~ 6476 Washington Street, Yountville; 707-944-2626, fax 707-944-0605. BUDGET TO MODERATE.

Philippe Jeanty, formerly of Domaine Chandon, now runs a classic French bistro on Yountville's main drag. Escargot, pâtés, lamb tongue, kidneys, sweetbreads, salad Nicoise and the inevitable *haricot verts* are typical offerings at **Bistro Jeanty**, along with seafood and some heavier dishes. As far as appearance goes, this two-room wonder is right out of the French countryside. ~ 6510 Washington Street, Yountville; 707-944-0103, fax 707-944-0370. MODERATE TO DELUXE.

Colors like terra cotta, mustard and other earth tones symbolize the kitchen's intent at **Livefire**, where almost everything is cooked in a smoker or rotisserie. The emphasis is on chicken, duck, game hens and outstanding fish, as well as knockout ribs and chicken sausage. ~ 5518 Washington Street, Yountville; 707-944-1500, fax 707-944-1504. MODERATE.

Bouchon is a glamorous and glorified bistro, with lots of sparkle in the decor and on the menu. Entrées lean to *coq au vin*, *entrecote avec frites*, braised lamb chops, sole meuniere, onion soup, roast chicken, sautéed seasonal vegetables, fruit tarts and soufflés. Yet its most unusual feature may be its late-night dining—as late as 2 a.m. as a courtesy to night owls such as workers from area restaurants. ~ 6534 Washington Street, Yountville; 707-944-8037, fax 707-944-2769. MODERATE TO DELUXE.

For Mexican dining, cruise into **Compadres**. The brick-lined restaurant is an unusually pretty setting for Americanized south-of-the-border specials. It's especially popular for brunch. ~ 6539 Washington Street, Yountville; 707-944-2406, fax 707-944-8407. MODERATE.

Set in an old building, **The French Laundry** features contemporary American cuisine with a classic French influence. Fare may include braised beef cheek and veal tongue with baby leeks, pan-roasted squab, and herb-roasted monkfish tail. The food is excellent, the wine list extensive, and the prix-fixe menu changes nightly. It's very popular; reservations are a must. No lunch Tuesday through Thursday. ~ 6640 Washington Street, Yountville; 707-944-2380. ULTRA-DELUXE.

Mustards Grill is an ultramodern brass-rail restaurant complete with track lighting and contemporary wallhangings. There's an attractive wooden bar and paneled dining room, but the important features are the woodburning grill and oven. Here the chefs prepare rabbit, grilled pork chops, smoked duck, and skirt steak. This eatery specializes in fresh grilled fish like sea bass, mako shark, spearfish and salmon. ~ 7399 St. Helena Highway, Yountville; 707-944-2424, fax 800-901-8098. MODERATE TO DELUXE.

A capacious room, with a wall of windows overlooking herb gardens and the Mayacamas Mountains, sets the tone for the flavorful menu at **Brix**. The cuisine here has more of an Asian influence than most Napa Valley restaurants. Try the Black n Blue seared ahi with wasabi aioli, stirfry noodles, salmon with miso or Asian spring roll and you'll get the picture. It's a fun list, with items like an Asian-infused fresh seafood trio "starter kit" for an appetizer, and main courses that run the gamut from mahimahi to pork medallions to a luscious mustard-glazed rotisserie chicken. ~ 7377 St. Helena Highway, Yountville; 707-944-2789. MODERATE TO DELUXE.

HIDDEN ▶   **Pometta's** is the saving grace of vacationers who just want something to eat, not a five-star dining experience. An ultra-casual favorite with locals, this deli serves up sandwiches and salads and hot dishes like chicken. You can tote your meal out or enjoy it here on picnic tables. ~ 7787 Route 29, Oakville; 707-944-2365. BUDGET.

First and last word in Napa Valley elegance is **Auberge du Soleil**, a hillside dining room overlooking the vineyards. Modern in design, this gourmet hideaway is a curving stucco structure with a wood-shingle roof. The circular lounge is capped by a skylight-cum-cupola and the dining area is an exposed-beam affair with an open fireplace. Even architecture such as this pales in comparison with the menu, which changes seasonally. Lunch might begin with the Seven Sparkling Sins appetizer (which includes foie gras, caviar and truffled quail eggs), then move on to a pan-seared foie gras and roasted duck sandwich. Dinner entrées include oak barrel–roasted sterling salmon, rack of lamb, and thyme-roasted pheasant; vegetarians might choose grilled asparagus and wild-mushroom lasagna. There's also an extensive wine list. ~ 180 Rutherford Hill Road, Rutherford; 707-967-3111, fax 707-963-8764; www.aubergedusoleil.com. ULTRA-DELUXE.

SHOPPING   Almost by definition, shopping malls are unattractive. **Vintage 1870** is a rare exception to a modern rule. Housed in the historic

Groezinger Winery, a massive brick building smothered in ivy, it contains several dozen fashionable shops. Wooden corridors, designed with an eye to antiquity, lead along two shopping levels. There are clothing stores galore and several restaurants, as well as specialty shops offering arts-and-crafts products. ~ 6525 Washington Street, Yountville; 707-944-2451, fax 707-944-2453.

Across the street, the **Groezinger Wine Company** features hard-to-find premium wines from California, Oregon and Washington. ~ 6528 Washington Street, Yountville; 707-944-2331, 800-356-3970, fax 707-944-1111.

The most charming shop in Yountville is **Mosswood**, which has a whimsical selection of home and garden accessories ranging from birdhouses and wind chimes to weathervanes, linens and knobs and pulls. ~ 6550 Washington Street, Yountville; 707-944-8151.

The restaurant **Brix** has room for one of the best wine shops in the area, with hundreds of choices (all the whites are available chilled) at prices not much above what you'd pay in a grocery store—that is, if you could find Grgich Hills chardonnay and some lesser-known sangioveses in your average Safeway. ~ 7377 St. Helena Highway, Yountville; 707-944-2789.

On Friday night **Compadres Restaurant** features jazz bands. ~ 6539 Washington Street, Yountville; 707-944-2406.   **NIGHTLIFE**

The place to be with the in crowd is at the piano bar at the posh **Auberge du Soleil**. Sooner or later, everyone who is anyone shows up. The bar offers an excellent selection of ports and other after-dinner drinks and the fireplace adds a cozy note on chilly evenings. ~ 180 Rutherford Hill Road, Rutherford; 707-963-1211, 800-348-5406.

LAKE HENNESSEY RECREATION AREA ⛴ 🛶 Located about   **PARKS**
five miles east of Rutherford, this lake provides water to the city of Napa. You can fish here but you can't rent a boat. There are picnic grounds and the scenery—lots of oak trees blanketing the surrounding hills—is wonderful. ~ East of the Silverado Trail along Route 128.

◆◆

WHERE THE WINERIES ARE

If you set out for a morning or afternoon of winetasting—a full day is not recommended—a good approach, logistically speaking, is to drive north on Route 29 and south on the Silverado Trail. The bulk of the wineries can be found on one road or another, with a handful up in the hills or along some of the narrow roads that run east–west between the two main thoroughfares.

▼▼▼▼▼▼▼▼▼▼▼▼▼
Outdoor Adventures

GOLF

As you might expect in this agricultural preserve, there are a number of golf courses. Golf is a year-round sport in this temperate valley, and while the resort courses are always expensive, public and semiprivate courses tend to be affordable. You should make reservations for weekend play.

The nine holes at **Chimney Rock Golf Course** are ideal for the sand-phobic. It has but two sand bunkers and the par-36 course is fairly flat. There's a pro, a shop and a restaurant at this semiprivate course. ~ 5320 Silverado Trail, Napa; 707-255-3363.

The 18-hole **Napa City Municipal Golf Course** is surrounded by Kennedy Park and rents clubs and carts. ~ 2295 Streblow Drive, Napa; 707-255-4333.

The Chardonnay Club has 27 championship holes arranged Scottish links-style on a par-72 course. There's a driving range, pro shop and club house. ~ 2555 Jameson Canyon Road, Napa; 707-257-8950.

TENNIS

Tennis courts are far and few between outside of the big resorts. However, public courts can be found in the city of Napa.

There are six tennis courts at the centrally located **Napa High School**, but they are not lighted for night play. ~ 2474 Jefferson Street, Napa; 707-253-3715.

On the north side of Napa, **Vintage High School** maintains eight courts for public use. ~ 1375 Trower Avenue, Napa; 707-253-3715.

BALLOON RIDES

A hot-air balloon ride is the best way to get a bird's-eye-view of the Napa Valley. These rides depart daily at the crack of dawn, weather permitting, and usually conclude with a champagne brunch. Expect to pay about $185 for most outings.

Adventures Aloft, the oldest company of its kind in Napa, departs from Vintage 1870. ~ 6525 Washington Street, Yountville; 707-944-4408; www.nvaloft.com. **Napa Valley Balloons** has a flotilla of more than a dozen balloons so there's almost always room for a couple more people. ~ Yountville; 707-944-0228.

BIKING

The flat terrain that characterizes most of this area is ideal for cycling. If you like hills, head out Route 128 to Pope Valley Road; you'll work up a sweat. If you like the looks of the Oakville Grade linking Napa with Sonoma, think again. It's a rugged climb up from the Napa side.

A bike ride through the Lower Chiles Valley will give you quite a workout. A tough 48 miles (roundtrip) if you start in Yountville, this one's best done in the early morning hours before the sun and the traffic heat things up. It's a hilly, scenic ride but one that will take you perilously close to Lake Berryessa. Head over to the Silverado Trail and go north until you turn east on Route 128 East. Then it's north on Chiles and Pope Valley Road and southwest on lower Chiles Valley Road. Return via Route 128 West.

For something easier, try the **14-mile loop** around Yountville and the Stags' Leap district. Though you can pick up the route anywhere, you might begin at Route 29 and Oak Knoll Avenue. Pedal east across Big Ranch Road to the Silverado Trail, then head left and up to Yountville Cross Road, which zigzags to Yountville. Hook up with Washington Street and take it south to California Drive. Go west, under the highway, then south on Solano Avenue, which leads back to Oak Knoll Avenue. By heading east again, crossing Route 29, you will shortly arrive back where you started. There is a bike lane along most of the Silverado Trail.

Fans of mountain biking are welcome at **Skyline Wilderness Park**. Most of its 25 miles of trails are open to both hiking and mountain biking. Elevation ranges from 130 feet to 1100. Admission. ~ 2201 West Imola Avenue, Napa; 707-252-0481.

Bike Rentals   Bikes can be rented at the **Napa Valley Cyclery**, which is also a good source of biking routes. ~ 4080 Byway East, Napa; 707-255-3377.

HIKING

With most open space devoted to vineyards, you won't find a lot of formal trails in this portion of Napa. Your best bet is in the parks; walking along major thoroughfares is a really bad idea. All distances listed for hiking trails are one way unless otherwise noted.

One easily accessible trail is the Trancas to Lincoln segment (2.5 miles roundtrip) of the **Napa River Trail**. From Route 29, turn east on Trancas Street and travel 1.5 miles (or go half a mile east of the Silverado Trail). There is a hiker access sign on the west side of the Napa River, where you will start your hike, all of it easy and almost all of it level. This is not a wild trail; you're never far from houses but you can find blackberry, ivy and wild grape as well as other flora thriving under live oak and bay trees. Get out your camera as you approach the end (before your return trip); there are some wonderful photo ops on the trail not far from an RV park. ~ Napa Parks and Recreation; 707-257-9529.

Skyline Wilderness Park has about 25 miles of hiking trails, ranging in elevation from 130 to 1100 feet. One of the most popular here is **Lake Marie Road** (2 miles). To reach the trailhead, take Imola Avenue east to where it ends at 4th Avenue. From the south corner of the parking lot, a signed trail turns to the right (just before a native plant garden); follow the grassy path west, turning left at the road. You will pass between two small lakes before the road begins to climb. Along this trail are fruit trees once cared for by patients at Napa State Hospital. Remain on the trail until you reach Lake Marie.

THREE

Northern Napa Valley

In a valley where 90 percent of the arable land is zoned for agricultural use, beauty is merely a matter of degree. Yet the stretch of Napa Valley from around St. Helena north to Calistoga is, if anything, slightly more gorgeous than the rest. The freeway terminates at Yountville, where Route 29 continues north as a two-lane road. On either side, from the Howell Mountains on the east to the Mayacamas on the west, rows upon rows of grapevines provide a vista that evolves through the seasons, from the green of spring and summer to the rust and gold of fall. Even in winter, the gnarled vines are picturesque, more so when wild mustard comes into bloom, carpeting the valley in brilliant yellow blossoms in January and February.

Locals call the area north of Rutherford "up valley," an area that encompasses two towns—St. Helena and Calistoga—engulfed by prize real estate. Especially if you're a vintner. This is where some of the country's famed wine pioneers made their name—Louis Martini, Charles Krug, and the Beringer Brothers among them. You can visit these wineries today, as well as a plethora of newcomers. The area is also home to two state parks, the valley's best shops and some of Wine Country's premier restaurants. Visitors can feast on freshly baked bread and pick up deluxe supplies for a picnic in the park or at any of a number of wineries that provide tables for expressly this purpose.

With millions of dollars sunk into vineyards and Napa Valley wines fetching record prices in retail stores as well as at auctions (especially the prestigious local auction each June), there are of course plenty of millionaires in the area. Yet at one level, this is farm country. When the scene threatens to become just a bit too precious, try to remember: these are farmers. And there are plenty of regular folks living here as well.

The Wappo Indians got here first, and though white explorers came across present-day Napa as early as 1823, the influx of pioneers did not begin until a British surgeon named Edward Bale arrived and built a flour mill near present-day St. Helena in 1846. He married into General Mariano Vallejo's family and received a Spanish land grant of some 20,000 acres, practically the entire acreage of the upper valley. Today, visitors picnic beside the Bale Grist Mill, now a state historic park three miles north of St. Helena.

Nearby is the oldest continuously operating winery in the valley, bonded in 1876. Frederick Beringer founded the winery and built the Rhine House, virtually a shrine to his German home. Another former Beringer home, the Hudson House, is now home to the winery's Culinary Arts Center.

Long before becoming famous as a wine region, Napa was a sought-after tourist destination for quite another reason. We have Sam Brannan to thank for that. In 1859, he founded Calistoga, at the northern end of the Napa Valley, envisioning it, correctly, as a resort that would rival those on the East Coast. A century and a half later, however, Calistoga remains resolutely un-chic, despite counting numerous swank wineries among its chief attractions. The same underground hot springs that supply the bathwater for numerous day spas in Calistoga also fuel another of the town's quirky charms: its own version of an Old Faithful Geyser that continues to live up to its name.

Up the hill from Calistoga is another attraction right out of *Ripley's Believe It or Not!* A petrified forest sits a stone's throw from the highway, an intriguing destination for an afternoon stroll in the shade. Created by mighty eruptions from nearby Mount St. Helena, the forest is a natural wonder that brings to life the rich geological history of the region.

▼▼▼▼▼▼▼▼▼▼
St. Helena

One look at Main Street speaks a thousand words. It's wall-to-wall boutiques, with the occasional hotel (one) and several restaurants. For the most part, these are fine stores that might well survive even if there were no tourists, which speaks volumes about the net worth of the locals. A pretty street lined with 19th-century stone buildings, it becomes a virtual parking lot in the high season. The town, named for nearby Mount St. Helena, evolved after British surgeon Edward Bale arrived in California aboard a whaling vessel, virtually penniless. He received a Spanish land grant of about 20,000 acres, built a flour mill in 1896 some three miles north of present-day St. Helena and probably died a very, very rich man.

One of Napa's most famous visitors was the prolific author Robert Louis Stevenson. A couple of blocks from the heart of town is a museum devoted to the Scottish writer, who traveled through the area in 1880 en route to the hills beyond Calistoga.

SIGHTS

Dozens of wineries are located to the north, south, east and west, but visitors owe it to themselves to get out of their cars and meander through the heart of town. It's the only way to get a feel for the regional lifestyle and, after all, it's one of only three actual "downtowns" in the whole Napa Valley.

In the Victorian-style downtown area, the brick-and-stone IOOF **Building** looms several stories above the pavement, as it has for a century. ~ 1352 Main Street.

The cynosure of St. Helena is the **Ritchie Block**, a stone structure with brick-and-wood facade. Featuring more frills and swirls than a wedding cake, it is a study in ornate architecture. ~ 1331 Main Street.

The town's **Robert Louis Stevenson Silverado Museum** houses a collection of artifacts from Robert Louis Stevenson's life and his sojourn in the Napa Valley. Having visited Monterey and San Francisco, the Scottish author arrived in Calistoga in 1880. (Stevenson was en route to Hawaii and the South Seas, seeking a salubrious environment in which to escape his lifelong illnesses.) Among the memorabilia at the museum are manuscripts, letters, photographs and first editions, as well as personal effects left behind by the globe-girdling Victorian. Closed Monday. ~ 1490 Library Lane; 707-963-3757, fax 707-963-0971; e-mail rlsnhs@calicom.net.

While the way to see Napa wineries is to visit the smaller concerns, big sometimes *is* better. Take **Beringer Vineyards**, for example. The vintage product here is the Rhine House, an 1890s Tudor-style mansion. With its mansard roof and stone inlay, it is a masterwork of spires, turrets and gables. The interior, complete with tasting room, is illuminated through stained glass and paneled in hand-carved hardwoods. Among the winery's other features are 1000 feet of tunnels cut into the neighboring hillside by 19th-century Chinese laborers. The adjacent historic bottling room has been converted into a tasting room. You can take a tour, which covers several interesting parts of the operation, including the tunnels. ~ 2000 Main Street; 707-963-7115, fax 707-259-4510; www.beringer.com.

The **Sutter Home Winery**, which made a household name out of white zinfandel, makes many other wines intended for mass consumption as well. The winery is an attractive bevy of beautiful Victorian buildings, and their gift shop is one of the busiest in town. Founded in 1874 by a Swiss-German immigrant, it was bought by the Sutters in 1906 and is now owned by the Trinchero family. ~ 277 St. Helena Highway; 707-963-3104, fax 707-967-9184; www.sutterhome.com.

HIDDEN ▶ Not much port is made in this part of the world, but you can sample several versions at **Prager Winery and Port Works**. Obscured by the infinitely larger Sutter Home Winery, this cozy warren of barrel cellars, tasting room and spider webs is as different from mainstream wineries as merlot is from chenin blanc. The Prager family make their ports a little drier than the Portuguese do, so it's a great place to learn more about this underappreciated treat, which you're unlikely to find anywhere else but here and in a few Napa Valley restaurants. Tours by appointment. Tasting fee. ~ 1281 Llewelling Lane; 707-963-7678, 800-969-7678, fax 707-963-7679; www.pragerport.com.

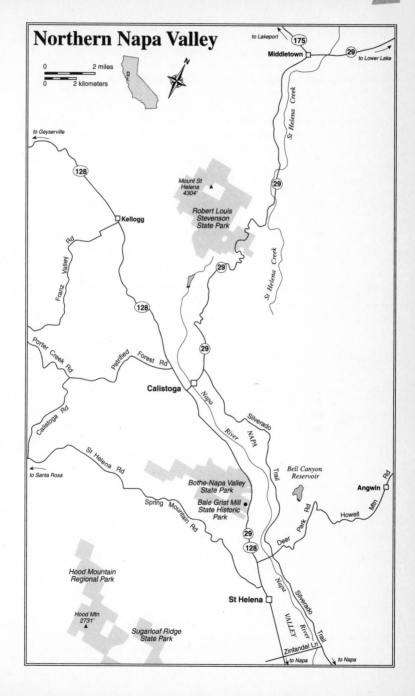

Northern Napa Valley

0 — 2 miles
0 — 2 kilometers

to Lakeport
175
Middletown
29
to Lower Lake

St Helena Creek

to Geyserville

128

Mount St
Helena
4304'

Robert Louis
Stevenson
State Park

Kellogg

29

St Helena Creek

Franz Valley Rd

Porter Creek Rd

128

29

Petrified Forest Rd

Calistoga

Napa

Calistoga Rd

St Helena Rd

River

Silverado

NAPA

to Santa Rosa

Spring Mountain Rd

Bothe-Napa Valley
State Park

Bale Grist Mill
State Historic
Park

Bell Canyon
Reservoir

Angwin

Deer Park Rd

Howell Mtn Rd

Hood Mountain
Regional Park

29
128

Trail

Hood Mtn
2731'

Sugarloaf Ridge
State Park

St Helena

Napa

Silverado

VALLEY

River

Trail

Zinfandel Ln

to Napa

to Napa

Headquartered in an 1885 winery, **V. Sattui Winery** is one of the most popular destinations in the valley. Wine critics don't think much of the wines—which are sold only here—but that doesn't deter the happy crowds who sample some of the ten wines and pick up deli items for a picnic in the shade by the highway. The enormous tasting room is in a barn almost obscured by vines; a dining area, aging cellars and the winery itself are housed in a historic stone building. ~ 111 White Lane; 707-963-7774, fax 707-963-4324; www.vsattui.com.

North of St. Helena, **Bale Grist Mill State Historic Park** is a picturesque stop. Sitting beside a tumbling stream, an 1846 waterwheel mill creates a classic scene. It was built for a Mexican land grantee and served as an early gathering place for farmers throughout the area. The mill is now partially restored and there are guided tours (weekends only). There's a visitors center plus a pair of raw wood buildings that housed the mill and granary. Admission. ~ Route 29; 707-942-4575, fax 707-942-9560; www.napanet.net/~bothe, e-mail bothe@napanet.net.

Not far past the old mill stream, a side road leads from Route 29 to **Tudal Winery**. Touted as one of the world's smallest wineries, it consists of a cluster of contemporary buildings surrounded by luxurious grape arbors. Tours and tasting at this family affair are by appointment. A walk around the entire winery will probably take a grand total of ten minutes, after which the owner may regale you for hours with tales of the Wine Country. Tasting fee. ~ 1015 Big Tree Road; 707-963-3947, fax 707-963-9288.

HIDDEN ►   It's easy to find **Litto Damonte's Hubcap Ranch**. Just take Howell Mountain Road east from the Silverado Trail in St. Helena to the hamlet of Pope Valley. Head north three miles until you see at least a thousand points of light. Those are Damonte's hubcaps, more than two thousand strong, adorning houses, barns, fences and pastures. Just to make sure you know who's responsible, Damonte has plastered his name on the barn in—what else—hubcaps.

LODGING   The only decent motel—in fact, apparently the only motel—in the area is **El Bonita,** a pretty little complex that sports window boxes and nicely landscaped grounds. The 41 rooms (some are in two-story buildings in the rear) are done up in pastels and florals more befitting a country inn. The pool is a rarity in these parts. ~ 195 Main Street; 707-963-3216, 800-541-3284, fax 707-963-8838. MODERATE.

HIDDEN ►   The **Inn at Southbridge** is just off the main drag in a complex that includes a restaurant, a winery and the Health Spa of Napa Valley. Spacious second-story accommodations are done in soothing Tuscan colors such as mustard and olive. Handcrafted furnishings bring some life to these somewhat lonely rooms. Room rates include continental breakfast and use of the adjacent health club. ~ 1020 Main Street; 707-967-9400, 800-520-6800, fax 707-967-9486. ULTRA-DELUXE.

The **Harvest Inn**, one of the few places to stay within walking distance of downtown, occupies four extensively landscaped acres amid a working vineyard; several lowrise buildings are linked by a network of pretty brick walkways. The 54 rooms are decorated in bright colors and feature amenities such as fireplaces and refrigerators. Two 24-hour swimming pools and hot tubs make

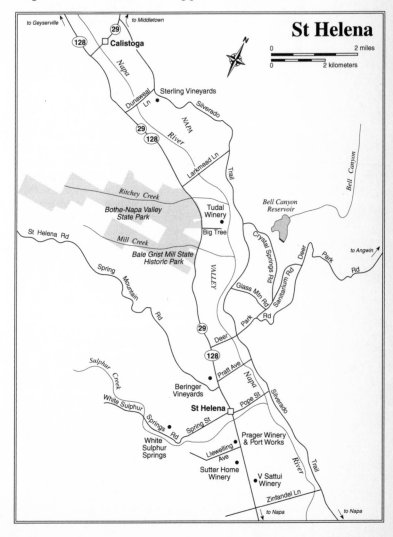

this a good choice if you are looking for a place to really unwind between winery excursions. Top of the line are three townhouse Spa Suites that command vineyard views. Continental breakfast is included. ~ 1 Main Street; 707-963-9463, 800-950-8466, fax 707-963-4426; www.harvestinn.com. DELUXE TO ULTRA-DELUXE.

In the center of town, **Hotel St. Helena** is a traditional false-front building dating to 1881. It features 18 guest rooms, all but four of which have private baths (the four share two European-style bathrooms down the hall). Many rooms include such decorative flourishes as caneback chairs, brass beds, antique armoires, marbletop vanities, and bent-willow headboards. Each is painted in warm pastel colors and plushly carpeted. Guests share an indoor reading room and sitting room with fireplace, plus other facilities like the hotel's wine bar. Continental breakfast is included. ~ 1309 Main Street; 707-963-4388, 888-478-4355, fax 707-963-5402. DELUXE TO ULTRA-DELUXE.

A gracious Victorian topped with a fanciful cupola affording 360° views of the Napa Valley, **Ink House Bed & Breakfast** attracts mostly straight guests but has a strong gay and lesbian following as well. The 1884 house is encircled by a wide veranda with white wicker chairs and offers seven antique-filled guest rooms, five with private bath. In addition to a full gourmet breakfast, wine and appetizers are served in the afternoon. There's an antique pool table in the basement, and mountain bikes are available for guests. ~ 1575 St. Helena Highway; 707-963-3890, fax 707-968-0739; www.napavalley.com/inkhouse, e-mail inkhouse bb@aol.com. MODERATE TO ULTRA-DELUXE.

HIDDEN ▶

Spread across 330 acres and claiming to be the oldest hot-springs resort in California, **White Sulphur Springs** dates to 1852. A deeply shaded creek and several walking trails run through the property, which also contains a redwood grove and a series of natural sulphur springs and pools. The cottages (five small, four large) and lodge-like carriage house possess a rustic charm. The former have private baths, knotty pine walls, kitchenettes, throw rugs and an ambience that borders between homey and funky. The latter share a bathroom, lounge and kitchenette with a fireplace. There are also "inn rooms" with private baths available at moderate cost. In the health spa you can treat yourself to a massage, an herbal facial, or a mud wrap. Or you can hop into the swimming pool, jacuzzi or sulphur soaking pool. ~ 3100 White Sulphur Springs Road; 707-963-8588, 800-593-8873, fax 707-963-2890; www.whitesulphursprings.com. MODERATE TO ULTRA-DELUXE.

Located at the end of a tree-shaded country road, **Meadowood** comprises 85 accommodations, a nine-hole golf course, two croquet lawns, two pools, tennis courts and a fitness center and spa. Guests may choose to stay in cozy cottages or in the Croquet Lodge; either way, they'll have comfortable furnishings and serene

Author Picks

CHAPTER FAVORITES

My mind and taste buds are transported to Tuscany at **Tra Vigne**, where a patio table under the olive trees is one of autumn's loveliest settings. *page 61*

I love making my way through the barrel cellars at **Prager Winery and Port Works** because it's one of those intimate, laidback experiences that are hard to come by in the upper Napa Valley. *page 56*

For ultimate relaxation, I head to the multiple pools at the **Calistoga Spa Hot Springs**, one of the few places where you can take a hot tub under the stars. *page 70*

I can't quite bring myself to actually buy those checked chef's pants, but there are plenty of other choices that intrigue me at the shop at the Culinary Institute of America's **Campus Store and Marketplace**. *page 64*

views of the grounds. ~ 900 Meadowood Lane; 707-963-3646, 800-458-8080, fax 707-963-3532; www.meadowood.com, e-mail reservations@meadowood.com. ULTRA-DELUXE.

Set in the Mayacamas Mountains, just 12 minutes from Napa's wineries and restaurants, the contemporary-style **Hilltop House** is an excellent place to spot deer, raccoons, rabbits, hawks and hummingbirds while enjoying the amenities of a 135-acre retreat. The four rooms are furnished with antiques, brass beds and down comforters, and offer panoramic mountain views. There's a large deck, a garden, a hot tub and a network of hiking trails. A full breakfast is included. ~ 9550 St. Helena Road; 707-944-0880, fax 707-571-0263 (call first). DELUXE TO ULTRA-DELUXE.

DINING

Tra Vigne can claim the most dramatic interior in the Wine Country. Soaring ceilings, unusual lighting, and festive displays of peppers and garlic make the setting as exciting as the menu. The theme here is regional Italian: chewy breads, bold pizzas, hearty salads, rabbit, chicken and grilled seafood dishes, and a first-rate wine list. ~ 1050 Charter Oak Avenue; 707-963-4444, fax 707-963-1233. MODERATE TO DELUXE.

Within the Tra Vigne complex, **Cantinetta** is an upscale Italian deli with a wood-paneled bar serving espresso, campari and wines by the glass. In addition to panini (Italian for sandwich), focaccia and the like, you'll find a changing array of picnic and heat-at-home items. ~ 1050 Charter Oak Avenue; 707-963-8888, fax 707-963-1233. BUDGET.

Gail's Café is an old-fashioned ice cream parlor and café, nostalgic to the max. A piano player greets you as you walk in the door, an incredible collection of antique signs decorates the walls, and the soda fountain dates from the 1900s. Besides shakes, sundaes and floats, Gail's serves espresso and cappuccino, burgers, salads and sandwiches. Breakfast and lunch served in winter; dinner served April through October. ~ 1347 Main Street; 707-963-3332, fax 707-963-1432; www.napavalley.com/gails, e-mail gailscafe@saber.net. BUDGET.

HIDDEN ►   **Tomatina** is a terrific place to bring the family. It's kid-friendly as well as budget-friendly, with thin-crust pizzas, pasta, salads and other easy-to-eat fare in an upbeat setting. Inexpensive wines are sold by the glass. ~ 1016 Main Street; 707-967-9999, fax 707-967-0495. BUDGET TO MODERATE.

Taylor's Refresher has been turning out burgers and dogs since 1949. Now you can get homemade tacos and burritos, and see how they taste with chocolate malts. Take your order to one of the nearby picnic tables. ~ 933 Main Street; 707-963-3486. BUDGET.

HIDDEN ►   It's obvious from the schedule that **Spring Street** is a restaurant for local folks rather than out-of-towners: It's open for lunch and dinner daily, brunch on Saturday and Sunday. The sandwiches include "crunchy tuna" (with chutney and almonds) and "Spanish Delight" (broiled cheese with avocado and green chiles). There are also specials like chile relleno casserole and corn chowder, plus an array of salads and wines. No dinner on Monday. ~ 1245 Spring Street; 707-963-5578. MODERATE.

For southern French and northern Italian–style cooking with a Pacific Rim influence, head to **Terra Restaurant**. You might be treated to appetizers such as fried rock shrimp, crab cabbage egg rolls, and *tataki* of tuna on the seasonally changing menu. Entrées feature exotic preparations of seafood, beef and squab. By way of ambience there are stone walls, terra-cotta features, and a wooden trim that lends an Asian overtone to this comfortable, Tuscan farmhouse–style dining room. Dinner only. Closed Tuesday. ~ 1345 Railroad Avenue; 707-963-8931. DELUXE.

One of the Napa Valley's best settings can be found tucked away behind the Freemark Abbey winery. **Brava Terrace** brings a bit of southern France to the valley with an open, airy dining room enlivened with contemporary art and a cozy fireplace. Grilled fish, cassoulet and produce still dewy from the garden star on a first-rate menu. ~ 3010 St. Helena Highway North; 707-963-9300, fax 707-963-9581. MODERATE TO DELUXE.

The Wine Spectator Greystone Restaurant at the Culinary Institute of America—just call it Greystone—is a cavernous restaurant in an 1889 National Historic Landmark in north St. Helena. The complex is a top-notch cooking school, but not to worry—the chefs are for real. The menu is devoted to Mediterranean cuisines, particularly tapas, mezze and antipasti from Spain, Italy, Turkey, North Africa and the Middle East. It's great fun to mix and match small dishes, with different wines to accompany each course. Flanked by century-old stone walls, the restaurant is large enough to have cooking, baking and grilling stations in full view, which provide a terrific distraction for fidgety kids. ~ 2555 St. Helena Highway; 707-967-1010, fax 707-967-2376; www.ciachef.edu/greyston/ghl3.html, e-mail wsgr@culinary.edu. MODERATE.

SHOPPING

For people living in northern Napa Valley, going on a shopping spree means heading for either St. Helena or Calistoga. Both towns combine local businesses with general merchandise stores. **Main Street**, St. Helena, is a falsefront boulevard lined with a hardware store, stationery shop, newspaper office, and grocery. Of interest to visitors are the boutiques, bookstore, jewelers and wine shop.

One of the most elegant stores in St. Helena is **Erika Hills**, an antique shop housed in a former church, where you can find a wide range of mostly imported treasures, from Limoges plates and Venetian glass to farmhouse furnishings. ~ 115 Main Street; 707-963-0919.

Feel guilty about leaving Junior at home? The shop for newborns to first-graders is **Sweet Pea**, which has some offbeat clothing you're unlikely to find at the mall. ~ 1309 Main Street; 707-963-1201.

Feel guilty about leaving Fido at home? You can assuage that feeling with a gift from **Fideaux**, a precious shop devoted to products and accessories for the upscale dog and cat. ~ 1312 Main Street; 707-967-9935.

If you want to learn more about wine, you can find plenty of help at **Main Street Books**, which has a decent selection of California travel books as well as many tomes on wine. Closed Sunday. ~ 1315 Main Street; 707-963-1338.

◆◆◆

MINDING YOUR BEESWAX

Outside town, **Hurd Beeswax Candles** has, since 1954, elevated candle-making to the level of art. The waxworks resemble statues rather than tapers; fashioned on the premises, they are formed into a myriad intricate shapes (some are also handpainted). In addition to a showroom, the adjacent candle factory provides an opportunity to watch wax being dipped, cut and rolled. There's also a demonstration beehive. ~ 3020 North St. Helena Highway; 707-963-7211, 800-977-7211, fax 707-963-4358.

Art on Main features original works by Northern California artists as well as prints, posters and ceramics. ~ 1359 Main Street; 707-963-3350.

You can decorate your home with all manner of Wine Country accessories from **Vanderbilt and Company,** a chic house-and-garden store with disposable supplies for a gourmet picnic as well as Italian handblown wine glasses, majolica pottery and other fine goods. ~ 1429 Main Street; 707-963-1010.

On the north side of town, you can find everything for the home cook (or the professional one) at the **Campus Store and Marketplace,** on the ground floor of the Culinary Institute of America at Greystone. ~ 2555 Main Street; 707-967-2311.

The **Napa Valley Olive Oil Manufacturing Co.** is more than a gourmet shopping spot: it's a sightseeing adventure as well. Housed in a former oil manufacturing plant, it contains the original press and crusher. Railroad tracks run along the cement floor, and posters of old Italia cover the walls. Today this tiny factory sells its own olive oil, along with delicious cheeses, salami, pasta and condiments. ~ 835 Charter Oak Avenue; phone/fax 707-963-4173.

Until 1960, Bothe-Napa Valley State Park was a private resort called Paradise Park, owned by Reinhold Bothe.

An extensive wine department, gourmet-to-go, exquisite produce, and every type of trendy condiment imaginable fills the cavernous **Dean & Deluca** store, a West Coast offshoot of the original in New York. ~ 607 Route 29; 707-967-9980.

At **Premium Outlets of St. Helena** you will find a shopping mall with clothing stores and an assortment of other shops. ~ 3111 North St. Helena Highway.

NIGHTLIFE   If they could roll up the sidewalks in St. Helena after dark, no doubt they would. There are few things to do at night in this town other than enjoy a fabulous meal.

The **1351 Lounge** resides in the old Cellar bar downtown, where old marble and other refined touches include burnished metal-topped tables and a green velvet curtain covering one wall. ~ 1351 Main Street; 707-963-1969.

PARKS   **BOTHE–NAPA VALLEY STATE PARK** 🚶🐴🛶 Rising from the valley floor to about 2000 feet elevation, this outstanding park is fully developed along one side, wild and rugged on the other. For those seeking to escape the Wine Country crowds, there are ten miles of hiking trails leading along steep hillsides through redwood groves. More than 100 bird species inhabit the area, including hawks, quail and six types of woodpecker. There are also coyotes, bobcats, deer and fox here. For guided horseback riding, call 707-996-8566. The park's developed area features spacious picnic groves, campgrounds, a swimming pool open in the summer, restrooms and showers (fee). Day-use fee, $5. ~ On Route 29 about five miles north of St. Helena; 707-942-4575, fax 707-942-9560; www.napanet.net/~bothe, e-mail bothe@napanet.net.

▲ There are 40 tent/RV sites and 9 walk-in sites; $15 per night, $20 on weekends. Reservations recommended; call 800-444-7275.

▼▼▼▼▼▼▼▼▼▼
Calistoga

Founded in 1859, Calistoga owes its origin and name to Sam Brannan. Brannan was the shrewd Mormon journalist and entrepreneur who first alerted San Francisco to the gold discovery. A decade later he saw liquid gold in Napa Valley's mineral springs and geysers. Determined to create a California version of New York's famous Saratoga spa, he named the region Calistoga. Indeed, its hot springs and underwater reservoirs were perfectly suited to a health resort.

Today Brannan's idea is carried on by numerous spas and health resorts. After imbibing at vineyards throughout the valley, visitors arrive in Calistoga to luxuriate in the region's mineral waters. I highly recommend that you sign up for "the works" at one of the local spas. You'll be submerged in a mud bath, led into a whirlpool bath then a steam room, wrapped head to toe in a blanket, and finally given a massage. By the end of the treatment, your mind will reside somewhere in the ozone and your body will be completely loose. (For a rundown on rubdowns, please see the "The Spas of Calistoga.")

The same geological factors that created the hot springs and other unusual features in this part of the Napa Valley also influence the landscape in another way.

In the surrounding countryside are some of the top vineyards in the state. The volcanic soil and climate are different here than in the lower portions of the Napa Valley, meaning the wines are unique. Days tend to be hotter and nights, cooler than elsewhere, thanks to the inland setting sheltered from most of the cold Pacific winds. And Calistoga is much farther from the tempering atmosphere of the San Francisco Bay that infiltrates the landscape around, say, Yountville. Two of the state's leading producers of sparkling wine are located here. For an overview, sign up for a hot-air balloon ride on a calm, fog-free morning. Almost all the points of interest around here relate, in some way, to towering Mount Helena.

Though it's been tamed considerably, **downtown** Calistoga still looks like a backdrop for a movie about the Wild West. Falsefront buildings dominate the streetscape on the main drag, interspersed with century-old brick buildings. The town's proximity to Mount St. Helena has given rise to a booming industry based on hot springs and mud baths and the attendant spa treatments.

SIGHTS

Other points of interest are the **Sharpsteen Museum** and adjacent **Sam Brannan Cottage**. Dedicated to Calistoga's original settlers, the museum displays tools from a blacksmith's shop and an early California kitchen. Sam Brannan's cottage is furnished in period fashion with Victorian furniture and a glorious old piano. The highlight of the entire display, however, is an elaborate diorama portraying Brannan's health resort in miniature. Representing Calistoga circa 1865, it contains everything from railway station to racetrack, hotel to distillery. ~ 1311 Washington Street; 707-942-5911, fax 707-942-6325; www.napanet.net/vi/sharpsteen.

One of the first wineries that you'll encounter as you enter Calistoga makes some of the state's most cherished sparkling wines. When Robert Louis Stevenson visited the **Schramsberg Vineyards**, he tasted 18 different wines. Today you'll have to settle for a tour (by appointment) of this historic facility. The road up to Schramsberg burrows through a dense forest before arriving at the original owner's home. The winery has added several buildings since Stevenson's day and now specializes in sparkling wine, but the old tunnels and cellars remain. Tasting fee. ~ Schramsberg Road; 707-942-2414, fax 707-942-5943; www.schrams berg.com, e-mail schramsberg@aol.com.

On the east side of the valley is an unusual small winery run by physician Ralph Wermuth. (When people ask him why he gave up medicine, he likes to tell them, "The medicine didn't work.") Not for the **Wermuth Winery** the endless chasing of this season's hottest new varietals. Instead, sample the colombard, gamay and other less-familiar wines. And get Ralph to sign your bottle. ~ 3942 Silverado Trail; 707-942-5924.

At **Clos Pegase** the tasting room is a post-modern affair designed by architect Michael Graves that features Honduran mahogany flourishes and antique glass decorations. There's a sculpture garden and fine works of art shown throughout the premises. A glass wall exposes the upright tank room where vintners make cabernet sauvignon, merlot and chardonnay. Tasting fee. ~ 1060 Dunaweal Lane; 707-942-4981, fax 707-942-4993; www.clos pegase.com, e-mail cp@clospegase.com.

Of the Napa Valley's most intriguing wineries is 160-acre **Château Montelena**. Tours by appointment lead to a castle that overlooks a lake landscaped in classic Chinese style. Oh, by the way, you'll also find a tasting room known for its chardonnays and cabernets. Tasting fee. ~ 1429 Tubbs Lane; 707-942-5105, fax 707-942-4221; www.montelena.com.

HIDDEN ►   **Robert Pecota Winery** is a family-run operation in what is probably Napa's northernmost wine-growing parcel, 40 acres highly suited to red wines. Pecota and two of his daughters are in charge, turning out 21,000 cases a year of cabernet sauvignon,

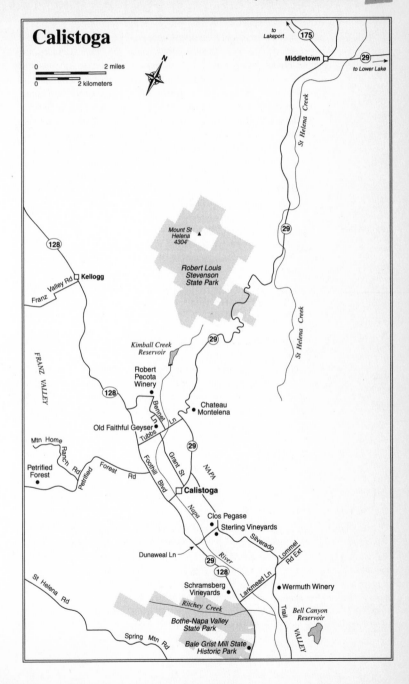

Calistoga

0 — 2 miles
0 — 2 kilometers

N

to Lakeport

175

Middletown

29

to Lower Lake

St Helena Creek

29

128

Kellogg

Franz Valley Rd

Franz

Mount St Helena 4304'

Robert Louis Stevenson State Park

St Helena Creek

29

FRANZ VALLEY

Kimball Creek Reservoir

Robert Pecota Winery

128

Bennett Ln

Chateau Montelena

Old Faithful Geyser

Tubbs Ln

Foothill Blvd

Grant St

NAPA

29

Mtn Home

Petrified Forest Rd

Ranch Rd

Petrified Forest

□ **Calistoga**

Napa

Clos Pegase

Sterling Vineyards

Silverado

Lommel Rd Ext

Dunaweal Ln

29

128

River

Larkmead Ln

St Helena Rd

Schramsberg Vineyards

● Wermuth Winery

Trail

Bell Canyon Reservoir

Ritchey Creek

Bothe-Napa Valley State Park

VALLEY

Spring Mtn Rd

Bale Grist Mill State Historic Park

merlot, cabernet franc and petite verdot—premium Bordeaux varietals. Tours by appointment only. ~ 3299 Bennett Lane; 707-942-6625, fax 707-942-6671; www.robertpecotawinery.com, e-mail rpecota@aol.com.

About three and a half million years ago, when nearby Mount St. Helena was an active volcano, the magma itself exploded. Evidently, eruptions from this firepit leveled an entire redwood grove, which transformed over the ages into a **Petrified Forest**. Located six miles up the mountain southwest of Calistoga, this eerie spot contains a succession of fallen giants. Redwoods measuring over 100 feet long and 8 feet in diameter lie along the forest floors, perfectly preserved in stone. Unfortunately, the place has the trappings of a tourist trap. Admission. ~ 4100 Petrified Forest Road; 707-942-6667, fax 707-942-0815.

LODGING

This unpretentious town has relatively few stuffy digs, at least compared to the rest of the Napa Valley. It's home to many modest lodgings that offer mineral baths as well as numerous bed and breakfasts.

If a room proves hard to reserve, or you need assistance with other bookings, several agencies offer reservation services. These can prove very convenient during peak tourist periods, or if you want to reduce long-distance calls. If interested, contact **Accommodations Referral**. Closed Saturday and Sunday. ~ 1407 Main P8466, fax 707-963-9595.

The **Calistoga Inn & Brewery** has reasonably priced rooms that include a continental breakfast. This 18-room hostelry sits atop a restaurant and pub that serve their own Napa Valley Brewing Company beer. The European-style accommodations are small but tidy, carpeted wall-to-wall, and plainly decorated. The furniture is nicked and baths are shared, but each room does have its own sink. ~ 1250 Lincoln Avenue; 707-942-4101, fax

THAR SHE BLOWS!

It's corny but decidedly wonderful to visit the **Old Faithful Geyser** about two miles northwest of town. It's only a pale resemblance to the huge one in Wyoming by the same name, but this version spews a satisfying jet stream of boiling water as high as 60 feet in the air. The show recurs about every 40 minutes, depending on varying climatic conditions. It's a vivid reminder of the power of nearby Mount St. Helena. Admission. ~ 1299 Tubbs Lane, Calistoga; 707-942-6463, fax 707-942-6898; www.old faithfulgeyser.com, e-mail geyser@ap.net.

707-942-4914; www.napabeer.com, e-mail calistoga@napabeer. com. BUDGET TO MODERATE.

Several Calistoga spas also provide overnight accommodations. **Indian Springs Hotel Resort,** located on the same grounds as the town's original resort, offers bungalow-style cottages (actually duplexes) with kitchenettes. Guests are welcome to use the spa's 98° mineral pool (it's 92° in the summer), tennis courts, shuffleboard, croquet, hammocks and bicycles. Indian Springs also features mud baths, steam baths, massages and facials, making it an excellent resting place for the health-minded. ~ 1712 Lincoln Avenue; 707-942-4913, fax 707-942-4919; www.indiansprings calistoga.com. ULTRA-DELUXE.

Built in 1914, the renovated **Mount View Hotel** has the aura and feel of a classic small-town hotel. It's a 29-room affair with a dining room and lounge downstairs and Victorian flourishes throughout. The lobby is spacious and elegant, featuring a fireplace and contemporary artwork. Guest rooms are nicely decorated with a mix of Victorian and modern touches. In addition, there are three cottages, each with a private hot tub. Guests are free to use the hotel's pool and spa. ~ 1457 Lincoln Avenue; 707-942-6877, 800-772-8838, fax 707-942-6904. DELUXE TO ULTRA-DELUXE.

Cosseted by elm trees, the 16 bungalows at the **Cottage Grove Inn** are the most chic in Calistoga, with luxurious touches like front porches, two-person hot tubs, mini-refrigerators, CD players and VCRs as well as skylights. Furnishings are plush and thoughtfully arranged. Continental breakfast is included. ~ 1711 Lincoln Avenue; 707-942-8400, 800-799-2284, fax 707-942-2653; www. cottagegrove.com. ULTRA-DELUXE.

Calistoga Spa Hot Springs is a jewel disguised as a plain old motel. The 57 rooms are contemporary and quite attractive, some with well-equipped kitchenettes. (Try to book a corner room on the upper level if you like a little extra space.) The pull here is a multitude of pools of varying sizes and temperatures. ~ 1006 Washington Street; 707-942-6269, fax 707-942-4214. BUDGET TO MODERATE.

Even in the over-touristed Napa Valley, there's a way to leave the crowds behind—head for the hills. Travel several miles upslope from Calistoga and you'll find **Mountain Home Ranch**. Once there, you may never make it back to the wineries. This is a fully equipped resort with a dining room, swimming pools, picnic areas, a tennis court and a fishing lake. It rests on 300 acres threaded with hiking trails. Accommodations range from rustic cabins, which are self-maintained and require bedding and towels, to all-weather cabins to rooms in the main lodge. Rates include a buffet breakfast. ~ 3400 Mountain Home Ranch Road; 707-

Text continued on page 72.

The Spas of Calistoga

The town of Calistoga is ground zero for the warm mineral-bath industry in California. A mixture of ash from nearby Mount Helena and natural water bubbling up hot from beneath the earth make for some very relaxing mud baths. Sitting in a tub of piping hot lava with a whiff of sulfur in the air may sound odd to the uninitiated, but to the converted, there's nothing better in terms of relaxation and detoxification. The spas in this small town in northern Napa Valley have more than mud baths. They offer just about every kind of body treatment known to man.

Calistoga Spa Hot Springs is a dream for water babies. Four outdoor pools of varying sizes and temperatures share a spacious courtyard to one side of the treatment rooms. All are filled with naturally heated mineral water, from the 18-inch deep wading pool to the L-shaped swimming pool to the large octagonal hot tub shaded by a pretty gazebo roof. If you're booking a treatment, you can use the pools for only $5 extra. Other day visitors are welcome for a modest fee on weekdays (a little more on weekends); series tickets are also sold, one of the better deals in spa land. House specialties are the mud and mineral baths, available in combination with a steam bath and blanket wrap and/or massage. The complex is built on the site of Dr. Aalder's Hot Mud Baths, dating from the 1920s and pictured in photographs that line the hallway to the spa section. Today the place has a vaguely art deco ambience that perfectly suits its off-the-main-drag location. This is one of the few spots where night bathing is offered. ~ 1006 Washington Street; 707-942-6269; www.calistogaspa.com.

Calistoga Village Inn and Spa is another possibility. They offer the unique powdered mustard bath as well as the more standard steam baths, blanket wraps, and facials. ~ 1880 Lincoln Avenue; 707-942-0991, fax 707-942-5306; www.greatspa.com, e-mail greatspa@napanet.net.

Housed in a mid-19th-century bank building, the **Lincoln Avenue Spa** has a certain panache thanks to details such as beautiful woodwork and green tile in the steam room. Which is pretty cool, too, if you're used to either the old-fashioned steam tubs (with doors) or even group steam rooms. Here the contraption looks very much like one of those sunning booths. There are several nice touches here such as mint, green tea, sea mud and herbal wraps and a number of facial treatments. Massages run a little high; the best bargain is the 90-minute deluxe special. ~ 1339 Lincoln Avenue; 707-942-5296.

The Mount View Spa has just room for one love seat in the pretty little waiting room, where sponged blush walls create the illusion of a glow (watch out for those prices). Located in the back of the Mount View Hotel, between the lobby and the pool area, the European-style spa is the most elegant in town, perhaps because it has no traditional mud baths. ~ 1457 Lincoln Avenue; 707-942-5789, 800-772-8838.

Dr. Wilkinson's Hot Springs is the granddaddy of Calistoga mud bathing. Facilities here are not glamorous—except for the nearby salon adjunct—but travelers familiar with some of the no-frills European-style spas will feel at home. ~ 1507 Lincoln Avenue; 707-942-4102.

Nance's Hot Springs dates back to 1923 but looks fresh and contemporary. Rows of camp-style beds are separated by curtains for privacy, perfect for napping after an old-fashioned mud bath, a mineral whirlpool bath and mineral steam, or perhaps before a half-hour or full-hour massage. The weekday deals here are outstanding, with a tub and a half-hour massage going for only $31. The motel is likewise reasonable, with doubles beginning at $55 weeknights and $75 weekends for a room with HBO, a kitchenette and use of the indoor hot mineral pool. There are sex-separated facilities for bathing. ~ 1614 Lincoln Avenue; 707-942-6211.

Indian Springs looks like a motor court you might have found in the desert in the 1950s—a wonderful mix of white, blue and red-orange that sets it apart from every other place in town. Neat bungalows march around the horseshoe driveway, evoking road trips from childhood. But this is a savvy place with some truly cool touches such as old-fashioned bathing suits displayed in Plexiglas frames and white beadboard walls in the treatment rooms. The mud at Indian Springs is not mixed, so it's startlingly black. The property, which has been here since the 1860s, is situated on three thermal geysers on 16 acres of ancient volcanic ash and has been welcoming guests to this very bathhouse since 1913. Along with the mud and mineral baths, Indian Springs offers upscale treatments such as facials, body polishes, nail care and Swedish massage, most available à la carte or as part of a package. The fantastic raised pool, estimated to be two times Olympic size, is open only to spa and bungalow guests. ~ 1712 Lincoln Avenue; 707-942-4919.

942-6616, fax 707-942-9091; www.mtnhomeranch.com, e-mail info@mtnhomeranch.com. BUDGET TO DELUXE.

Meadowlark Country House is a beautiful 19th-century home with 20 acres of wooded grounds. Out beyond the mineral pool, hot tub and sauna (enclosed, clothing optional) you can watch horses being trained for jumping events. Each of the seven rooms features contemporary or English country antique furniture, comforters and a view of forest or meadow. A generous breakfast is served each morning and you will find the serene veranda a great place to catch up on your reading. ~ 601–605 Petrified Forest Road; 707-942-5651, 800-942-5651, fax 707-942-5023; www.meadowlarkinn.com. DELUXE TO ULTRA-DELUXE.

It may not be for everyone, but **Harbin Hot Springs** is a popular place, as witnessed by the weekend crowds. Seven natural springs feed the warm, hot and cold mineral-water pools of this New Age retreat center. You may stay in a dormitory, a retreat room, an ultra-deluxe cabin, or camp out and relax and soak in the clothing-optional pools, hike on trails through the hills, and enjoy quiet conversation with the other guests. There's a café serving breakfast and dinner or you can bring your own vegetarian food to cook in the communal kitchen. Also on the vast property are a health food store and bookstore. ~ Harbin Springs Road, Middletown; 707-987-2477, fax 707-987-0616; www. harbin.org. MODERATE TO ULTRA-DELUXE.

DINING

For its size, Calistoga has the most varied restaurant scene of any town in the Napa Valley. You'll find a wide range of moderately priced places to dine, as well as a couple of budget choices.

Named for the official state dog of Louisiana, **Catahoula Restaurant and Saloon** offers a blend of the Gulf Coast with the cream of California. Along with andouille sausage pizza pie, arugula salad with teleme, and seafood file gumbo are plenty of unabashedly Cajun-inspired items such as Southern fried rabbit with dirty rice and collard greens and pork porterhouse steak with red-eye gravy (a Southern staple) and "soft sexy grits." Diners are seated in a spacious room decorated with portraits of various Catahoulas; a separate bar serves as a holding pen for hungry patrons. ~ 1457 Lincoln Avenue; 707-942-2275, fax 707-942-5338. MODERATE.

If you want a place where you will feel instantly at ease, slide into a booth in the bar at **Brannan's Grill**. In a great big dining room softened by mica light shades and skylights, American regional cuisine is served up in hearty and handsome portions. The best item on the menu is the quail salad appetizer but heavier fare—Yankee pot roast, Fisherman's Wharf cioppino, fried oyster po'boy sandwich and half-pound filet with "expensive" mushrooms—is more the norm. ~ 1374 Lincoln Street; 707-942-2233, fax 707-942-2299. MODERATE TO DELUXE.

Wappo Bar Bistro dishes up dazzling food that spans the globe with Asian noodles with shiitake mushrooms, Thai shrimp curry, Ecuadorean braised pork, osso bucco, chiles rellenos with walnut pomegranate sauce, and Turkish mezze (that hard-to-find treasure that in this case includes herb and cheese-stuffed eggplant sandwich, white bean salad, carrots, golden beets, shaved fennel, cracked green olives, hummus, yogurt sauce and, believe it or not, more). Closed Tuesday. ~ 1226 South Washington Street; 707-942-4712, fax 707-942-4741. MODERATE.

The **All Seasons Café** is a Wine Country classic—a little bit bistro, a lot California. Marble tables set on a black-and-white checkerboard floor seem small once you pile them up with organic greens, local game birds, wild mushrooms and various pastas and imaginative main courses. The wine list, like the adjacent wine shop, is chock-full of regional. No lunch on Wednesday. ~ 1400 Lincoln Avenue; 707-942-9111, fax 707-942-9420. MODERATE.

The setting is informal and the menu Italian: informal as in sawdust floor and exposed-rafter ceiling; Italian as in pasta and pizza. At **Bosko's**, they don't even bother to change the menu from lunch to dinner. Day or night, you'll find fresh pasta dishes like fettuccine with scallops and mushrooms, linguini with shrimp and clams, and spaghetti with meatballs. Or you can have a meatball, sausage, or Italian ham sandwich. The wine list is actually longer than the menu, but the meals they offer are good and filling. ~ 1364 Lincoln Avenue; 707-942-9088, fax 707-942-9661; www.napavalley.com/restaurants/bosko. BUDGET TO MODERATE.

Stop by the **Smokehouse Cafe** in the historic California Depot for down-home Southern-style country cooking. The atmosphere is funky and lots of fun, with white oak floors, wooden tables, and an eclectic collection of cooking utensils hanging on the walls. Barbecue is what's happening here, and the place smokes all its own meats and makes its own sausages. The juniper-smoked salmon is a special treat. Closed Tuesday in January and

INTO THE WOODS

For an easy walk, half of which is wheelchair-accessible, examine the **Petrified Forest Loop** inside the only petrified redwood forest in the world. The original trail is half-a-mile long; a newer half-mile trail is open for tours on Sunday afternoon or by appointment. Admission. ~ 4100 Petrified Forest Road, Calistoga; 707-942-6667.

February. ~ 1458 Lincoln Avenue; 707-942-6060, fax 707-963-2123. MODERATE.

HIDDEN ►   **Triple S Ranch** has been pleasing local palates since the 1960s. Head north of Calistoga into the Sonoma Mountains to find this unique eatery in an early 1900s barn. It's one of those timeless places that can't be categorized. Animal trophies, cookie jars, tin trays, bottles and old tools decorate the walls. Red-and-white checked tablecloths adorn tables laden with huge portions of fried chicken, baked ham, steak, lobster and other hearty fare. The onion rings are legendary. Meals include a relish plate, soup or salad, drink and dessert. After dinner, you can play a game of bocce ball or horseshoes. Closed Monday. ~ 4600 Mt. Home Ranch Road, four miles north of Calistoga; 707-942-6730, fax 707-942-4250. MODERATE TO DELUXE.

SHOPPING   All the stores in Calistoga are lined up along Lincoln Street. It's a mixed bag that includes some women's and children's clothing boutiques, a bookstore and two top-notch places to buy regional and international wines.

The historic **Calistoga Depot** has been converted to a mall. Within this former railway station are assorted stores, including the **Calistoga Wine Stop** (707-942-5556, 800-648-4521), housed in an antique railroad car. ~ 1458 Lincoln Avenue.

Books on wine and regional attractions are among the specialties at the **Calistoga Bookstore**, but you can also find the latest novels and some New Age titles. ~ 1343 Lincoln Avenue; 707-942-4123.

All kinds of handcrafted jewelry, in all sorts of price ranges, is the stock in trade at **The Artful Eye**. ~ 1333 Lincoln Avenue; 707-942-4743.

NIGHTLIFE   The northern end of the Napa Valley is quite a bit less chi-chi than the southern part. What nightlife there is tends to be more down-home—sometimes actually loud.

The **Mount View Hotel** has an old-time saloon. With a blue wood ceiling, green beams, wooden booths, and hardwood floors, this bar is certainly original. ~ 1457 Lincoln Avenue; 707-942-6877, 800-772-8838.

Jazz, blues and country-and-western bands rock the Calistoga Depot's **Smokehouse Cafe** on Friday, Saturday and Sunday evenings. ~ 1458 Lincoln Avenue; 707-942-6060.

PARKS   **ROBERT LOUIS STEVENSON STATE PARK** 𝄐 On the slopes of Mount St. Helena northeast of Calistoga, this sprawling parcel inspired many scenes in Stevenson's *The Silverado Squatters*. This is where the author and his bride spent their honeymoon in

1880, in an abandoned bunkhouse that belonged to the Silverado Mine. Few of the park's 3300 acres are developed, except for a couple of lengthy hiking trails. It's worth the climb to one of two summits for one of the best vantage points in the Wine Country. ~ Route 29; 707-942-4575.

CALISTOGA RANCH CLUB 🏃 🚲 🏊 ⛵ This privately owned facility spreads across 167 acres in Napa Valley's eastern hills. Home to recreational vehicles as well as tent campers, it features hiking trails, picnic areas, a fishing lake (bass and bluegill await), an Olympic-sized swimming pool, restrooms, a laundry and a snack bar. There are also rustic cabins and self-contained Airstream trailers to rent. ~ Located at 580 Lommel Road, the campground lies off Silverado Trail about four and a half miles from town; 707-942-6565, 800-847-6272, fax 707-942-6902.

▲ There are 144 tent/RV sites; $20 for two people per night for tent sites, $27 for full RV hookups. Cabins cost $54.15 per night; trailers cost $93.35.

Outdoor Adventures

RIDING STABLES

Napa Valley Trail Rides offers excursions in the Bothe–Napa Valley State Park between St. Helena and Calistoga. These guided trail rides last about an hour and a half and follow a path through the redwoods beside a spring-fed stream. Most of the trail is flat, with a couple of slight climbs. Riders of all levels are welcome. ~ 707-996-8566; www.winecountrytrailrides.com.

GOLF

There's not much in the way of golf courses in this neck of the woods.

Duffers will have to settle for the nine holes at the **Mount St. Helena Golf Course**. It's a par-34 public course with a snack bar and golf shop. The 2670-yard course is flat and easy to walk; fairways are narrow and lined with trees; only one hole has water. ~ Napa County Fairground, Calistoga; 707-942-9966.

BIKING

The key to happy pedaling in the Napa Valley is to keep away from Route 29. There are side roads that go virtually straight up hillsides as well as flat places on lightly trafficked roads. A couple of bike shops can give you their own suggestions; rentals run usually about $7 an hour or $25 for the whole day.

A bike trail runs along the Silverado Trail from Soscol Avenue all the way to Calistoga, but the only safe riding is north of Trancas Street.

Bike Rentals **St. Helena Cyclery** rents 24-speed hybrid bikes, ideal for comfortable rides, by the hour or by the day. The helpful staff can tailor outings to suit your needs, from winery tours to short, flat rides in a nearby residential area. ~ 1156 Main Street, St. Helena; 707-963-7736.

Getaway Adventures has a shop in downtown Calistoga; they offer guided bike tours throughout the Wine Country. Closed Wednesday. ~ 1117 Lincoln Avenue, Calistoga; 707-942-0332, 800-499-2453; www.getawayadventures.com.

HIKING

It's worth doing some strenuous hiking to get the most stunning Wine Country views, but there are a number of moderate trails as well. Poison oak is a consideration almost everywhere in warm weather, as are ticks, so dress accordingly. All distances listed for hiking trails are one way unless otherwise noted.

The best hiking destination in the St. Helena vicinity is Bothe–Napa Valley State Park. The moderate **History Trail** (1.2 miles) begins at the picnic area and passes the Pioneer Cemetery, where members of the Tucker family are buried beyond a white picket fence. At a three-way junction, the middle path heads up sharply through a mixed forest of madrone, tan oak, black oak and Douglas fir. From the peak of the trail, you descend to Mill Creek and pass a stone dam built by Edward Bale's daughter. The trail leads to the historic Grist Mill, from which you can return to the start.

The moderately difficult **Coyote Peak Trail** (1.5 miles) heads away from Ritchey Creek, then climbs up to 1170 feet elevation for scenic views of the Napa Valley.

Ritchey Canyon Trail (3.9 miles) starts off easy on an 1860 roadbed that wanders beside a stream and is shadowed by redwoods and firs. Farther along, the trail becomes moderate and leads past a small cascade that flows into a small canyon.

A tranquil hike along Ritchey Creek can also be found on **Redwood Trail** (1 mile). In spring, redwood orchids and trilliums add to the beauty of this tree-shaded pathway.

The **South Fork Trail** (.9 mile) is a moderately strenuous hike that circles the rim of Ritchey Creek and arrives at a vista point overlooking the canyon.

The **Ritchey Canyon Trail** and **Upper Ritchey Canyon Trail** (4.2 miles total) combine for a moderate hike. Ritchey Creek flows beside the early part of the trail, which leads to the old Hitchcock house (home to the family of San Francisco's famed Lily Hitchcock Coit). You can venture off the trail along small paths that lead to the creek; keep an eye out for the crayfish that thrive here. Trees flower in the springtime, making it one of the loveliest times for a visit. The trail leads to the state park boundary, where you will make an about-face for the return trip.

FOUR

Sonoma Valley

Fresh air, good soil, plenty of sunshine, abundant agricultural possibilities, natural hot springs—these things have attracted residents to this valley throughout history, from the Wappo Indians thousands of years ago to transplanted San Franciscans last week. The same conditions that favor the creation of award-winning wines also happen to appeal to human beings. The fact that the city of Sonoma is only 50 miles from the Golden Gate Bridge means this location has the best of at least two worlds.

Human settlement in the Sonoma Valley has been traced back some 12,000 years, following the great migration from Asia across the Bering land bridge and then southward from Alaska. Among them were the Wappo, Mayakmahs and Wintuns in the north portion, closest to the Mayacamas Range; Miwoks along the coast; Pomos in the southern portion of the valley; Patwins in the southeast; and Koskiwok closest to San Francisco Bay. The population of these tribes probably approached 5000. They lived in tule-thatched huts, traded among each other, cleared land to ferret out more game and found restoration in the natural hot springs.

As the missionaries and explorers came north from Mexico in the early 19th century, they found an ideal mission site that they named San Francisco Solano de Sonoma. Founded in 1823, the settlement was the last and northernmost of the 21 California missions. It took the Franciscan fathers a scant few years to convert the locals to their religion, but the harshness of the regime led to unrest. The Mexican government decided to secularize the mission and sent one of their top men, General Mariano G. Vallejo, to carry out the assignment. Vallejo was successful in transforming the settlement into a pueblo; he laid out the central plaza, built barracks and wound up acquiring a great amount of land, money and influence.

By the 1840s, however, an influx of American settlers from the other side of the Sierra Nevada led to the end of Mexican power. By 1848, Mexico ceded all of California to the United States. By 1850, California became a state, with Vallejo elected to the state senate. Despite his efforts to retain Sonoma as the county seat, Santa Rosa won out in 1854 (a result still challenged by some historians). Adding insult to injury, residents of the current county seat removed all the county records in the middle of the night, and many Sonomans today feel that was the end of their town's political clout.

But the valley had other resources. The Franciscan fathers had planted, among other things, mission grapes. The history of premium grapes, however, follows a different plot. The behemoth that is the modern California wine industry has its roots in the Sonoma Valley, but while mission grapes were grown here and elsewhere in the state, the first European varietals were introduced in Sonoma by Count Agoston Haraszthy. He arrived here in 1857, established the Buena Vista Winery and, in the early 1860s, returned to Europe to tour wine-producing regions there. He sent hundreds of premium grape cuttings back to be planted in his extensive acreage on the east side of the valley.

As more Europeans, especially Italians, arrived in Sonoma, they carried on their traditions from the old country. By 1876, Sonoma Valley was turning out more than two million gallons of wine a year. In 1904, Samuele Sebastiani, who had emigrated from Tuscany in 1895 at the age of 21, purchased a small Sonoma wine cellar, married a local girl and dreamed up the concept of shipping volumes of wine in railroad tank cars—an improvement over shipping it in freight cars. Little did he know that he was beginning a dynasty that would lead to the present, when the fourth generation of Sebastianis are likewise occupied in the family business. However, like everywhere else in the Wine Country, phylloxera threatened to completely douse the burgeoning industry in the valley. The coup de grace came in 1919 with Prohibition, although many locals found ways to circumvent the restrictions against producing alcoholic beverages.

It was around this time that Jack London, the most prolific and best-paid author of his era, arrived in the valley and put it on the map in *The Valley of the Moon*, a novel that mythologizes the region. Remains of his fantastic Glen Ellen estate are now part of a California historical park.

By the early 1930s, two men found another agricultural product that would thrive in Sonoma—cheese. Celso Viviani and Tom Vella were among the pioneers; their scions run successful cheese businesses in downtown Sonoma to this day. Along with an increasing number of artisanal bakers, the cheesemakers and winemakers with shops in downtown Sonoma make it easy to assemble a picnic to enjoy on the grounds of the historic plaza, where more than 200 species of trees provide bountiful summertime shade and duck ponds delight generation after generation.

Begin your tour on Route 12/121, the two-lane road that leads into town from San Francisco and other points south. (If by chance you are arriving from Napa or other points east, your first stop should be at the Visitors Bureau, located within the plaza on 1st Street East.)

▼▼▼▼▼▼▼▼▼▼▼▼▼▼▼▼

Southern Sonoma Valley

Even if there were no wine industry, Sonoma would make a worthwhile destination because of its historical significance and small-town charm. The 19th-century structures built by General Vallejo now form part of a multi-part state park, most of which faces the downtown plaza. It was Vallejo who laid

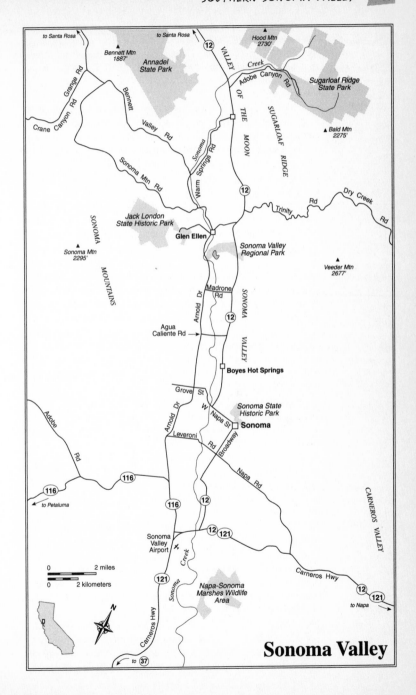

to Santa Rosa
to Santa Rosa

12

Hood Mtn
2730'

Bennett Mtn
1887'

Annadel
State Park

Creek

Adobe Canyon Rd

Sugarloaf Ridge
State Park

Grange Rd

Crane Canyon Rd

Bennett

Valley Rd

VALLEY

OF

THE

MOON

SUGARLOAF

RIDGE

Bald Mtn
2275'

Sonoma Mtn Rd

Sonoma Warm Springs Rd

12

Trinity Rd

Dry Creek Rd

SONOMA

Jack London
State Historic Park

Glen Ellen

Sonoma Valley
Regional Park

Veeder Mtn
2677'

Sonoma Mtn
2295'

MOUNTAINS

Madrone
Rd

Arnold Dr

12

SONOMA

VALLEY

Agua
Caliente Rd

Boyes Hot Springs

Adobe

Rd

Grove St

Arnold Dr

W Napa St

Sonoma State
Historic Park

Sonoma

Leveroni Rd

Broadway

Napa Rd

116

116

116

12

CARNEROS

VALLEY

to Petaluma

Sonoma
Valley
Airport

12

12 121

Sonoma Creek

0   2 miles
0   2 kilometers

Carneros Hwy

Napa-Sonoma
Marshes Wildlife
Area

12

121

to Napa

121

Carneros Hwy

N

to 37

Sonoma Valley

out the eight-acre plaza, still in existence today, that defines the city's core. Many of the adobe and falsefront buildings dating from that era have evolved into shops, restaurants, offices and hotels that help make the town one of northern California's premier tourist destinations.

SIGHTS

If you're not familiar with the Sonoma Valley, make your first stop the **Sonoma Valley Visitors Bureau.** Located just inside the entrance to the Viansa Winery, this small adobe structure is a well-stocked outpost of the main bureau downtown, and can help you select brochures, maps and books as well as souvenirs. ~ 25200 Route 121, Sonoma; 707-935-4747; www.sonomavalley. com, e-mail info@sonomavalley.com.

Approaching the Sonoma Valley from San Francisco via Route 12/121, one of the first wineries you'll come across is the **Viansa Winery & Italian Marketplace.** Occupying the knoll of a small hill with a commanding view north to much of the valley, Viansa belongs to Vicki ("Vi") and Sam ("an-Sa") Sebastiani. The name is familiar to most American wine drinkers because the Sebastianis have been making wine in Sonoma longer than almost anyone. Viansa celebrates the family's Italian heritage with the Tuscan-looking estate, the wines and the foods. The marketplace is the size of a dining hall and is stocked with all kinds of comestibles and condiments (many set out for sampling) as well as wines available for tasting. Free self-guided tours. ~ 25200 Route 121, Sonoma; 707-935-4700, 800-995-4740, fax 707-996-4632; www. viansa.com, e-mail tuscan@viansa.com.

HIDDEN ►

Within plain sight of the winery and, to a lesser extent, the highway, the **Viansa Wetlands** are testimony to Sam Sebastiani's commitment to the environment. The 90-acre preserve attracts all manner of waterfowl–great blue herons, cinnamon teal, widgeons, mallards, pintails, geese, egrets and swans among them— as well as snipe, dowitchers, sparrows, turkey vultures, hawks and eagles, depending on the time of year. Ninety-minute tours (fee) are offered on alternate Saturdays from February through June. Closed July through January. ~ 25200 Route 121, Sonoma; 707-935-4700, 800-995-4740, fax 707-996-4632; www.viansa. com, e-mail tuscan@viansa.com.

Across the highway from Viansa, the tasting room at **Cline Cellars** is housed in an award-winning restored farmhouse dating to the mid-19th century. The winery is known for its Rhone varietals, including mourvedre, viognier and syrah. Picnic tables are set in the shade beside the nearby duck ponds and rose gardens. ~ 24737 Route 12/121, Sonoma; 707-935-4310, 800-546-2070, fax 707-935-4319; www.clinecellars.com, e-mail epcline@sonic.net.

About a mile north, **Gloria Ferrer Champagne Caves** can be glimpsed from the highway. This sparkling wine facility, an American sister to the Ferrer family holdings in Spain, was an instant hit with its first wines. The Ferrers carved caves (typical in their native country) out of the hillside for storing premium sparkling wines. The wines are available for purchase or for tasting (nominal fee) either indoors or on a wide patio with lovely views of the surrounding countryside. Tasting fee. ~ 23555 Route 121, Sonoma; 707-996-7256, fax 707-996-0720; www.gloriaferrer.com.

From these caves, it's about a ten-minute drive to downtown **Sonoma**, a Spanish-style town of 8200 people. And the spot to

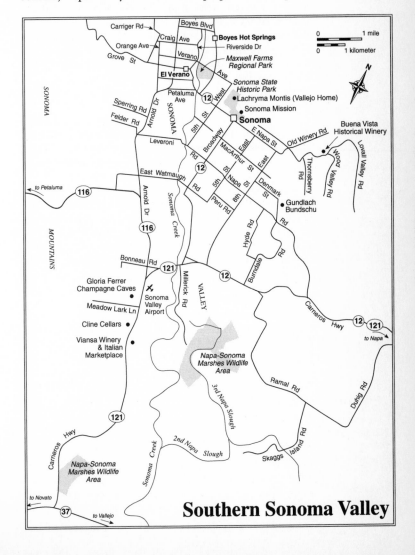

Southern Sonoma Valley

begin this tour-within-a-tour is the **Plaza**, bounded by 1st Street East, 1st Street West, Spain and Napa streets. The center of Sonoma for more than 150 years, this shady park is an excellent picnic place. The largest plaza in the state, it contains a playground, an open-air theater, a duck pond and a rose garden. At the **Sonoma Valley Visitors Bureau** there are maps and brochures of the area. ~ 453 1st Street East, Sonoma; 707-996-1090; www.sonomavalley. com, e-mail info@sonomavalley.com

Spanish adobes, stone buildings, and falsefront stores surround the historic square. Mission San Francisco Solano, or **Sonoma Mission**, stands at the southeast corner. Founded in 1823, this was the last and most northerly of the 21 California missions. With its stark white facade, the low-slung adobe houses a small museum. There are dozens of paintings portraying other California missions; the chapel has also been painted brilliant colors and adorned with carved wood statues. ~ 1st Street East and East Spain Street, Sonoma.

The **Sonoma Barracks**, across the street, were built with Indian labor during the 1830s to house the troops of Mexico's General Mariano Guadalupe Vallejo. A two-story adobe with sweeping balconies, it's now a museum devoted to early California history. ~ 1st Street East and East Spain Street, Sonoma.

Next door, the **Toscano Hotel** is furnished in 19th-century fashion with woodburning stoves, brocade armchairs, and two gambling tables with poker games in progress. Dating to 1852, this wood-frame structure was built as a general store but later used to house Italian workers. ~ 20 East Spain Street, Sonoma.

The only remains of General Vallejo's 1840 house, **La Casa Grande**, is the servant's house with its sagging adobe facade. ~ East Spain Street between 1st Street East and 1st Street West. Together with the mission and other antique buildings encircling the plaza, it is part of **Sonoma State Historic Park**; all these noteworthy places can be toured for a single admission price. ~ Sonoma; 707-938-1519, fax 707-938-1406; www.napanet.net/~sshpa, e-mail sshpa@napanet.net.

TIME OUT FOR TRAINS

Kids who tire of all the dusty history will appreciate a visit to **Train Town**. Miniature steam engines chug around a ten-acre park, passing over trestles, through three tunnels, and arriving at a scale-model Western town. Also visit the petting zoo, antique carousel, and cabooses. Closed Monday through Thursday. Admission. ~ 20264 Broadway, Sonoma; 707-938-3912.

Just north of the plaza stands the **Depot Park Museum**, where the displays commemorate railway history and the Bear Flag uprising when Americans revolted against General Vallejo in 1846. You can also see Sonoma as it was at the turn of the 20th century. Closed Monday and Tuesday. ~ 270 1st Street West, Sonoma; phone/fax 707-938-1762; www.vom.com/~depot, e-mail depot@vom.com.

About a half mile west of the town square, you'll find another antique structure. **Lachryma Montis** was the home General Vallejo built in 1852, after the United States had assumed control of California. Vallejo successfully made the change to American rule, becoming a vintner and writing a five-volume history of early California. Something was lost in the transition, however, and this yellow Victorian house with pretty green shutters fails to evoke images of a Mexican general.

Nevertheless, it's well worth touring. Every room is appointed in 19th-century style, as though Vallejo were expected to arrive any moment. The old pendulum clock still swings and the dinner table is set. Out back, the cookhouse contains personal effects of the Chinese cook and ducks flap around the pond. Part of Sonoma State Historic Park, it also features a cactus garden, a mini-museum and a picnic area. Admission. ~ At the end of 3rd Street West; 707-938-1519, fax 707-938-1406.

While Vallejo was settling into his American-style home, Count Agoston Haraszthy, a Hungarian aristocrat, moved to Sonoma and founded **Buena Vista Historical Winery** in 1857. Popularly known as the "father of the California wine industry," he eventually imported 100,000 vines from Europe. Today the actual winemaking occurs at the vineyard estate in the Carneros area, but you can taste sample vintages in the old stone winery and take a self-guided tour around the grounds. Now a historical monument, the winery also has picnic tables for the crowds that visit. ~ 18000 Old Winery Road, Sonoma; 707-938-1266, 800-678-8504, fax 707-939-0916; www.buenavistawinery.com.

A short drive south and east leads to another of the oldest wineries in California. Five generations have worked at **Gundlach Bundschu** since 1858, though there was a long hiatus from Prohibition until the 1970s. Zinfandel and merlot are some of G-B's best products, aside from a series of hilarious wine posters. Cave tours are offered on weekends in summer; picnic grounds are open year-round. ~ 2000 Denmark Street, Sonoma; 707-938-5277, fax 707-938-9460; www.gunbun.com, e-mail wino@gunbun.com.

LODGING

Small historic hotels can be found on and near the plaza, as can bed-and-breakfast inns. From the Carneros to the northern edge of town is a smattering of very nice motels with comfortable furnishings and quirky charm. While the top places cost well over $200 a night, you can find happiness for half that at some smaller establishments, especially from January through March when demand is down. That's the only time any budget accommodations are available.

Claiming a corner of a busy intersection near the Gloria Ferrer Champagne Caves, the **Vineyard Inn** is a classic Mission Revival–style motor court. It has 24 adjoining bungalows, each with a private entrance off the landscaped courtyard. The suites have a wetbar and refrigerator; some have whirlpool tubs. Extras include a barbecue area and small pool. Continental breakfast is included. ~ 23000 Arnold Drive, Sonoma; 707-938-2350, 800-359-4667, fax 707-938-2353. MODERATE.

A massive remodeling of a historic mansion led to the creation of **MacArthur Place**, which also has accommodations in a series of contemporary cottages and two-story buildings. Some rooms are outfitted with DVD players and whirlpool baths. Decor throughout is chic country, with sophisticated color schemes in shades such as olive and lemon. A full-service spa is located near a swimming pool amid the extensively landscaped grounds. The inn's restaurant specializes in top-quality steak. ~ 29 East MacArthur Street, Sonoma; 707-98-2929, fax 707-933-9833; www.macarthurplace. com. ULTRA-DELUXE.

The **Swiss Hotel**, an adobe building circa 1840, is a five-room hostelry that features rooms with private baths and a refrigerator. One has a four-poster bed and pine furniture, others have a variety of antique and modern pieces. The hotel rests on the town's central plaza and contains a bar and restaurant downstairs. ~ 18 West Spain Street, Sonoma; 707-938-2884, fax 707-938-3298. DELUXE TO ULTRA-DELUXE.

Sonoma's plaza boasts another historic hostelry, the **Sonoma Hotel**, which dates to around 1872 and is a 16-room facility decorated entirely with French Country furnishings. The lobby has a stone fireplace and the adjoining lounge features a hand-carved bar. Combining history with comfort, this vintage hotel is worth a visit. Continental breakfast is included, as is complimentary wine service. ~ 110 West Spain Street, Sonoma; 707-996-2996, 800-468-6016, fax 707-996-7014; www.sonomahotel.com, e-mail sonomahotel@aol.com. DELUXE TO ULTRA-DELUXE.

The 1869 **Thistle Dew Inn**, located a block west of the town plaza, is a dream-come-true for fans of the bungalow style. Arts and Crafts furniture looks like it came with the house; a cottage in the rear adds another three rooms. An outdoor hot tub can be used almost year-round. Full breakfast is included. ~ 171 West Spain Street, Sonoma; 707-938-2909, 800-382-7895, fax 707-996-8413; www.thistledew.com, e-mail tdibandb@aol.com. DELUXE TO ULTRA-DELUXE.

Author Picks

CHAPTER FAVORITES

When I need to relax and renew my appreciation of the valley, I pay a visit to **Jack London State Historic Park**, where a leisurely stroll to the Wolf House ruins is an inspiration. *page 89*

When I've had my fill of Wine Country cuisine and my taste buds crave a change, I head for **La Salette**, where I can savor Portuguese, African and Caribbean dishes found nowhere else in the area. *page 92*

It seems that I'm often wracked by indecision whenever I encounter the selection of fresh-picked tomatoes, luscious strawberries and other summertime treats at the **Sonoma Certified Farmers Market**, my favorite place to shop. *page 88*

With fragrant rose gardens, fabulous views and cozy accommodations, I could get used to the landed gentry life at **Beltane Ranch**, which captures the essence of a Wine Country stay. *page 92*

The **El Dorado Hotel**, also located on the square, is a small gem. Originally an adobe built in 1843, this refurbished stucco establishment offers 26 small- to moderate-size rooms. Appointed with four poster beds, peach down comforters, Mexican tile floors, and California/Spanish–style furniture, each has a private balcony. There's also a heated swimming pool. Continental breakfast is included. ~ 405 1st Street West, Sonoma; 707-996-3030, 800-289-3031, fax 707-996-3148; www.hoteleldorado.com, e-mail info@hoteleldorado.com. DELUXE TO ULTRA-DELUXE.

DINING

There are a dozen places to eat on or just off the Sonoma plaza. A handful of decent establishments are scattered throughout the area, though as yet you won't find any restaurants in the Carneros district in the southern part of the valley.

On the west side of the valley is a local hangout known as **Juanita Juanita**. This is ultra-fresh Mexican food in a place that redefines ambience to mean children's drawings on the wall, plastic cutlery and plates, and dozens of small bottles of all kinds of hot sauces lined up along the counter. The super quesadilla and the daily dinner specials are the best deals, though you really can't go wrong regardless. ~ 19114 Arnold Drive, Sonoma; 707-935-3981. BUDGET.

Sonoma Cheese Factory is *the* spot to stop on the way to the picnic grounds. In addition to a grand assortment of cheeses, it sells wines, sandwiches and gourmet specialty foods. There's also a small outdoor patio for diners. In back, where store gives way to factory, you can watch Jack cheese being made. ~ 2 West Spain Street, Sonoma; 707-996-1931, 800-535-2855; www.sonomajack.com, e-mail retail@sonomajack.com. BUDGET.

In 1911, Agostino Pinelli sacrificed a thousand gallons of his red wine to put out the great Sonoma fire that burned a chunk of downtown property.

Marioni's Restaurant, located right on the plaza, is an attractive split-level dining room with adjoining bar. Decorated with American Indian rugs and paneled in dark wood, it features a steak and seafood menu. Dinner includes steak and lobster, seafood specials, prime rib, and vegetable casserole. At lunch (not served in the winter) there are sandwiches, soups and salads, plus several egg dishes. ~ 8 West Spain Street, Sonoma; 707-996-6866, fax 707-935-6508. MODERATE.

The seasonal menu is short at **Heirloom,** where the focus is on American food, particularly Wine Country treats such as regional cheeses and freshly picked produce. Argentine ribeye with cardoon and potato gratin and a roast half-chicken with a sage and butternut sauce are typical entrées here on the ground floor of the Sonoma Hotel. The liveliest tables are in the spacious bar area; more subdued seating is available in a back room or on an enormous shaded patio in the rear. No lunch on weekdays. ~ 110 West Spain Street, Sonoma; 707-939-6955, fax 707-996-7014. MODERATE.

The General's Daughter is a gloriously restored yellow Victorian that once belonged to General Mariano Vallejo's daughter. High-ceilinged rooms, decorated with paintings of oversized farm animals and lots of greenery provide an appropriately residential atmosphere. The kitchen has faltered since it opened in the early 1990s but there is much to like on the wide-ranging California-cuisine menu, particularly among the appetizers. This is the place to bring an aunt or a group for a sedate Sunday brunch. ~ 400 West Spain Street, Sonoma; 707-938-4004, fax 707-938-4099. MODERATE TO DELUXE.

If you prefer Mexican cuisine, try **La Casa.** Located just off the plaza, this colorful restaurant offers a full menu from south of the border. There are margaritas and other tequila drinks at the bar, plus a bill of fare ranging from snapper Veracruz to chile verde to chimichangas. ~ 121 East Spain Street, Sonoma; 707-996-3406, fax 707-996-0842. BUDGET TO MODERATE.

Savor the flavors of Tuscany at **Cucina Viansa,** a classy Italian deli and marketplace accented with a black-and-white tile floor and marble countertops. A selection of cold pasta salads, rotisserie meats (marinated rabbit, leg of lamb), and Italian specialties (polenta lasagna, grilled torta) can be ordered to go or enjoyed on one of the café tables overlooking the Sonoma

Copia → Napa

French laundry

Mustards

Terra (St. Helena)

Model Bakery (chocolate
Rolls)

Opus 1
Coppola — museum

Dean & Deluca — near
Mustard's
past Yountville

Travina

QUAKER

Susan

Printed on post consumer recycled paper.

Mission. Oenophiles can visit the adjoining wine bar featuring vintages from Viansa Winery. ~ 400 1st Street East, Sonoma; 707-935-5656, fax 707-935-5651. BUDGET.

If you dine at **Della Santina** on a mild day, head to a table on the brick-lined back patio. This Italian favorite is the only place in town to order petrale sole and sand dabs (occasionally available). There are other daily fish and veal specials as well as classic northern Italian dishes: lasagna, tortellini, cannelloni and so on; rabbit, duck, turkey, pork and chicken rotate on the rotisserie. Della Santina's is especially known for its gnocchi; here a bowl of the little dumplings runs less than $10. The wine list, of course, incorporates Italian as well as California vintages. ~ 133 East Napa Street, Sonoma; 707-935-0576, fax 707-935-7046. MODERATE.

Don't let the simplicity of the menu fool you. The half-dozen or so main courses at **Café La Haye** are the result of sophisticated chefs who manage to create delectable dishes in a postage stamp–size kitchen. Chicken, beef, pasta and daily fish and risotto selections get the deluxe treatment in this split-level storefront restaurant just off the Sonoma plaza. No dinner on Sunday. Closed Monday. ~ 140 East Napa Street, Sonoma; 707-935-5994. MODERATE.

Deuce is an American bistro housed in a rambling Victorian cottage where elaborate wood carvings hark back to the hippie era. Start with fried calamari or rock shrimp rolls and move on to tender local duck breast, dry-aged club steak or seafood options such as Pacific halibut. Patio seating is delightful in decent weather, and always an option to consider early in the evening before moving indoors. Desserts are scrumptious, especially the chef's special Meyer lemon pot de crème, made with extra-rich duck eggs. ~ 691 Broadway, Sonoma; 707-933-3823, fax 707-933-9002. MODERATE.

SHOPPING

The old Spanish town of Sonoma contains a central plaza around which you'll find its best shops. Stroll the square (bounded by 1st Street East, 1st Street West, Spain and Napa streets) and encounter gourmet stores, boutiques, a designer lingerie company, antique stores, poster galleries, and a brass shop. Many of these establishments are housed in historic Spanish adobes.

Slightly west of the square, **Wild Thyme Café** is out-and-out adorable, with a tempting collection of international cheese and organic local produce. Take-out meals are also available. ~ 165 West Napa Street, Sonoma; 707-996-0900; www.wildthymecafe.com, e-mail wildthyme@vom.com.

Robin's Nest specializes in discount kitchen accessories and gifts such as Italian bowls and platters. ~ 116 East Napa Street, Sonoma; phone/fax 707-996-4169.

One place to consider is the **Arts Guild of Sonoma**, containing works by local artisans. Here are paintings, ceramics and jewelry. ~ 140 East Napa Street, Sonoma; 707-996-3115.

A nearby mall, **El Paseo de Sonoma** contains more off-street shops. ~ 414 1st Street East, Sonoma.

The Sign of the Bear, a gourmet cook's general store, pays homage to the California lifestyle. The shop sells everything from nutmeg to napkin rings, gadgets to glassware, cookware to make just about anything and cookbooks to teach you how to do it. ~ 435 1st Street West, Sonoma; 707-996-3722.

You'll find organic produce, flowers and crafts, along with foodstuffs such as cheeses, honey and ostrich meat, at the **Sonoma Certified Farmers Market**, held every Friday at Arnold Field (1st Street West) from 9 a.m. to noon. From late May into early October, the farmers market also takes place Tuesday evenings right on the plaza (Broadway at Napa Street) from 5:15 p.m. until dusk. ~ 707-538-7023.

NIGHTLIFE As in the Napa area, Sonoma Valley nightlife revolves around summer events at the wineries. Check local calendars for concerts, theatrical performances, and other special programs. If that seems uninteresting, or if it's not summertime, you'll have to rely on hotel and restaurant bars for entertainment. There's a particularly good one at the **Heirloom** on the town plaza. The building dates to the mid-1800s and the lounge is filled with French Country furnishings and fixtures. ~ 110 West Spain Street, Sonoma; 707-996-2996.

With old photos adorning its walls, the bar of the historic **Swiss Hotel** is a favorite meetingplace of locals and travelers alike. ~ 18 West Spain Street, Sonoma; 707-938-2884.

Cucina Viansa offers live music on Friday and Saturday nights. ~ 400 1st Street East, Sonoma; 707-935-5656.

Northeast of Sonoma's city center, it's Oktoberfest all year at **Little Switzerland,** where you can dance the polka and waltz and pretend you're in another time and place. There's live music every Sunday from 5 p.m. to 9 p.m. Join your partner on the main dancefloor inside or in the beer garden outside. Dinners of steak, pasta and chicken are also served. Reservations recommended. Open Sunday only. Cover. ~ Corner of Riverside Drive and Grove Street, El Verano; 707-938-9990, fax 707-938-8748.

PARKS **MAXWELL FARMS REGIONAL PARK** A paved path encircles most of this centrally located park, where early morning finds many older people taking their constitutionals, some with dogs in tow. Parents bring their offspring to burn off energy in the playground and the grassy infield is ideal for games of Frisbee. ~ Route 12 at Verano Avenue, Sonoma; 707-565-2041.

From the northern Sonoma city limits to Santa Rosa, a ribbon of two-lane road runs through the scenic Valley of the Moon. The farther north you drive, the fewer commercial buildings and the more open space, with vineyards in the foreground and Sonoma and the Mayacamas mountains forming the borders. This is prime grapegrowing country and has been even before the days that Jack London lived and farmed here, when he was writing some of his best-selling novels.

Northern Sonoma Valley

Just north of Sonoma, **Boyes Hot Springs** blossomed as a summer resort area popular with San Franciscans who traveled by train from the city. Now this unincorporated town is experiencing a mini-renaissance, thanks in large part to the expansion of the Sonoma Mission Inn. If the Napa Valley is Stevenson country, however, Sonoma Valley belongs to Jack London. A world adventurer and self-described "sailor on horseback," London was not the type to settle down. Illegitimate son of an astrologer, he was in turn an oyster pirate, socialist, gold prospector, and internationally renowned author. But settle he did, a few miles northwest of Sonoma in the town of **Glen Ellen**.

SIGHTS

> After Jack London's untimely death, his wife built the House of Happy Walls and opened the property to wealthy vacationers as Jack London's Beauty Ranch.

Calling this area "the valley of the moon," London and his wife Charmian acquired a 1400-acre ranch and began construction of the Wolf House, an extraordinary mansion with 26 rooms and nine fireplaces. In 1913, when nearly completed, London's dream house mysteriously burned. Three years later, after producing 51 books and becoming America's first millionaire author, he committed suicide at age 40.

Today, at **Jack London State Historic Park**, you can wander the old estate. At the east end of the park, the House of Happy Walls, occupied by Charmian after her husband's death, is a museum containing first editions and original manuscripts. London's study is adorned with the original artwork for his stories, and many keepsakes from his world adventures are here. A half-mile path leads past the author's grave, simply marked by a stone boulder, to the west side of the park and the tragic ruins of the Wolf House, a monument to a lost dream. Nearby, the cottage where London lived and wrote from 1911 until his death in 1916 still stands. Admission. ~ 2400 London Ranch Road, Glen Ellen; 707-938-5216, fax 707-938-4827.

Children and wine connoisseurs alike will enjoy the 45-minute tractor-pulled tram tour through the 85-acre **Benziger Family Winery**. This scenic facility, just to the west of Jack London State Historic Park, also boasts a peacock aviary, an art gallery and a redwood-shaded picnic area. Tastings of their chardonnays, cabs, merlots and pinot blancs, among others, are available in the tasting room. ~ 1883 London Ranch Road, Glen Ellen; 707-935-3000, fax 707-935-3016; www.benziger.com, e-mail greatwine@benziger.com.

A bit of history awaits at the **Valley of the Moon Winery**, which sits on 60 acres that were once part of General Vallejo's 48,000-acre land grant. A winery has operated at this location since 1876, and portions of the farmhouse-style winery still possess the original stone and concrete walls. Tours of the winery are available daily at 10:30 a.m. and 2 p.m.; food and wine pairings are featured on weekends starting at noon. ~ 777 Madrone Road, Glen Ellen; 707-996-6941, fax 707-996-5809; www.valleyofthe moonwinery.com, e-mail luna@valleyofthemoonwinery.com.

Kenwood, a residential community straddling the highway, has no real downtown to speak of. A few stores and top-notch wineries line the scenic highway.

Route 12, the Sonoma Highway, travels north through Sonoma Valley, past miles of vineyard and forest. Numerous small wineries dot this rustic area, including **Kenwood Vineyards**. Backed up against the mountains in a group of redwood buildings, the winery was founded in 1906. The current owners, who took over in 1970, instituted the French style of fermenting small batches of wine individually. You can taste the results of their experiment any day, and daily tours are available at 11:30 a.m. and 2:30 p.m. ~ 9592 Sonoma Highway, Kenwood; 707-833-5891, 800-536-9663, fax 707-833-1146; www.kenwoodvineyards.com, e-mail info@heckestates.com.

The strikingly beautiful **Château St. Jean Winery** sits beside a colonnaded mansion built during the 1920s. The winery has added several similar buildings, including one with an observation tower from which to view the surrounding countryside. Wine, not extraordinary vistas, is the business here, and the winery has won several awards for its chardonnays and Johannisberg rieslings. You can taste these and other varietals and take a self-guided tour of the grounds. It's also a nice place to bring a picnic. ~ 8555 Sonoma Highway, Kenwood; 707-833-4134, 800-478-5326, fax 707-833-4200; www.chateaustjean.com.

LODGING This area offers some unusual choices, from full-service resorts to small B&Bs. You certainly won't come across any chain lodging in this part of the Valley of the Moon. Some quasi-legal B&Bs operate on a word-of-mouth basis, but you won't find them reviewed here.

The **Sonoma Mission Inn and Spa** lives up to its name, in all three senses of the word. The pale pink stucco facade on this gracious Mission Revival–style hotel harks back to the days when American Indians enjoyed the natural mineral waters of this area. The 198 accommodations are appointed in earthy tones, with wooden shutters and ceiling fans adding a hint of the plantation; some rooms have fireplaces. A full-service spa, an 18-hole golf course and two swimming pools add up to one of the best retreats in the Wine Country. ~ 18140 Route 12, Boyes Hot Springs; 707-938-9000, 800-862-4945, fax 707-938-4250; www. sonomamissioninn.com. ULTRA-DELUXE.

A short drive from downtown Glen Ellen leads to the **Glenelly Inn**, one of the few properties around here that was actually

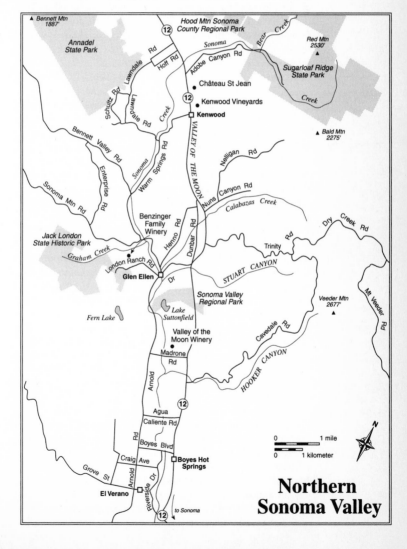

Northern Sonoma Valley

built, in 1916, to serve as an inn. Most of the inn's eight rooms are on the small side, but touches like a hot tub, a common room with a cobblestone fireplace and breakfast tables in the shade of old oak trees lure guests out of their quarters. The inn also runs five off-site rental cottages that are more expensive. ~ 5131 Warm Springs Road, Glen Ellen; 707-996-6720, fax 707-996-5227. DELUXE.

The most elegant accommodations in Glen Ellen can be found at the **Gaige House Inn**, built as a private residence in the 19th century. Most of the 13 rooms are decorated with traditional antiques, but a pair on the lower floor in the back are done up in chic fashion with African accents. A full country breakfast is served in the large, bright dining room on the ground floor or on the terrace near a large pool flanked with white umbrellas and magnolia trees. ~ 13540 Arnold Drive, Glen Ellen; 707-935-0237, 800-935-0237, fax 707-935-6411. ULTRA-DELUXE.

The **Beltane Ranch** is a century-old farmhouse converted into an easygoing inn. Backed by hundreds of acres that climb up the slopes of the Mayacamas Mountains that border the Napa Valley, the five rooms in this pretty yellow B&B are furnished with well-worn antiques as well as some swings and hammocks on the two-story wraparound porches. There's also a two-room cottage with its own patio. Tennis courts and private hiking trails beckon after the full breakfast, which is included. ~ 11775 Route 12, Glen Ellen; 707-996-6501. MODERATE TO DELUXE.

Wonderfully located for visiting wineries in both Kenwood and Glen Ellen, **Muir Manor** offers four upstairs accommodations (two share a bath) in a 1913 Sonoma County Historic Landmark. Established on what was a 40-acre fruit orchard, the inn is within walking distance of wineries and restaurants. ~ 8790 Route 12, Kenwood; 707-833-6996; www.muirmanor.com, e-mail info@muirmanor.com. MODERATE.

DINING The town of Glen Ellen has emerged as the culinary star of this neighborhood, with a cluster of excellent choices along downtown's "restaurant row." Less fancy fare, usually Mexican or Italian, is also available; true bargains can be found at taquerias in Boyes Hot Springs.

When no one in your dining party can agree on where to eat, it may be time to try a place that serves African, Brazilian and Portuguese dishes. **La Salette** is the masterpiece of chef Manny Azevedo, whose heritage and wide-ranging travels have inspired an unusual menu. Salt cod with onions, oven-roasted salmon, Mozambique prawns with tomatoes and grilled plantain are usually on a menu that changes slightly with the seasons. Tasteful paintings and sculpture by a local artist enliven the off-white walls in this room-and-a-half restaurant, with some patio seating for balmy evenings. Closed Monday and Tuesday. ~ 18625 Route 12, Sonoma; 707-938-1927.

The Restaurant at Sonoma Mission Inn presents innovative but unpretentious fare in an elegant dining room of dark, highly polished woods. Prepared with local produce, entrées may include salmon steamed in banana leaves and served with lemon rice pilaf; ostrich medallions; and dijon-marinated rack of lamb. Formal attire for men and women is required. Dinner only. ~ Sonoma Mission Inn, 18140 Route 12, Boyes Hot Springs; 707-938-9000, fax 707-938-4250; www.sonomamissioninn.com. ULTRA-DELUXE.

A less formal option is **The Big 3 Diner** at Sonoma Mission Inn. This bistro-style eatery serves tasty, healthful fare with a northern Italian influence. You'll find pastas, pizzas and salads on the lunch and dinner menu, while breakfast features freshly baked goods, pancakes and egg dishes. ~ Sonoma Mission Inn and Spa, 18140 Route 12, Boyes Hot Springs; 707-938-9000, fax 707-938-4250; www.sonomamissioninn.com. MODERATE.

The Ferguson Observatory at Sugarloaf Ridge State Park (707-833-6979) boasts a 40-inch telescope and offers public viewing nights.

The Bistro at Glen Ellen sits just down the road from Jack London's estate. The dining room is a plate-glass facility overlooking forest and stream. In addition to views, there are ample lunch and dinner menus at reasonable prices. Entrées include risotto with shrimp and butternut squash, braised lamb, chicken and spinach ravioli and char-broiled salmon. ~ 13740 Arnold Drive, Glen Ellen; 707-996-4401, fax 707-996-0850. MODERATE TO DELUXE.

Mustard-yellow walls, mismatched yellow chairs and changing art exhibits set a sort of bohemian tone at **The Girl & The Fig**. In the scant year it's been open, word has spread fast that this here is a menu—and a wine list—to be reckoned with. You will indeed find figs, both fresh and dried, in an offbeat salad with arugula, goat cheese and pecans; a selection of cheese courses; and, most impressive, an imaginative wine list long on Rhone varietals and bereft of chardonnay and cabernet sauvignon. ~ 13690 Arnold Drive, Glen Ellen; 707-938-3634. MODERATE TO DELUXE.

The most consistently good food in the northern Sonoma Valley is served in the dining rooms and on the patio at the **Kenwood Restaurant and Grill**. Management doesn't change the menu much except for specials; everyone must be pleased with the crab cakes, locally raised chicken, lamb and steak dishes, as well as with a longtime favorite, sashimi, which is a rarity in the Wine Country. A fireplace in the long bar room is ideal for a late-afternoon lunch. ~ 9900 Route 12, Kenwood; 707-833-6326. MODERATE TO DELUXE.

Family owned and operated, **Cafe Citti** is an Italian trattoria set amongst the vineyards of Kenwood and extremely popular with Sonoma Valley locals, who love its casualness and friendly atmosphere. Flowers and candles on the tables add a bit of romance. The Italian chef serves up a variety of pastas; rotisserie chicken stuffed with fresh herbs, garlic and rosemary; and weekend specials. He also makes his own mozzarella cheese and biscotti. ~ 9049 Sonoma Highway, Kenwood; 707-833-2690. MODERATE.

SHOPPING   On the way to Jack London State Historic Park, be sure to stop in at the **Jack London Bookstore**. An important resource center for London scholars and fans, it contains numerous first editions of the author's works. Closed Tuesday. ~ 14300 Arnold Drive, Glen Ellen; 707-996-2888; e-mail jlondon@vom.com.

The **Olive Press** is a unique source of local olive oils, many of them pressed on the premises. In addition to the oils, some of which are always available for sampling, you'll find table top merchandise such as plates, platters and bowls. ~ 14801 Arnold Drive, Glen Ellen; 707-939-8900.

NIGHTLIFE   Out in Jack London country, the **Jack London Saloon** is a pretty, brick-faced barroom that draws a mixture of locals and visitors. Fashionably decorated with Tiffany-style lamps and old movie posters, it's a good drinking place. ~ Jack London Lodge, 13740 Arnold Drive, Glen Ellen; 707-996-3100, fax 707-939-9642.

PARKS   **LARSON PARK** Four tennis courts, a softball diamond and an open field are the only attractions at this neighborhood complex. A handful of picnic tables sit in the shade beside little Sonoma Creek. There are restrooms near them. ~ Off Dechene Street, Boyes Hot Springs; 707-565-2041.

JACK LONDON STATE HISTORIC PARK 🚶 Occupying much of a ranch once farmed by the famous author, this park ranges over hilly terrain. The central attractions are a museum, the House of Happy Walls, and the remains of the house that Jack built, Wolf House. Parking fee, $6. ~ 2400 London Ranch Road, Glen Ellen; 707-938-5216, fax 707-938-4827.

SONOMA VALLEY REGIONAL PARK 🚶 🚲 Both paved and unpaved trails crisscross this parcel, parts of which are shaded. Two miles are paved for bike riding as well as walking. If you hike off the pavement in warm weather, wear boots or keep an eye out for the occasional rattlesnake. Popular with dog owners, the 162-acre park also has a special one-acre play area for off-leash pets near the Route 12 parking lot. Day-use fee, $2. ~ Route 12, Glen Ellen; 707-565-2041.

SUGARLOAF RIDGE STATE PARK 🚶 🚲 🐎 ↲ Within this 3000-acre facility lie two different ecological systems as well as 25 miles of hiking trails along which to explore them. There are chaparral-coated ridges (you can see San Francisco and the Sierra Nevada from the top of Bald Mountain), plus forests of maple, laurel, madrone and alder. Sonoma Creek tumbles through the park; you can try for trout here. Spring brings a profusion of wildflowers, and autumn is another popular season in the park. Horse rentals are available from the Sonoma Cattle Company (707-996-8566). Facilities include picnic areas and restrooms. Day-use fee, $5. ~ Located east off Route 12 between Sonoma and Santa Rosa, the park is at 2605 Adobe Canyon Road in Kenwood; phone/fax 707-833-5712.

A There are 49 sites; $15 to $16 per car per night. Camping here is a reasonably priced lodging option for a visit to the Wine Country and is popular with Bay Area families. Call 800-444-7275 for reservations.

Outdoor Adventures

GOLF

You'll find greens in Sonoma at the championship 18-hole **Sonoma Mission Inn Golf & Country Club.** Fees include carts; clubs are available for rent. They enforce a strict dress code and mandatory soft-spike policy. ~ 17700 Arnold Drive, Sonoma; 707-996-0300, fax 707-996-8464; www.sonomamissioninn.com.

RIDING STABLES

The hills and valleys of the Wine Country provide wonderful opportunities for equestrians. Slide into the saddle and saunter through the forest on a guided journey offered by **Sonoma Cattle Company & Napa Valley Trail Rides.** They operate horseback-riding trips three times a day year-round at Sugarloaf Ridge State Park in Kenwood and from May through October at Jack London and Bothe–Napa Valley state parks in Napa. A moonlight ride in Sugarloaf four or five days before a full moon is an unforgettable experience. They also offer box-lunch and barbecue-dinner rides. ~ P.O. Box 877, Glen Ellen, CA 95442; 707-996-8566, fax 707-938-8366; www.thegrid.net/trailrides.

TENNIS

Two public courts are located in a corner of **Maxwell Farms Regional Park.** They are free and available on a first-come, first-serve basis. ~ Route 12 at Verano Avenue, Sonoma; 707-565-2041.

GETTING AWAY

For those wanting to enjoy the Wine Country air, **Getaway Adventures** operates weekend and six-day biking trips through the Napa, Sonoma and Alexander valleys, as well as hikes through Calistoga to Mt. St. Helena. ~ 1117 Lincoln Avenue, Calistoga; 707-942-0332, 800-859-2453; www.getawayadventures.com, e-mail info@getawayadventures.com.

BIKING   A two-mile **bike path** links Route 12 (at Verano Avenue) with Depot Park in downtown Sonoma. Paved and flat, it's too narrow for automobile traffic and thus perfect for cyclists and strollers who only have to cross a few streets along the way.

Although you will see some cyclists on Route 12, they are foolhardy. A better thoroughfare is **Arnold Drive**, which runs parallel to the highway from Petaluma Avenue north through the town of Glen Ellen, where it terminates at Route 12. Near that intersection is a beautiful country lane called **Dunbar Road**. This is a less-traveled route that connects Glen Ellen to Kenwood, on the west side of Route 12.

At Sugarloaf Ridge, try the nine-mile **Bald Mountain Trail** to Gray Pine and then through the meadow loop. You'll pass open meadows sprinkled with oak trees.

Bike Rentals   A couple of blocks north of the Route 12 end of the paved bike path is the **Good Time Bicycle Company**, which rents, repairs and sells bicycles. The shop is a terrific source for suggestions about places to pedal and offers guided tours of the area. ~ 18503 Route 12, Sonoma; 707-938-0453.

HIKING   Thanks to the hills and mountains that define the Sonoma Valley, the hiking here provides some of the best views of any trails in the Wine Country. All distances listed for hiking trails are one way unless otherwise noted.

Trails at Jack London State Historical Park include the walk to the **Wolf House ruins**, a gravel trail (1.5 miles roundtrip) that begins at the House of Happy Walls, the park's visitors center that is located about 350 feet from the parking lot. Along the way you'll see oaks and madrones and a plethora of wildflowers. A much more rigorous outing climbs **Sonoma Mountain** (8 miles roundtrip), takes four or five hours and rises 1800 feet. The trailhead is located off the parking lot.

The trails at **Sugarloaf Ridge State Park** (707-833-5712) provide opportunities to explore ridges and open fields. Every spring, wildflowers riot throughout the meadows. The park's most popular walk is along **Creekside Nature Trail** (.8 mile roundtrip). This self-guided stroll begins at the day-use picnic area and carries past stands of oak, alder, ash, maple, and Douglas fir. Watch for several species of lichen *and* poison oak! If you are up for a steep climb, try **Bald Mountain Trail** (2.7 miles), which leads to the top of the mountain. At an elevation of 2729 feet, the summit offers spectacular views of the Sonoma and Napa valleys and, on a clear day, San Francisco and the Golden Gate Bridge, the Sierras, and St. Helena. The climb begins at the day-use parking lot near the campground, which is already 1000 feet in elevation.

FIVE

Northern Sonoma County

Covering some 1600 square miles, Sonoma County is too large to tour in a day or even a weekend. It takes less than 15 minutes to drive from Santa Rosa to Healdsburg via Route 101 and only another 20 to reach Cloverdale, but once you veer off into side roads, you will be driving at only about 35 mph.

The secret to touring the area north of Santa Rosa does, after all, lie along country lanes on either side of the highway. At the center of this area is Healdsburg, a country town centered on a plaza and dating back to 1854. The Russian River flowing beside this booming small city long ago inspired many urban types to establish summer homes on its banks, and there are plenty of river rats living here full time as well.

Northern Sonoma County extends from Santa Rosa, northeast of the Sonoma Valley, north to Cloverdale. The area includes major grapegrowing regions such as the Alexander Valley and the Dry Creek Valley. The Russian River region lies to the west and is covered in Chapter 6. Although Santa Rosa is the county seat and has the biggest urban area in the entire Wine Country, it has very few wineries itself.

Because there is a town of Sonoma, a valley called Sonoma and a county named Sonoma, some visitors become confused. Just as people say "New York" when they should say "New York City," a lot of northern Californians say "Sonoma" and could mean the town, the valley or the entire county. All we can say is, get used to it. It will all make sense in short order.

Sonoma is one of the fastest-growing counties in the Bay Area though it has lagged behind San Francisco and the San Jose area. The first to arrive here were the Miwok and Pomo tribes, who crossed the land bridge from Asia into present-day Alaska. The first white men to arrive came aboard a Spanish ship with the explorer Francisco de Bodega y Cuadro, who was looking for San Francisco Bay. Instead, they hit landfall on the Sonoma coast in the fall of 1775.

But it was the Russians, not the Spanish, who established the first outpost, settling on a bluff to the north and building a fort there in order to protect their lucrative fur trade. They also began moving inland to warmer weather, but after the Mexican missionaries established a mission in the Sonoma Valley in the 1820s, the stage was set for the Mexican to prevail over the Russians as well as the native Indians. Most of Sonoma was still frontier country but, like most of the state, the arable portions were divided into ranchos under Mexican rule. General Mariano Vallejo, who had come to secularize the mission system, cemented his power base through his ability to apportion ranchos in the region. In the process, he convinced his widowed mother-in-law, Dona Maria Carrillo, to join the family. She settled near Santa Rosa Creek in 1837 and built the first European home in the Santa Rosa Valley.

The future town grew up around that adobe home and by 1854—four years after California became a state—wrested the county seat from the town of Sonoma. By the end of that decade, Santa Rosa boasted 100 buildings and 400 citizens. In the process of expanding, the new city boosted the fortunes of the surrounding area. A bit north, Harmon Heald settled on the Sotoyome Rancho, sold lots and helped start the town that bears his name. In 1854, Colonel A. C. Godwin opened Geyserville's first store. Italians, Swiss, British, Irish, Germans and others arrived to develop northern Sonoma. In the process, they established farms and planted vineyards using grapevines brought, by and large, from their native countries. The horticulturist Luther Burbank settled in Santa Rosa; his home and gardens are open to the public today.

Santa Rosa was well-positioned to further its leadership in the world of commerce by the time premium grapes became big business in the area. The valleys on all sides of Santa Rosa are filled with top-notch wineries eager to welcome visitors into their tasting rooms. Today, high technology, in the form of major-league companies such as Hewlett-Packard as well as numerous start-ups, is challenging wine's role as the number-one regional industry. All it takes is one Friday-afternoon rush-hour commute experience to convince anyone of what a boomtown Santa Rosa—along with its satellite communities—has become.

▼▼▼▼▼▼▼▼▼▼
Santa Rosa

Santa Rosa, the largest city in Sonoma County (with nearly 150,000 residents) and the county seat, is home to a burgeoning high-tech industry that has put it on the list of the country's best places to live and work. The downtown area is a hodgepodge, however. Route 101 dissects the city, separating the Historic Railroad Square district from the retail and office complexes of the rest of downtown. The county offices are another neighborhood entirely, located half a mile from the center of town.

SIGHTS

This is not a major tourist destination; it just sits in the middle of one. Still, there are some unusual attractions worth checking out.

Santa Rosa is known worldwide as the home of Luther Burbank, the great horticulturist who worked miracles on plant life, creating the Santa Rosa plum, Shasta daisy and hundreds of other hybrids. His legacy remains in full bloom at the **Luther Burbank Home & Gardens**, where visitors can stroll through gardens filled with the descendants of his plant "inventions" and tour the Victorian house where he lived for 20 years. The house is open

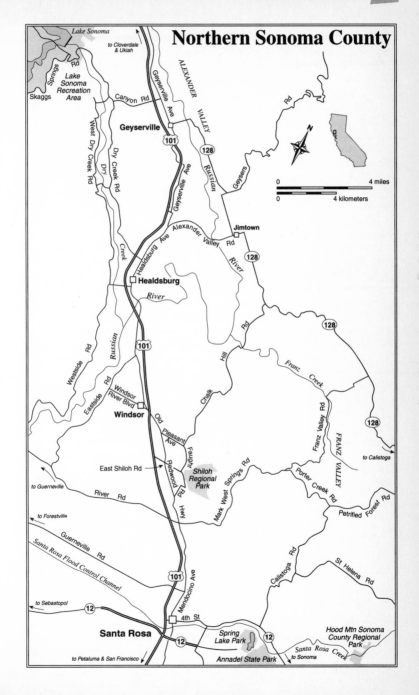

Northern Sonoma County

Tuesday through Sunday from April through October. Admission to tour the house. ~ Santa Rosa and Sonoma avenues; 707-524-5445, fax 707-524-5827; www.lutherburbank.org, e-mail burbank home@flash.netdex.com.

On the western edge of downtown, **Historic Railroad Square** was once a busy commercial and transport center. Today its buildings, some of which survived the great 1906 earthquake that destroyed much of the city center, contain antique and specialty shops and restaurants. ~ 4th and Wilson streets, located west of Route 101 and east of the railroad tracks.

The old Santa Rosa Depot has been restored and turned into a visitors center. Stop by the **Santa Rosa Convention & Visitors Bureau** for more information about the town. ~ 9 4th Street; 707-577-8674, 800-404-7673, fax 707-571-5949; www.visitsanta rosa.com.

Housed in a former 1909 post office, the **Sonoma County Museum** provides a historical and cultural perspective on the region with changing exhibits, some of them designed especially for kids. The museum includes the Hart Collection of early California art, the Sonoma County history exhibit, and the Dixon Collection of metal jewelry and sculpture. Closed Monday and Tuesday. Admission. ~ 425 7th Street; 707-579-1500, fax 707-579-4849; www.pressdemo.com/scmuseum, e-mail scm@pon.net.

The prolific creativity of North American Indians—basketry, jewelry, sculpture, pottery and textiles—is on display at the **Jesse Peter Museum**, located at Santa Rosa Junior College. Also showcased is art from Africa, Asia and the Pacific. Closed Saturday and Sunday, and from mid-June to mid-August. ~ Bussman Hall, Santa Rosa Junior College, 1501 Mendocino Avenue; 707-527-4479, fax 707-527-1861; www.santarosa.edu/museum.

HIDDEN ► Nearby, the **Santa Rosa Rural Cemetery** allows visitors a glimpse of the town's former inhabitants, including victims of the 1906 earthquake. ~ Franklin Avenue and Monroe Street.

HIDDEN ► **Paradise Ridge Winery** offers visitors a bit of California lore along with its chardonnay, merlot, cabernet sauvignon and sparkling blanc de blanc. The location adjoins land where the Fountaingrove winery once stood. The winemaker there was the first Japanese winemaker in the U.S., the son of a samurai whose fascinating life is the subject of an exhibit at Paradise Ridge. There's also a sculpture grove on the property. ~ 4545 Thomas Lake Harris Drive (off the Fountaingrove Parkway near Route 101); 707-528-9463.

HIDDEN ► If you've never seen actual airplane engines or ejection seats up close and sans plane, you can't miss them at the **Pacific Coast Air Museum**. This small museum, right next to the airport, also exhibits scale models, flight suits and a variety of aeronautical

gadgetry. Closed Monday. ~ 2330 Airport Boulevard; 707-575-
7900, fax 707-545-2813; www.pacificcoastairmuseum.org.

For a wild diversion, head into the hills in search of **Safari** ◄ HIDDEN
West. Here, on hundreds of acres, onyx, antelope, zebras, Watusi
cattle, peacocks, giraffes and many more rescued, endangered or
threatened species roam in safety. Four-wheel-drive tours let visitors get close enough for excellent photographs at this accred-

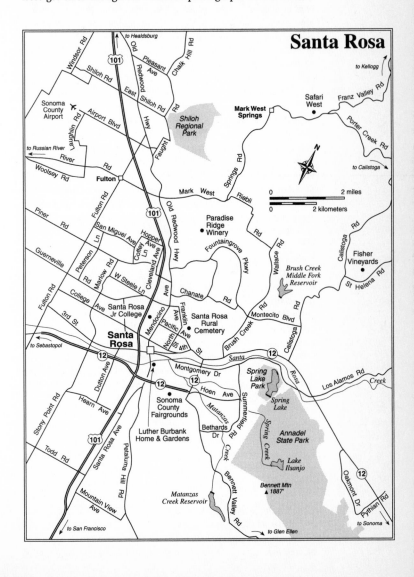

ited private zoo, where only the birds are in cages. Admission. ~ 3115 Porter Creek Road; 707-579-2551.

Up in the mountains outside Santa Rosa, hidden along country lanes, lies **Fisher Vineyards**. Tucked into a fold in the hills and surrounded by redwood forest, this picturesque winery is a family-style operation. The main building, a lofty board-and-batten structure, was built with wood cut and milled on the site. It follows a contemporary California design and overlooks the surrounding vineyards. Planted primarily with cabernet sauvignon, chardonnay, and merlot vines, the winery produces a small but delicious quantity of wine each season. Visiting by appointment only. ~ 6200 St. Helena Road, Santa Rosa; 707-539-7511, fax 707-539-3601.

LODGING   While small inns abound in the small towns in this section, there are few in the big city of Santa Rosa. You can find a couple of sizable hotels, however, as well as a smattering of motels.

Conveniently located on the border of east Santa Rosa, the **Flamingo Resort Hotel** is close to two shopping centers as well as the county fairgrounds, yet not far from the wineries of the Sonoma Valley. It has a very '50s feel to it, but the 170 rooms (most of which are on the ground floor) are well-maintained. The landscaping is attractive and links the disparate buildings. A big swimming pool and a restaurant are among the amenities; guests also have access to the fitness center and tennis courts. ~ 2777 4th Street; 707-545-8530, 800-848-8300, fax 707-528-1404; www.flamingoresort.com. DELUXE TO ULTRA-DELUXE.

You can stay in the heart of Santa Rosa's fascinating Historic Railroad Square at **Hotel La Rose**, built in 1907 by the same Italian stonemasons who were responsible for the depot across the street. It has been listed on the National Register of Historic Places and is a member of Historic Hotels of America. English country style describes the decor, with dark greens and rose-red colors. Some guest rooms sport four-poster beds, others brass beds. The fourth-floor attic rooms have sloping ceilings, and some are brightened by skylights. An outdoor spa is available to guests. ~ 308 Wilson Street; 707-579-3200, 800-527-6738, fax 707-579-3247; www.hotellarose.com, e-mail reservations@hotellarose.com. ULTRA-DELUXE.

One of the best deals in town is the **Sandman Motel**, where 112 rooms on two floors are attractive if not spectacular. Amenities far surpass those of most motels—a heated pool, hot tub, laundry room and a refrigerator in each room. It's not in a pretty location, but it is close to shops and restaurants and the Sonoma County Civic Center. ~ 3421 Cleveland Avenue; 707-544-8570, fax 707-544-8710. BUDGET TO DELUXE.

HIDDEN ►   The **Fountaingrove Inn** on the north side of Santa Rosa is one of very few non-chain hotels in the area. Its low-rise structure of

Author
    Picks

CHAPTER FAVORITES

I'm always impressed when I wander through the **Luther Burbank Home & Gardens**, looking at the artifacts and reviewing the life story of the horticulturist who presented us with more than 800 strains of fruits, vegetables, grasses and flowers. *page 98*

The Wine Country is an ideal setting for B&B inns, none more lovely than the **Haydon Street Inn**, where the vantage from the wraparound porch whisks me into a scene from Wilder's *Our Town*. *page 110*

If you, like I, prefer to avoid the crowds, head north and west of Healdsburg along Dry Creek Valley Road. Though the warm hillsides are ideal for zinfandel vines, this area is also known for sauvignon blanc. The best place to sample some is at **Dry Creek Vineyard**. *page 108*

It's exhilarating to ride the range in an open-top jeep and get close to zebras, giraffes and endangered animals like the oryx at **Safari West**, a cross between the African bush and a regular zoo. *page 101*

stone and redwood has 126 modest but comfortable guest rooms. Amenities include a swimming pool, a hot tub and a restaurant as well as a complimentary continental breakfast. ~ 101 Fountaingrove Parkway; 707-578-6101, 800-222-6101, fax 707-544-3126; www.fountaingrove.com, e-mail pmeiger@fountaingrove inn.com. DELUXE.

Now that the 50 acres of surrounding vineyards have matured, the **Vintners Inn** blends in with the landscape. Spacious accommodations are decorated in European country style, with antiques and comforters. Little piazzas and open landscaping between two-story townhouses create a luxurious ambience. Breakfast is included. ~ 4350 Barnes Road; 707-575-7350, 800-421-2584, fax 707-575-1426; www.vintnersinn.com, e-mail info@vintners inn.com. ULTRA-DELUXE.

DINING

It's hard to think of any type of cooking that isn't available in the Santa Rosa vicinity, from burgers to Thai food to haute cuisine. Few restaurants here can match the upscale offerings in Sonoma and Napa; on the other hand, same-day reservations are usually possible. Good ethnic deals can be found in the vicinity of the Santa Rosa Junior College campus.

Hank's Creekside Café is a cozy spot near the corner of Farmer's Lane where many of the city's movers and shakers come for power breakfasts of crab-cake Benedict, pancakes and a wide selection of sausages including a Cajun version and a British banger. Lunch is a bit more pedestrian, with a mix of sandwiches, burgers, salads and homemade chili. At night, the room is transformed with candles and flowers into a totally different restaurant known as **Emile's Creekside Bistro**, run by a completely different chef. Filet mignon with red wine sauce and gorgonzola and *coq au vin* are the type of dishes described on the chalkboard menu at what is indeed a French-style bistro. No dinner on Monday and Tuesday. ~ 2800 4th Street; 707-575-8839. BUDGET TO DELUXE.

Sonoma County alone encompasses roughly 1600 square miles, far more than the entire state of Rhode Island.

A popular standby in the Railroad Square neighborhood, **Mixx** features an eclectic menu in an art deco room defined by an impressive mahogany-and-oak bar. This is a good spot to order a bunch of small plates to share, especially if you like to experiment with Italian, Californian, Cajun and Indian foods. Heartier fare includes Sonoma duck and grilled lamb. Closed Sunday. ~ 135 4th Street; 707-573-1344, fax 707-573-0631. MODERATE TO DELUXE.

The Wine Country is not a theme park, appearances to the contrary. If you need proof, sample the exquisite Chinese cuisine at **Gary Chu's**. This excellent restaurant depends on the locals who love it. The decor is understated in shades of gray with abstract underwater murals etched in aqua on black. The menu, however, is not. Chu's gives diners a taste of Chinese-California haute cuisine with refined fare such as walnut prawns in a sweet, cream apple dressing, sea scallops with champagne sauce and Mongolian lamb. Service is impeccable, the wine list filled with good choices, and the location central to downtown shops and theaters. Closed Monday. ~ 611 5th Street; 707-526-5840, fax 707-526-3102. MODERATE.

Look for the brick storefront that heralds **El Capitan**. This colorful but very modest spot turns out fresh burritos and other fast Mexican food, with daily specials that lean towards the vegetarian. ~ 544 Mendocino Avenue; 707-545-9576. BUDGET.

If you have a lot of mouths to feed, mosey over to **Ludy's BBQ Grill and Catering**. The kids will like the chuckwagon fare in this Western-themed place. Ribs, chicken, links, fish-and-chips and burgers make this a popular place for real food at real-world prices. And it's open until 10 on Friday and Saturday. ~ 1901 Mendocino Avenue; 707-541-7427. BUDGET TO MODERATE.

You cannot find fresher or tastier Thai food than what comes out of the kitchen at **Jhanthong Banbua**. Located in front of a motel near the Santa Rosa Junior College campus, this pretty place knocks itself out with service and a menu with something for everyone. Particularly fine are the pad thai and anything with shrimp. ~ 2400 Mendocino Avenue; 707-528-8048. MODERATE.

As Mediterranean as the cold wind for which it's named, **Mistral** is in fact a warm and gracious restaurant that, more than most, aims to please. The extensive menu—braised mahimahi, *fritto misto*, grilled pork tenderloin—is often augmented with a one-night-only tasting dinner. The interior room is nicely divided with area carpeting and demi-columns, but on even half-decent days, it's nicer on the huge patio. Mistral prides itself on its wine list, which features 175 bottles to choose from and 40 wines by the glass. No lunch Saturday and Sunday. ~ 1229 North Dutton Avenue; 707-578-4511, fax 707-578-0703. MODERATE TO DELUXE.

One of the first Wine Country restaurants to champion the region's natural resources, **John Ash & Co.** continues that mission long after its namesake departed the kitchen. Produce from nearby fields, fish from the sea and locally made cheeses and breads still star on the menu; for example, Laura Chenel and Bellwether Farm cheeses, roasted pears, Sonoma greens, fresh-picked herbs appear in many appetizers and entrées, along with locally raised beef, pork and chicken. Two large rooms, with high ceilings and plenty of windows, overlook a patio where patrons dine in the shelter of a wisteria-entwined arbor. ~ 4330 Barnes Road; 707-527-7687, fax 707-527-1202. DELUXE TO ULTRA-DELUXE.

◄ HIDDEN

At the **Willowside Café**, plank floors and a galvanized copper-topped bar greet visitors, who are lucky if they can nab one of the 15 table seats; otherwise, there are a few seats at the bar. This roadside wonder whips up some of the most extraordinary food in Santa Rosa. Choices change daily on the short menu that is likely to serve dishes like quail with lotus and pineapple or guinea fowl confit with a red chile crêpe. An excellent wine list incorporates French as well as regional vintages. Closed Monday and Tuesday. ~ 3535 Guerneville Road; 707-523-4814. MODERATE TO DELUXE.

SHOPPING

Before there were malls, there were low-rise shopping complexes like **Montgomery Village**, where locally owned stores tended to serve the upscale customer. Here you can find several mini-blocks of shops, all housed in wood structures painted dark brown. Among them are **The Competitor** (707-578-5689), which has the Wine Country's best selection of men's and women's clothing and accessories for both golf and tennis. **Copperfield's Books** (707-578-8938) is a comfortable, well-stocked store big on regional titles. For fancy home accessories, the place to browse is **Ireko** (707-579-3700), which almost qualifies as an art gallery thanks to the high quality of its merchandise. ~ Magowan Drive at Farmers Lane.

In and around Railroad Square, west of downtown and Route 101, you can find an assortment of offbeat stores, particularly antique shops. One of the best is **Whistle Stop Antiques**, where more than 35 dealers in antiques and collectibles are spread out over 10,000 square feet. ~ 130 4th Street; 707-542-9474.

Artifacts specializes in furniture and estate items but has a sideline of cookbooks and used cookware. ~ 107 4th Street; 707-566-7127.

It's Halloween all year long at **Disguise the Limit**, where you can find the paraphernalia to be a clown, a queen or an alien from outer space. Also here are toys and a few magic tricks to put up your sleeve. ~ 100 4th Street; 707-575-1477.

The **Santa Rosa Farmer's Market** is held every Wednesday and Saturday morning year-round in the parking lot at the Sonoma County Veterans Memorial Building (or inside, if it's raining). Growers from all over the region bring their produce, flowers and crafts for one of the liveliest markets in the Wine Country, located just off Route 12 east of the intersection with Route 101. ~ 1351 Maple Avenue.

Santa Rosa Wednesday Night Market is open from May through September in the downtown blocks around 4th and D streets, which are blocked to automobile traffic from about 5 to 10 p.m. These nights take on the flavor of a street fair on balmy summer nights, when couples and family make an evening of strolling and shopping. ~ 4th Street at Courthouse Square.

NIGHTLIFE **Planeteria Furia** is a Latin dance club featuring salsa and cumbria (its slower sibling) music on Friday nights, followed by country music (Latin-style) on Saturday. Cover. ~ 528 7th Street; 707-578-4445.

The **Santa Rosa Inn** seems to be the city's only gay bar, though straights should feel comfortable here. Deejay music keeps the dancefloor filled on Friday and Saturday nights, usually starting late in the evening. ~ 4302 Santa Rosa Avenue; 707-584-0345.

One of the few places in the area featuring live rock and blues, **The Old Vic** attracts a mixed crowd of 20-somethings and baby boomers. Cover. ~ 731 4th Street; 707-571-7555.

SYMPHONY AND THEATER The **Santa Rosa Symphony** frequently attracts sell-out crowds to its performances at the Luther Burbank Center. The season runs from October until May on Friday and Saturday nights and Sunday afternoons (with seven different concerts presented three times each); two summer festivals are offered in addition to the regular subscription series. ~ 50 Mark West Springs Road; 707-546-8742.

The **Sonoma County Repertory Theater** produces dramas and comedies (and once in a while, a musical) at two locations, one in Santa Rosa and the other in Sebastopol. Choices range from classics to cutting-edge during the year-round season. ~ 415 Humboldt Street, Santa Rosa; 707-544-7278; 104 North Main Street, Sebastopol; 707-823-0177.

The **Summer Repertory Theater** is a high-energy group that stages six different major plays and musicals in the space of two months in June, July and August. The SRT sticks to the tried-and-true but has a reputation for top-notch production values. ~ 1501 Mendocino Avenue; 707-527-4343.

There are some 47 parks in the Santa Rosa area, from pocket parks to places large enough to accommodate horseback riders and campgrounds.

PARKS

ANNADEL STATE PARK 🚶🛶 Possessing a wealth of possibilities, this 5000-acre facility has 39 miles of trails through meadow and forest. A volcanic mountain flanks one end of the park and a lake provides fishing for black bass and bluegill. There's also a marsh where many of the area's 160 bird species flock. Blacktailed deer and coyotes roam the region. The park has picnic areas and toilets. Day-use fee, $2. ~ Off Route 12 about five miles east of Santa Rosa; 707-539-3911, fax 707-538-0769.

SPRING LAKE PARK 🚶🚴🐴⛵🛶 One of the most popular in the region, this 314-acre park is on the east side of Santa Rosa. The lagoon is open in summer only; it has lifeguards. Non-power boats can be rented and fishing is allowed; the lake is stocked with catfish, trout, bluegill and bass. However, if you want to go horseback riding, you have to bring your own mount. The park has picnic areas and toilets. Parking fee, $4. ~ 5390 Montgomery Drive; 707-539-8092.

▲ There are 31 campsites, no electricity or water; $16 per night.

FULTON COMMUNITY PARK 🚶🚴 A creek runs through this partially undeveloped park, situated on former vineyard and orchard grounds on the west side of Santa Rosa. Popular activities include strolling and picnicking beneath oak trees; BMX enthusiasts, armed with shovels, often create their own dirt mounds in the undeveloped portion for jumps. Facilities here include a playground, a skate park, a picnic area and restrooms. ~ 725 Fulton Road; 707-543-3292.

◄ HIDDEN

SKATING IN THE PEANUTS GALLERY

The Redwood Empire Ice Arena may be the only sports facility ever created by a cartoonist. Built in 1969 by the late Charles Schulz of *Peanuts* fame for his children, the Olympic-sized arena is open year-round from 6 a.m. until 10:30 p.m. Snoopy's Gallery and Gift Shop, also part of the facility, sells Snoopy memorabilia, books, clothing, and life-size comic strip characters. ~ 1667 West Steele Lane, Santa Rosa; 707-546-7147, fax 707-546-3764.

▼▼▼▼▼▼▼▼▼▼▼▼▼▼▼▼▼▼▼▼▼▼
Healdsburg and Points North

North of Santa Rosa, the county of Sonoma includes the towns of Windsor, Healdsburg, Geyserville and Cloverdale, which is on the border with Mendocino County. There is more open space the farther north you travel, but every week—or so it seems—more and more grape vines are planted within sight of the main highway.

SIGHTS
It's about 25 miles via Route 101 from Santa Rosa to the city of **Healdsburg**. Once known as the "buckle in California's prune belt"—a moniker derived from the days when orchards, not vineyards, dominated the landscape—this town has evolved into a lively 'burg, with a flourishing downtown packed with shops, restaurants and lodgings. The center of activity is **Healdsburg Plaza**, a park landscaped with palm and oak trees where people really do picnic. On summer weekends, free concerts are occasionally offered here.

At the **Healdsburg Chamber of Commerce** you can pick up maps, brochures and other information on the region. ~ 217 Healdsburg Avenue, Healdsburg; 707-433-6935, fax 707-433-7562; www.healdsburg.org, e-mail hbgcham@pacbell.net.

The **Healdsburg Museum** is housed in the revamped Carnegie library two blocks from the plaza. You'll find permanent displays on regional history, including rare Pomo baskets as well as 19th-century artifacts such as tools and clothing; changing exhibits tend to focus on a single subject. Closed Monday. ~ 221 Matheson Street, Healdsburg; 707-431-3325.

Healdsburg is centrally located for exploring several wine appellations, including Dry Creek Valley and the Alexander Valley. The roads linking the wineries provide some of the most pleasant driving anywhere in the Wine Country.

Dry Creek Valley, a luxurious landscape of vineyards and forest, stretches to the west of Healdsburg, and has two small wineries warrant special attention. **Dry Creek Vineyard** sits in an ivy-covered building surrounded by shade trees. There's tasting every day and the winery provides picnic tables for guests. Among the excellent wines produced are chenin blancs, fumés, cabernets, chardonnays, merlots and zinfandels. ~ 3770 Lambert Bridge Road, Healdsburg; 707-433-1000, 800-864-9463, fax 707-433-5329; www.drycreekvineyard.com, e-mail dcv@drycreekvineyard.com.

Along the far rim of Dry Creek Valley rises **A. Rafanelli Winery**, a classic family-style enterprise. David A. Rafanelli, whose roots go far back in the wine industry, owns the place and does much of the work himself along with his wife, Patty. Planting primarily zinfandel and cabernet grapes, they produce excellent wines in limited quantities. The winery itself consists of an old barn behind the family home. Backdropped by forested hills, it overlooks the valley and surrounding countryside. Tours and tasting are by appointment. ~ 4685 West Dry Creek Road, Healdsburg; 707-433-1385, fax 707-433-3836.

One of the top gardens in the Wine Country can be found on the grounds of the **Ferrari-Carano Vineyards & Winery**, the last winery on Dry Creek Road before it ends at Lake Sonoma. Another highlight is the impressive underground barrel-aging cellar. Wind up a visit in the hospitality center called Villa Fiore, where fume

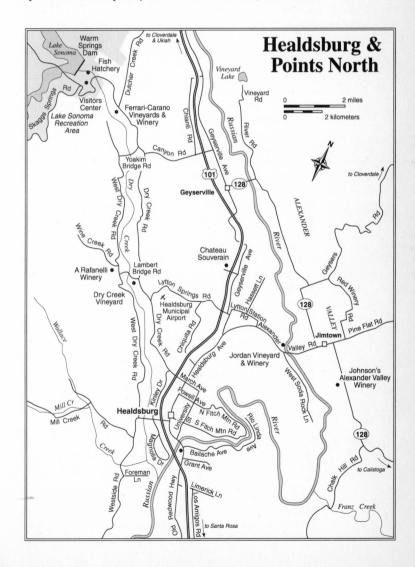

blanc, chardonnay, merlot and cabernet sauvignon are among the best options for tasting. ~ 8761 Dry Creek Road, Healdsburg; 707-433-6700.

East of Healdsburg lies the **Alexander Valley**, a region whose wines are gaining an increasingly fine reputation. Because of its warm climate, the valley is sometimes compared with the Bordeaux area of France. Its vintages, however, have a quality all their own.

The 1924 theater pipe organ at Johnson's Alexander Valley Winery is used for the winery's occasional concerts.

Jordan Vineyard & Winery is a lavish facility built along the lines of a Bordeaux château, and the winery is housed in a grand building that overlooks the Alexander Valley. Electronic gates protect the grounds, and no signs mark the entranceway. So a tour of the estate is a rare experience, providing a glimpse into a winery whose elegance matches its excellence. Tours are by appointment. Closed Sunday and for two weeks at Christmas. ~ 1474 Alexander Valley Road, Healdsburg; 707-431-5250, fax 707-431-5259.

A long road leads to an unpainted redwood barn at **Johnson's Alexander Valley Winery**. There is a wealth of modern equipment around the place, which produces fine pinot noirs and cabernets. Owned by a father-daughter team, the little winery offers tasting anytime. ~ 8333 Route 128, Healdsburg; 707-433-2319, fax 707-433-5302; www.johnsonwines.com, e-mail the winery@johnsonwines.com.

A short drive north on Route 101 takes you to the exit for **Chateau Souverain**, an almost palatial structure where even the tasting room has a view. This winery is known for cabernet sauvignon, merlot and sauvignon blanc, in particular. ~ Independence Lane, Geyserville; 707-433-8281, fax 707-433-5174; www.chateausouverain.com.

Route 101 streams north past Ukiah and several more wineries. A more interesting course lies along **Route 128**, which leads northwest from Cloverdale through piedmont country. En route, the two-lane road meanders like an old river, bending back upon itself to reveal sloping meadows and tree-tufted glades. It's a beautiful country drive through rolling ranch land. Sheep graze the hills and an occasional farmhouse stands along the roadside, its windows blinking sunlight at solitary cars.

LODGING   Numerous country inns dot the area, including some in the hearts of towns, some in rural areas and some practically across the street from vineyards. There are no large hotels in the northern part of the county, but you can find a couple of inexpensive motels.

A few blocks off the Healdsburg plaza sits the **Haydon Street Inn**, a lovely bed and breakfast set in a vintage 1912 house. Each room is beautifully appointed with antique furniture and artistic wallhangings. Both the private rooms and the common areas are quite spacious. The tree-shaded lawn, comfortable living room, and wraparound front porch are a perfect expression of Main Street, America. Serving a full breakfast and afternoon refreshments, the inn has eight rooms in the main building and the separate carriage house, all with private baths; several rooms feature jacuzzi tubs. ~ 321 Haydon Street, Healdsburg; 707-433-5228, 800-528-3703, fax 707-433-6637. DELUXE TO ULTRA-DELUXE.

The **Healdsburg Inn on the Plaza** occupies two floors above a street-level gallery in what was once a Wells Fargo bank. All the rooms are drastically different, but most are done up in pastels with touches such as lace curtains and Victorian antiques. Four of the ten rooms overlook the leafy park, but the inn's best feature is the terrace where breakfast is served. ~ 110 Matheson Street, Healdsburg; 707-433-6991, 800-431-8663, fax 707-433-9513; www.healdsburginn.com. MODERATE TO DELUXE.

Another Victorian choice is the **Camellia Inn**, which retains many of its original architectural details such as 12-foot ceilings and twin fireplaces in the double parlor. Guest accommodations located in the main house are traditional with chandeliers, oriental rugs and period antiques, though a few rooms are quite small; newer additions tend to be feature more contemporary decor. A major-league breakfast is served in the formal dining room. Camellias bloom copiously during the winter and a pool in the back is a most welcome sight after a hot day of winetasting. ~ 211 North Street, Healdsburg; 707-433-8182, 800-727-8182; www.camelliainn.com, e-mail lucy@camelliainn.com. DELUXE TO ULTRA-DELUXE.

Built in the early 1900s as a private summer retreat, the **Madrona Manor Country Inn** is a charming example of Gothic Victorian architecture, complete with a balconied porch, turrets and gables. The best rooms are in the main house; they are spacious (two upstairs sport a shared veranda) and furnished in serious antiques, including chaises longues and armoires. There are an additional 12 accommodations in several outbuildings on an eight-acre site as well as a carriage house. Guests enjoy the pool and a breakfast buffet. The on-site restaurant whips up eclectic California cuisine. ~ 1001 Westside Road, Healdsburg; 707-433-4231, 800-258-4003, fax 707-433-0703; www.madronamanor. com. ULTRA-DELUXE.

The **Hope-Merrill House** is a perennial favorite, an appealingly comfortable inn with oodles of Victorian touches. A dozen guest rooms on two floors in this late-19th-century building are cozily decorated with antiques and period replica wallpaper. Unusual for a B&B, it has a pool in the garden. Across the street is the Hope-Bosworth House, with an additional four rooms. ~ 21253 Geyserville Avenue, Geyserville; 707-857-3356, fax 707-857-4673. MODERATE TO DELUXE.

HIDDEN ►   If you're yearning to retreat back into the '60s, check out **Isis Oasis**, a ten-acre hideaway that combines bed-and-breakfast facilities with massage, tarot readings, and past-life experiences. Set in the tiny town of Geyserville, this New Age camp offers an array of accommodations. You can check into a yurt, a "tower house lodge," or a three-room honeymoon cottage; wander the Egyptian-style grounds, which include a pyramid and obelisk; and luxuriate in the hot tub, sauna and swimming pool. There is also a zoo with exotic animals and birds, and an Egyptian meditation temple. ~ 20889 Geyserville Avenue, Geyserville; 707-857-4747, 800-679-7387, fax 707-857-3287; www.isisoasis.org, e-mail isis@saber.net. MODERATE TO DELUXE.

DINING   You could dine for a week just by patronizing the restaurants on and near the Healdsburg plaza. Most of the places described below are locally owned and operated and offer an eclectic choice of experiences and prices.

Bistro Ralph is a small but chic place that locals patronize on a regular basis. The food is interesting and adventurous, yet recognizable. You might call it California home-style, featuring fresh produce and fish and some heartier fare in a minimalist setting. The place is known for its imaginative wine offerings. ~ 109 Plaza Street, Healdsburg; 707-433-1380. MODERATE.

Felix & Louie's occupies a cavernous space with horizontal sails across the high ceiling and a metal-topped bar set in front of the wood-fired pizza oven. The order of the day here is hearty Italianate fare, from bruschetta to pizza to fish and baby-back ribs, plus a sumptuous lasagna that defies its bland description as vegetarian. The full bar somewhat compensates for an unimpressive wine list with only a couple of by-the-glass choices. On nice nights, join the locals seated out back on the hidden patio. ~ 106 Matheson Street, Healdsburg; 707-433-6966, fax 707-433-1974. BUDGET TO MODERATE.

In a revamped bungalow a couple of blocks off the plaza, the **Acre Café & Lounge** calls its food "Sonoma kitchen garden cuisine." Vegetarians can have a field day here, but meat eaters won't starve since there's chicken, steak and seafood. Closed

FARM FRESH

From May through October, every Saturday morning at the North Plaza parking lot, the **Healdsburg Farmers Market** is a smorgasbord of berries, stone fruit, lettuces and artisanal cheeses and other goodies for the picnic basket. ~ North and Vine streets, Healdsburg; 707-431-1956.

Monday and Tuesday. ~ 420 Center Street, Healdsburg; phone/
fax 707-431-1302. MODERATE TO DELUXE.

For a quick, inexpensive bite, take a side street off the plaza and
head to **El Farolito Mexican Restaurant**. The menu is basic—
tostados and tacos—but you can eat here or ask for take-out and
enjoy your meal on a bench in the park. ~ 120 Plaza Street,
Healdsburg; 707-433-2897. BUDGET.

The **Café at the Winery** boasts one of the best restaurant views ◀ **HIDDEN**
in northern California. With expansive windows and a sizable
patio, it can accommodate nature lovers in any weather. You may
want to sample wines in the tasting room (perhaps picking up
one to enjoy with dinner). Elegant dishes such as grilled salmon,
roast leg of lamb, pâté and a goat-cheese-and-leek tart befit the
semi-formal decor. Closed Monday through Thursday. ~ 400
Chateau Souverain Drive, Geyserville; 707-433-3141. MODERATE
TO DELUXE.

Healdsburg's plaza is flanked with a dozen or more shops, with **SHOPPING**
things for kids as well as gourmet foods and home furnishings
and accessories.

One of the best sources for regional guides and wine-related
books as well as literature is **Toyon Books**. ~ 104 Matheson
Street, Healdsburg; 707-433-9270.

A Friend in the Country stocks elegant tabletop merchandise,
along with small lamps, linens, pillows and knickknacks. ~ 114
Matheson Street, Healdsburg; 707-433-1615.

The Healdsburg branch of Napa's renowned **Oakville Grocery**
is bigger than the original, with an awesome assortment of condiments and wine along with fresh produce, juices and cheese. ~
124 Matheson Street, Healdsburg; 707-433-3200.

Healdsburg Avenue boasts more antique stores than any
other street in town and probably even the county. Some 20 dealers peddle their wares at **Healdsburg Classics**, which is known
for patio furniture as well as traditional pieces. ~ 226 Healdsburg Avenue, Healdsburg; 707-433-4315.

Northern Sonoma County is pretty quiet at night, but on Saturday **NIGHTLIFE**
nights there is always a live band (rarely is there a cover), which
may be blues, Latin jazz or something else, at the **Bear Republic
Brewing Company**. ~ 345 Healdsburg Avenue, Healdsburg; 707-
433-2337.

LAKE SONOMA 🚶🚴🐎⛵🏕🚤 More than 50 miles **PARKS**
of shoreline define this lake, created by the construction of Warm
Spring Dam. Add the land acreage to that of the water, and you
get 17,000 pretty much unspoiled acres. The visitors center has
Pomo Indian and natural history displays and a fish hatchery; it's

the place to pick up hiking trail maps (there are 40 miles of trails) and fishing guides. The only real beach is at the Yorty Creek Recreation Area. ~ Skaggs Springs Road, Geyserville; 707-433-9483.

▲ There are 113 campsites ($10 to $16 per night) and 2 group areas ($80 per night); some campsites are close enough to the lake to boat in. There's also backcountry camping; the required permits can be obtained at the visitors center.

Outdoor Adventures

Lake Sonoma offers numerous secluded coves along its 53 miles of shoreline. Anglers can go for bass, channel catfish, red ear perch or Sacramento perch. A boat ramp and a full-service marina are available for those who decide to rent a boat. ~ Dry Creek Road; 11 miles north of Healdsburg; 707-433-2200.

FISHING

From November through March, fisherpeople can try for steelhead trout from the banks of the **Russian River** near Healdsburg.

WATER SPORTS

During the spring, summer and early fall, canoes are a popular mode of transportation on the Russian River. **W. C. Trowbridge Canoe Trips** has them available for half- and full-day outings. ~ 20 Healdsburg Avenue, Healdsburg; 800-640-1386.

BALLOON RIDES

In business since 1974, **Flambuoyant Hot Air Excursions** take off from Healdsburg and soar above Sonoma Valley, offering views of Alexander and Dry Creek valleys, the Russian River, and more. Afterward, riders are treated to brunch. Capacity of four to eight people; they specialize in private flights. ~ 250 Pleasant Avenue, Santa Rosa; 707-838-8500, fax 707-838-8900.

SKATING

Skaters and rollerbladers can drop in for some air at **Santa Rosa Skatepark**, equipped with three connecting bowls as well as snake runs, halfpipes and curbs. Helmets are required. ~ Fulton Community Park, 725 Fulton Road, Santa Rosa; 707-543-3292.

Ice skating enthusiasts strap on their blades at the **Redwood Ice Arena**, open year-round. ~ 1667 West Steele Lane, Santa Rosa; 707-546-7147, fax 707-546-3764.

GOLF

Play a challenging game at the public 18-hole **Windsor Golf Course**. ~ 6555 Skylane Boulevard, Windsor; 707-838-7888. **Oakmont Golf Club** features a par-72 championship course and a par-63 executive court. This tree-lined, semiprivate club rents clubs and carts. ~ 7025 Oakmont Drive, Santa Rosa; 707-539-0415, fax 707-539-0453.

BIKING

The **Joe Rodota Trail**, which is used for walking as well as pedaling, runs alongside Route 12 between Route 101 and Sebastopol before petering out. However, you can pick up the trail again north of town off Route 116 and ride into Graton. The sum of these parts is about 3 miles, virtually all of it flat; the prettiest section is between Sebastopol and Graton.

Bike Rentals   In the Santa Rosa area, head to **Dave's Bike Sport**. If you're not in the mood to buy a bike, you can rent road or mountain bikes, as well as helmets and locks. They also do repairs. ~ 353 College Avenue, Santa Rosa; 707-528-3283. **Spoke Folk Cyclery** includes helmets, locks and backpacks with their rental bikes (hybrid, tandem, road). You can buy a bike and accessories, as well as have repairs done. ~ 249 Center Street, Healdsburg; 707-433-7171.

All distances listed for hiking trails are one way unless otherwise noted.

HIKING

Once inhabited by Pomo and Wappo Indians, **Annadel State Park** is a mix of forest and meadow laced with 39 miles of hiking paths. ~ 707-539-3911. The **Warren B. Richardson Trail** (2.7 miles) wanders through a forest of Douglas fir en route to Lake Ilsanjo. Spring brings redwood orchid blossoms, adding a rare experience to an already splendid hike.

Marsh Trail (3.6 miles) climbs the side of Bennett Mountain and offers grand views of Lake Ilsanjo as well as nearby mountain ranges. For a trip to an old quarry site where cobblestones were once excavated, head down the aptly named **Cobblestone Trail** (2 miles).

SIX

Russian River Area

With its headwaters in Mendocino County, the Russian River rambles south through north central California to Healdsburg. Here it turns west toward the sea, as the surrounding landscape changes from rolling ranch land to dense redwood forest. The area around Guerneville, where the river begins its headlong rush to the Pacific, has enjoyed a rebirth as a gay resort area.

Earlier a family vacation spot, the Guerneville–Forestville–Monte Rio area became a raffish home to bikers and hippies during the '50s and '60s. Then in the '70s, gay vacationers from San Francisco began frequenting the region. Today, the Russian River is San Francisco's answer to Fire Island. There are many gay resorts in and around Guerneville, and almost without exception every establishment in town welcomes gay visitors. The area is still also a popular family resort area.

This stretch of the river offers prime fishing and canoeing opportunities. As the river rumbles downslope, it provides miles of scenic runs past overhanging forests. Black bass, steelhead, bluegill, and silver salmon swim these waters, and there are numerous beaches for swimming and sunbathing. From Santa Rosa, the winding, two-lane River Road follows the northern edge of the Russian River, taking you to the ocean, where it dead-ends at Goat Rock Beach.

The first people known to live in the lower Russian River were the Miwok and Pomo Indians, who established a number of villages where the bigger towns stand today. They called the river Shabaikai, or "Big Snake," after its shape. The Russian trappers and Aleuts from Alaska landed in Bodega Bay in 1809, but the area was already claimed by the Mexican government as part of Alta (upper) California. The American and European settlers arrived in the early 1850s and in short order began logging. One look at the towering redwoods was probably all it took to make them realize they had their own kind of gold mine, just as prospectors from all over the world were depleting the Sierra foothills of the real thing. (George Guerne, for whom Guerneville is named, ran a thriving saw mill on the banks of the river.) One tree in particular achieved special fame. Felled on the south side of the river in 1873, this 3000-year-old specimen stretched 275 feet—so large it was used to fashion "The Church Built from One Tree" in nearby Santa Rosa.

Eventually, the stands of redwoods were diminished to the point that other crops, including prunes, hops and tobacco, were raised in the early 1900s. Railroads anticipated the area's becoming a desirable getaway from San Francisco and began running excursions to the Russian River. Before long, hotels, resorts and summer cottages were built to house all the warm-weather visitors.

Some visitors were of a different stripe altogether. A group of San Francisco newspapermen, who had the habit of calling themselves "Bohemians," had been gathering for summer retreats in Marin County before regularly renting a 160-acre redwood grove near Monte Rio on the river in 1882. They bought the property in 1898, redubbed it Bohemian Grove, and laid the groundwork for one of the world's most famous private clubs. The all-male Bohemian Club, based in San Francisco, claims more than 2000 members. While "the Grove" encampment each summer still includes artists and scriveners, members and guests have included William Randolph Hearst, Ronald Reagan, Henry Kissinger, Richard Nixon, Bob Hope and other famous and powerful men. You can tell when each summer session is about to begin by counting the number of private jets landing at the Sonoma County Airport.

What used to be an ultra-rural hideaway is now surrounded by small towns up and down the river. And there are more visitors than ever before, eager to experience the area's climate and growing conditions, found to be well suited to a number of grape varieties. After the Europeans, especially the Italians, discovered Sonoma, it was but a matter of time before grapes were planted. (Actually, the Russians planted grapes as early as the 1830s, but very little is known about what they were or what became of them.) Families named Martini and Prati were the Russian River equivalent of the Sebastianis and the Simis elsewhere in the county and like those colleagues, their names still grace wineries today.

Family homes, weekend cottages and just plain shacks crowd the steep banks of the river as it meanders west past a series of towns, most of them barely on the map—and some seem in danger of actually sliding off. Cazadero, just over eight miles north of Guerneville, gets more rain than anyplace else in the county (an average of about 75 inches a year, half of what Guerneville gets). When winter rains swell the river—as well as the contributory creeks—some areas are routinely evacuated; many homes have been lost to water and mudslides over the past decade.

The rest of the year passes in peace, free of the damaging vagaries of Mother Nature. Although the area has become more of a year-round residential haven than it once was, the population swells noticeably in the summer, when river rafters and canoers and vacationers and daytrippers flock to the cool shade of the redwoods in this scenic region.

The entire Russian River region is an Eden of small farms, vineyards and orchards, though the famous Gravenstein apples are losing ground to grapes and other more profitable crops. As in Healdsburg and other areas, the land in this part of the Wine Country has witnessed a succession of crops, including orchards and hop fields. Today, it would seem that almost anything can grow in the fertile soil near the river. Summer and fall, the myriad two-lane roads buzz with cars filled with folks seeking to pick their own berries, hunt for pumpkins or fell their own Christmas trees. In the spring, these same roads make for dazzling drives, with the pink and white blossoms of fruit and nut trees brightening the otherwise dreary, late-winter landscape.

And of course, year-round, wine lovers poke around these same backroads, knowing that this is the Promised Land of Pinot Noir. Chardonnay is another grape known to thrive in the cool growing climate of the Russian River Valley, and the combination of the two results in some fine sparkling wine in this appellation.

▼ ▼ ▼ ▼ ▼ ▼ ▼ ▼ ▼ ▼ ▼ ▼
Sebastopol Area

This region of the Wine Country is also an apple-growing area. Small towns such as Sebastopol and Graton are surrounded by orchards and vineyards along with numerous nurseries specializing in roses or palm trees or other growing things.

Sebastopol is Sonoma's answer to the East Bay's Berkeley, a city with a lively arts scene and a reputation for environmental activism and quirky politics. If you were thinking of importing some heavy-duty weaponry into town, think again: Sebastopol has declared itself a nuclear-free zone. It has also become something of an antique-lover's mecca, with many shops in town and south of it along Route 116, known as the Gravenstein Highway (named for a variety of apple that thrives in the region).

SIGHTS

You'll have to keep your wits about you as you traverse Sebastopol. Even before so many streets were made one-way, it wasn't exactly a piece of cake to navigate the streets in the central town. If Sebastopol is your destination, fine; park where you can and you'll be within walking distance of anything downtown. If you're headed out to the coast or north to Guerneville, heads up! The signage is good and moreover the locals are long accustomed to giving directions. There's not a lot in the way of historic sites in town, but it's a lovely place to stroll, shop, have a sandwich—or stay on for an excellent dinner—and learn a little about regional history. The town was settled in 1852 but at last count still had less than 8000 residents.

Located in a restored 1917 railroad depot, the **West County Museum** houses books, magazines, newspapers, photographs, videotapes and audiotapes on regional history in its Triggs Reference Room. More archival material illuminating west Sonoma history appear in exhibits that rotate three or four times a year. Closed Monday through Wednesday. ~ 261 South Main Street, Sebastopol; 707-829-6711; www.wschs-grf.pon.net/wcm.htm.

Many farms allow visitors to wander the orchards and berry fields and **pick produce**. The **Sonoma County Farm Trails**, which sponsors the Gravenstein Apple Fair in August, publishes a map that will lead you to apples, pears, berries, cherries, peaches and vegetables. ~ P.O. Box 6032 Santa Rosa, CA 95406; 707-571-8288, 800-207-9464, fax 707-571-7719; www.farmtrails.org, e-mail farmtrails@farmtrails.org.

You can also pick up a Sonoma County Farm Trails map at the **Sebastopol Chamber of Commerce**, along with other helpful information on the area. ~ 265 South Main Street, Sebastopol; 707-823-3032, fax 707-823-8439; www.sebastopol.org, apples@sebastopol.org.

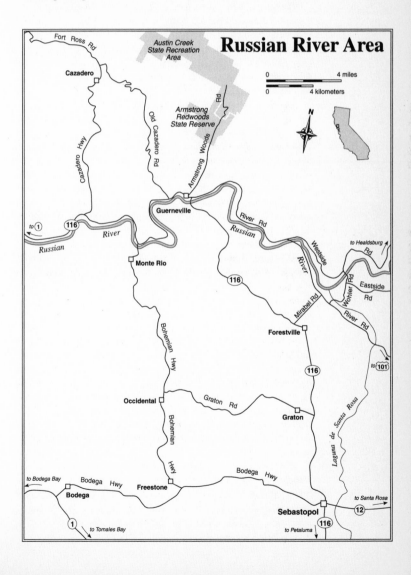

Russian River Area

Less famous than Santa Rosa's Luther Burbank home and gardens, the **Luther Burbank Gold Ridge Experiment Farm** has its own following. Here, on 18 acres, the legendary horticulturist built a cottage to live in while he conducted his experiments on Gravenstein apples, cherries, grapes, plums and lilies between 1895 and 1926. Access to the gardens is free, but reservations are required for guided tours. ~ 7781 Bodega Avenue, Sebastopol; 707-829-6711, fax 707-829-7041.

West of Sebastopol on Route 12 in the historic town of Freestone is **Osmosis Enzyme Bath & Massage**. While hot-springs soaks and mud baths are possible at countless locations, Osmosis claims to be the only place in North America offering Japanese enzyme baths, composed of cedar fiber, rice bran and more than 600 active enzymes. ~ 209 Bohemian Highway, Freestone; 707-823-8231, fax 707-874-3788; www.osmosis.com.

North of Sebastopol along Route 116 is **Graton**. Once a foundering town well off the tourist map, it has recently experienced a rebirth, thanks largely to the energetic ambitions of a local real-estate maven who undertook the restoration of many old buildings along the two-block main drag.

The former turn-of-the-20th-century Hotel Graton, for instance, was restored in 1998 and now comprises the tasting room of the **Blackstone/Martin Ray Winery**, where you can sample three different labels. Among their specialities are merlots, chardonnays, pinot noirs and cabs. Their winemaking facilities, located across the street, are available for tours by appointment only. ~ 9060 Graton Road, Graton; 707-824-2401, fax 707-824-2592; www.martinray-winery.com, www.blackstone-winery.com.

LODGING For a town its size, Sebastopol is surprisingly short on lodging, including the chain variety. But you can find a couple of nifty places to lay your head, and rooms are plentiful in nearby Santa Rosa.

A huge courtyard and landscaped garden make the **Sebastopol Inn** seem larger than its 37 rooms. Arranged in two two-story wings, the rooms and suites are sparkling fresh, done in country colors like blue and lemon and snappy ticking stripes; some have balconies or patios while others have jacuzzis. Other amenities include an outdoor pool and jacuzzi and an on-site coffeehouse. ~ 6751 Sebastopol Avenue, Sebastopol; 707-829-2500, fax 707-823-1535; www.thesebastopolinn.com, e-mail stay@thesebastopolinn.com. MODERATE TO DELUXE.

The two-story **Holiday Inn Express Hotel & Suites** has 82 standard rooms opening onto interior corridors. It's close to Main Street, within walking distance of shops and restaurants. Continental breakfast and a whirlpool are among the complimentary amenities. ~ 1101 Route 116, Sebastopol; 707-829-6677, fax 707-829-2618; www.lokhotels.com. MODERATE TO DELUXE.

Other lodgings lie in the towns to the west. Located on a 60-acre estate, the Mediterranean-style **Sonoma Coast Villa** offers unusual elegance for the countryside. Twelve accommodations are arranged on a single level, opening onto a courtyard. Most decor tends towards French and Italian country, but it's understated. The villa offers spa services and, on the weekends, complimentary soup and salad to guests who may not be in the mood to travel to a nearby town for dinner. Full breakfast is included. ~ 16702 Route 1, Bodega; 707-876-9818, 888-404-2255, fax 707-876-9856; www.scvilla.com, e-mail reservations@scvilla.com. ULTRA-DELUXE.

Located a few miles northeast of Bodega, the **Inn at Occidental** is a charming Victorian homestead encircled by a wide porch bedecked with pots of pink geraniums and white wicker rockers. The eight guest rooms are furnished with antique mahogany, pine beds, down comforters, and display cases of antique glass and pottery from the owner's private collection. A full breakfast is included, as is access to the garden jacuzzi. ~ 3657 Church Street,

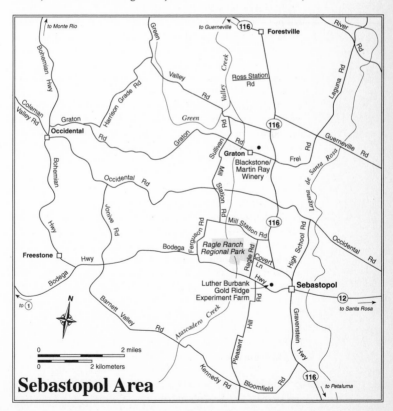

Sebastopol Area

Occidental; 707-874-1047, 800-522-6324, fax 707-874-1078; www.innatoccidental.com, e-mail innkeeper@innatoccidental. com. DELUXE TO ULTRA-DELUXE.

DINING   Aside from fast-food joints, there are fewer dining choices in Sebastopol than one might expect for a town its size, but the situation is improving. The good news is that there seems to be at least one to fit your budget.

Housed in a renovated 1907 bank building, the 40-seat **101 Main Bistro & Wine Bar** is graced with 30-foot-high ceilings warmed up with draped fabric. This inviting arrangement sets the stage for the most acclaimed food in town. The chef has his way with local meats and produce, from lamb and wild mushrooms to desserts on the order of a pear-and-goat-cheese tart. Diners accompany these refined delights with any of more than 100 regional wines, many of which are available by the glass. Closed Monday. ~ 101 South Main Street, Sebastopol; 707-829-3212, fax 707-829-8353. DELUXE.

Anyone who waxes nostalgic about food from the '50s will fall hard for **The Pine Cone**, a downtown standby that's withstood the test of time. All-American fare like tuna melts, hamburgers and honest-to-goodness creamy rich milkshakes might feel they're in a culinary time warp. By the time you've finished stuffing yourself, you may well be tempted to call the waitress "Mom." ~ 162 Main Street, Sebastopol; 707-823-1375. BUDGET.

Old-timers remember Mom's Apple Pie on the Gravenstein Highway. It's still there, but it's been shoved into a corner since the lunchroom was taken over by **Stella's Café**. It's an odd set-up but good news for people looking for tasty food and reasonably priced wines. Some dishes, like skewered vegetables with curry and ginger sauce, may make you forget all about meat, but you'll find that, too. Closed Tuesday. ~ 4550 Route 116, Sebastopol; 707-823-6637. MODERATE.

The old-timer in nearby Graton is the **Willow Wood Market Café**, which really is a market. If you could pick just one place to soak up the ambience of life in west Sonoma, this should be it. Ultra-casual, it offers some table-and-counter seating in front, amidst the shelves stocked with canned goods and New Age merchandise, as well as four additional tables in the rear and a few more on the pretty patio. Soups and salads are healthful and fresh (in season you might order a roasted beet and tomato soup), and all-American main courses on the small menu usually include fish or roast half-chicken with mashed potatoes. Closed Sunday. ~ 9020 Graton Road, Graton; phone/fax 707-823-0233. MODERATE.

SHOPPING   Downtown Sebastopol is home to a number of small stores, most one-of-a-kind and locally owned. Several antique collectives stand

Author Picks

CHAPTER FAVORITES

Of the many delights of the Russian River region, I'm most refreshed by an al fresco lunch with a view of the surrounding countryside at **Korbel Champagne Cellars**. *page 125*

When I think of summer, I think of floating along a river—in particular, the **Russian River**, snug in a canoe with a cold beverage and something soft on which to nap. *page 132*

I love sleeping upstairs in one of the *casas* at the **Applewood Inn**, where I'm surrounded by giant redwoods that give the illusion of camping out in a treehouse. *page 128*

One of my favorite instant mood-boosters is a visit to **Rosemary's Garden** to pick up sachets and pot-pourri to freshen suitcases, drawers and closets. *page 123*

on the Gravenstein Highway (Route 116) to the southeast, and there are a couple of places in Graton worth a peek.

The **Antique Society** is the biggest and the best of the area's many purveyors of previously owned items. Warehouse in size, it is dust-free, with beautifully arranged collections worthy of a Macy's window. There's even a department devoted to tansu chests. ~ 2661 Route 116, Sebastopol; 707-829-1733.

Rosemary's Garden is so well stocked with herbs, potpourri, ointments, soaps and the like that it almost takes your breath away. ~ 132 North Main Street, Sebastopol; 707-829-2539.

The place to shop for children is **HearthSong Toys**, which sells well-made toys and good-for-you games. ~ 156 North Main Street, Sebastopol; 707-829-0944.

One of the best-known places to shop for apples is **Walker Apples**, at the end of a country lane. Closed mid-November through July, the farm sells 23 varieties of apples the rest of the year. ~ Upp Road, Sebastopol; 707-823-4310.

◄ *HIDDEN*

Gravenstein, red and golden Delicious, Jonathan and Rome apples are available at **Dutton Ranch/Sebastopol Vineyards**. Prime time is August and September, so if you're visiting off-season it's a good idea to call ahead. The ranch offers winetastings and sells wines and gifts. There's also a picnic area open to the public. ~ 8785 Green Valley Road, Sebastopol; 707-829-9463; www.sebastopolvineyards.com.

Downtown Graton has a couple of extraordinary shops. **Cold Mountain Books** specializes in rare and used volumes. It's the kind of place you're likely to run across a book you had always meant to read or in fact did read a long time ago and want to do it again. And it's a great shop for browsing when you need inspiration. ~ 9050 Graton Road, Graton; 707-823-2881.

Patterson's Emporium may sound like something old and dusty, but nothing could be further from the truth. The assortment of gifts, gadgets, music and home accessories here include many items we've never seen anywhere else, making this attractive store worth going out of your way to visit. ~ 9040 Graton Road, Graton; 707-824-9600.

NIGHTLIFE   Compared to nearby Guerneville, there's not much action in Sebastopol but they don't exactly roll up the sidewalks at night, either.

Blues or rock bands are usually on stage at **Jasper O'Farrell's**, probably the top bar in this area. In fact, there's live music, no cover, seven nights a week, with reggae or Cajun bands making an occasional appearance. ~ 6957 Sebastopol Avenue, Sebastopol; 707-823-1389.

When the mood is right, the **Powerhouse Brewing Co.** offers live music on the weekends. The mix is eclectic—folk, zydeco, reggae, whatever—and if you've ever heard of the band, there's probably a cover charge. ~ 268 Petaluma Avenue, Sebastopol; 707-829-9171.

PARKS   **RAGLE RANCH REGIONAL PARK**   This 156-acre parcel encompasses oak woodlands, creeks and marshes. It's very popular with nearby residents, who avail themselves of a parcourse, a soccer field, ball fields, tennis and volleyball courts, and picnic areas outfitted with barbecue grills. Day-use fee, $3. ~ 500 Ragle Ranch Road, one mile north of Bodega Highway, Sebastopol; 707-565-2041.

▼▼▼▼▼▼▼▼▼▼▼▼
Guerneville Area

Guerneville is famous for its gay resorts but is still a family-friendly city. It straddles the Russian River, with virtually all its commercial development on the north bank. Forestville is next in size, with a small downtown lined with services and shops. The tiny towns like Monte Rio are a cross between quaint and funky and are by and large bedroom communities.

SIGHTS   As the biggest town on the river west of Route 101, it has the most restaurants, bars, shops and inns. **Guerneville** (pronounced gurn-vul) was settled in 1860, once known as Stumptown and later named after a Ohio native, George E. Guerne, who built a saw- and planing-mill there in 1864.

The Russian River is the main attraction in this neck of the red-woods. Near town are a number of wineries. The **Visitors Information Center** provides maps and brochures on facilities and water sports. ~ 14034 Armstrong Woods Road, Guerneville; 707-869-

9212, 800-253-8800, fax 707-869-9215; www.russianriver.org,
e-mail info@russianriver.org. The Center also operates the **Russian
River Region Visitors Bureau at Korbel Station**. ~ 13250 River
Road, Guerneville; 707-869-2772, fax 707-869-9215.

As you first arrive in downtown Guerneville you will come
to a traffic signal at the intersection of Armstrong Woods Road.
Turning north will take you to **Armstrong Redwoods State Reserve**,
where you undoubtedly will marvel at the grove of ancient redwoods dating back 1400 years and reaching heights of 300 feet.
Admission. ~ 17000 Armstrong Woods Road, Guerneville; 707-
869-2015, fax 707-869-5629.

Of course, Guerneville would never have developed into a resort destination had it not been for the waters of the Russian River.
The most popular spot around Guerneville to
plunge in for a swim or launch a canoe is **Johnson's Beach**. Located just two blocks from the heart
of downtown, this sunny waterfront strip is also
home to many summer events, including the renowned
Russian River Jazz Festival. ~ South end of Church
Street, Guerneville.

> The apple most identi-
> fied with the area, the
> Gravenstein, was in-
> troduced hereabouts
> by the Russians up
> in Fort Ross.

Founded in 1882 by three brothers, **Korbel Champagne
Cellars** produces today's most popular sparkling wines. On
any day of the week you may taste these award-winning bubblies
and sample their still wines and brandies. The tasting room and
attached gift shop offer nine different champagnes, some of
which are available nowhere else; also on the premises are a microbrewery and a gourmet delicatessen. While guided tours are
offered throughout the year, I recommend visiting during spring
and summer when the winery's century-old garden is alive with
roses, tulips and daffodils. ~ 13250 River Road, Guerneville;
707-824-7000, fax 707-869-2981; www.korbel.com, e-mail info
@korbel.com.

Dozens of wineries distinguish the Russian River region.
Several outstanding ones can be found along Westside Road and
smaller roads that are sometimes little more than a lane, while
others are located south on heavily traveled routes such as Route
116 (Gravenstein Highway). It's on this latter boulevard that you
will find **Russian River Vineyards Topolos** (most people simply
say Topolos, pronounced taupe-uh-lohs). This rambling complex is
known for its cutting-edge techniques such as biodynamic farming, which is believed to produce more vital crops by capitaliz-
ing on natural forces that tend to have minimal negative impact
on the land. But the real fun is in the tasting room, where a wide
array of wines, including some unusual varietals like Alicante
Bouschet, are available for sampling. Don't miss the port. ~ 5700
Route 116, Forestville; 707-887-1575, fax 707-887-1399; www.
topolos.com, e-mail topolos@topolos.com.

HIDDEN ►

Without doubt, one of the prettiest vineyard settings in all California belongs to **Iron Horse Vineyards**. The driveway snaking into this hidden spot is bordered with flowers, olive trees, and palm trees. Hills roll away in every direction, revealing a line of distant mountains. The winery buildings, painted barn-red, follow the classic architecture of American farms. Laid out around them in graceful checkerboard patterns are fields of pinot noir and chardonnay grapes. At harvest time these will be handpicked and then barrel-aged, for the emphasis at this elegant little winery is on personal attention. The outdoor tasting area boasts a view of green valley and is open seven days a week by appointment. ~ 9786 Ross Station Road, Sebastopol; 707-887-1507, fax 707-887-1337; www.ironhorsevineyards.com.

Found about a mile east off the Gravenstein Highway, **Martini & Prati** is just about the most unprepossessing winery in the county. Yet it has a distinct charm, once you get inside the tasting room that's been renovated into an adorable Italian marketplace. Here you can taste the very good and least expensive viognier made in California. The rest of the offerings are a mixed bag of Italian and California varietals. What's really great about this place is that you can purchase an empty jug and, depending on how busy everyone is, perhaps accompany a staff member into the barrel room and get the jug filled—dig this—for free. ~ 2191 Laguna Road, Santa Rosa; 707-823-2404; e-mail info@martiniprati.com.

LODGING

Gay resorts outnumber other accommodations in Guerneville, though everyone is welcome everywhere. A couple of secluded country inns add to the mix.

Resting on 15 waterfront acres on the edge of downtown Guerneville, **Fifes Resort** is the Russian River's largest gay resort. In addition to a restaurant and a bar, Fifes offers such facilities as a beach, a pool and volleyball courts, as well as a disco and gym. Accommodations are as varied as the sports activities. There are 100 budget-priced campsites as well as moderate-to-deluxe-priced individual cabins that were built in the 1920s and haven't changed much since then. Each is simply furnished with a queen-sized bed and without television or telephone. Some two-room cabins have a woodburning stove and a sofa bed in one room. ~ 16467 River Road, Guerneville; 707-869-0656, 800-734-3371, fax 707-869-0658; www.fifes.com, e-mail info@fifes.com. BUDGET TO MODERATE.

Fondly called "triple R," **Russian River Resort** offers 24 cheerfully decorated guest rooms situated around a clothing-optional hot tub area. Whereas most other resorts in the area can be described as rustic, this resort provides more modern, contemporary accommodations; each room is carpeted, has a private bath and cable TV (several have woodburning fireplaces as well). Throughout the year, the Russian River Resort organizes 15 to

20 events celebrating major holidays and festivities such as Women's Weekend. The guests are almost exclusively gay male but lesbians and gay-friendly straights are welcome. A restaurant is located on the premises. ~ 16390 4th Street, Guerneville; 707-869-0691, 800-417-3767, fax 707-869-0698; www.russianriver-resort.com, e-mail info@russianriverresort.com. DELUXE.

Catering primarily to gays and lesbians, **Highlands Resort** sits on three acres. Accommodations here come in many forms. Some are individual cabins with fireplaces, private baths, and kitchenettes; others are more standard motel-style rooms. The pool suite has a brass bed, a TV, a refrigerator and a view of the pool,

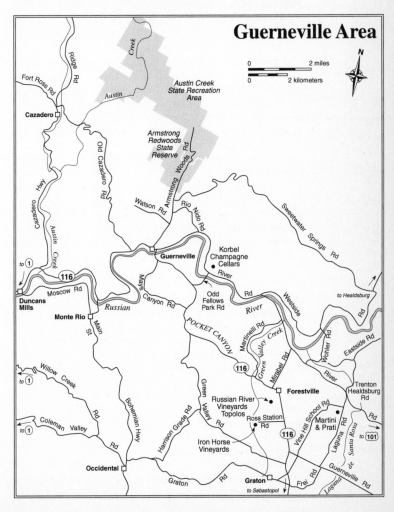

Guerneville Area

where sunbathing is *au naturel*. A hot tub, continental breakfast and a guest lounge with a piano, TV, VCR and books complete the amenities. There is also space for 20 tents. ~ 14000 Woodland Drive, Guerneville; 707-869-0333, fax 707-869-0370; www.high landsresort.com, e-mail muffins@highlandsresort.com. BUDGET TO DELUXE.

Spread over five wooded acres along the Russian River, **The Willows** is a gay and lesbian guesthouse resort with spots for tent camping and barbecuing on the grounds. The main lodge has 13 bedrooms, most with private baths, and a spacious living room with a stone fireplace, library and grand piano. The price tag includes breakfast, tea and coffee served in the morning and afternoon, as well as use of the canoes. ~ 15905 River Road, Guerneville; 707-869-2824, 800-953-2828, fax 707-869-2764; www. willowsrussianriver.com. MODERATE TO DELUXE.

Fern Grove Inn sits at the foot of a mountain and is a five-minute walk from town. The 20 mustard-colored craftsmen cottages were built in 1926 and are furnished with a mixture of antiques and contemporary styles. Some have jacuzzi tubs, and all suites have fireplaces or wood burning stoves. Guests enjoy breakfast, as well as sherry and port in the evenings. There's a two-night minimum on the weekends. ~ 16650 River Road, Guerneville; 707-869-9083, fax 707-869-1615. MODERATE TO ULTRA-DELUXE.

HIDDEN ► The prettiest accommodations in this neck of the redwoods belong to the **Applewood Inn**, hidden on a hillside in tiny Pocket Canyon. Belden House, the original family home built in 1922, has the older, more staid rooms, while two two-story *casas* across the courtyard offer more space that in some cases includes a small balcony. With a pool, hot tub and excellent restaurant (which uses produce from its own gardens), this estate, secluded among the redwoods, is the kind of place to which you can retreat and never leave the grounds until your visit is over. ~ 13555 Route 116, Guerneville; 707-869-9093, 800-555-8509, fax 707-869-9170; www.applewoodinn.com. DELUXE TO ULTRA-DELUXE.

Village Inn, a refurbished woodframe complex on the river, draws a mixed clientele. This cozy country inn, set amid redwood trees, has a homey, old-time feel. You'll also find a good restaurant and bar with river views. All rooms come with private bath and begin in the moderate range; ultra-deluxe price if you want a river view and deck. They're trim little units: clean, carpeted and decorated with an occasional piece of art. ~ 20822 River Boulevard, Monte Rio; 707-865-2304, 800-303-2303, fax 707-865-2332; www.village-inn.com, e-mail village@sonic.net. MODERATE TO DELUXE.

Huckleberry Springs Country Inn sits on 56 acres in the hills above Monte Rio. The most unique of its four cottages, the round Cherry Barrel, was formerly a building for curing cherries. It's lined with cedar wood, and, like the others, has modern art on the walls, a ceiling fan, a refrigerator and a wood stove. Guests who stay four nights get 50 percent off on the fourth and fifth nights. Closed December through February. ~ P.O. Box 400, Monte Rio, CA 95462; 707-865-2683, 800-822-2683; www. huckleberrysprings.com, e-mail mail@huckleberrysprings.com. ULTRA-DELUXE.

Fern Falls, set on two acres and another idyllic resort, attracts both gays and lesbians alike. Two cabins sport skylights and vaulted ceilings. Another is built around a giant oak tree. Each is furnished with antiques and has a kitchen with a stove, a microwave and a coffee grinder, as well as a mini-library and VCR. One cabin contains a baby grand piano. Outdoor showers provide a bathing experience you'll never forget. The scent of roses and fresh herbs permeates the gardens. The spa is perched under a massive bolder above the waterfall. Many guests say a stay here is a spiritual experience. Closed January. ~ P.O. Box 228, Cazadero, CA 95421; 707-632-6108, fax 707-632-6216. DELUXE TO ULTRA-DELUXE.

DINING

Restaurants around Guerneville are mostly casual, the exceptions being in the nicer inns. In summer, you'll find plenty of places that welcome diners in shorts, though shirts and shoes are always a good idea.

While even remote Guerneville now offers more than a couple of places to get an espresso, none are better than the **Coffee Bazaar**. Located on Armstrong Woods Road a block off the main strip, this cafe's food and beverages are tasty and affordable. There is a wide range of coffee creations and a generous selection of pastries each morning. Lunch choices include soups, salads, sandwiches, quiche, calzones and even lasagna; many vegetarian options are available. There is plenty of seating inside, but take a sidewalk table to peoplewatch. ~ 14045 Armstrong Woods Road, Guerneville; 707-869-9706; www.coffee-bazaar. com, e-mail dyoung@sonic.net. BUDGET.

WHAT'S IN A NAME

The Spanish called the 58-mile Russian River "San Ygnacio" in the early 1800s. The Russians who settled in Fort Ross up the coast referred to it as "Slavianka" (Slav woman). The first record of the Spanish version of the modern name came in 1843, when it was described in a petition for a land grant as "la boca del Rio Ruso," the mouth of the Russian River.

Situated on Main Street, **Sweet's River Grill** is big on atmosphere and satisfying food. Nearly all the seating is on the front patio, which is well-protected from the sun and is warmed by overhead heaters on chilly evenings. The full menu offers appetizers such as artichoke seafood dip or Cajun alligator sauté, and entrées include farm-raised venison, grilled ostrich, wild-mushroom puff pastry, and a variety of pastas. Brunch on weekends. ~ 16251 Main Street, Guerneville; 707-869-3383, fax 707-869-9274. MODERATE TO DELUXE.

The restaurant at **Fifes** is an intimate dining room with a stone fireplace, pine walls, and an exposed-rafter ceiling. There's also a sundeck for warm-weather dining. Fifes features a sophisticated California-cuisine menu that changes seasonally. Dinner includes scampi, steak, chicken curry, and prosciutto tortellini. Breakfast features eggs Benedict, while lunch combines sandwiches and salads with special entrées. Open for breakfast, lunch and dinner in the summer; dinner and weekend brunches only in the off-season. ~ 16467 River Road, Guerneville; 707-869-0656, 800-734-3371; www.fifes.com, e-mail info@fifes.com. MODERATE TO DELUXE.

Russian River wines are distinctive because a 70-foot-deep stratum of gravel lies beneath the valley, forcing vine roots to reach deeper for water and adding trace minerals that give the grapes a complex flavor.

If you're looking to have a cozy dinner away from downtown, head east out of town on River Road to **Burdon's**. Here you will find an elegant dining room with low lighting, white tablecloths and minimal decor. Chicken, steak and seafood predominate the menu, although there are a few pasta dishes. You'll also find prime rib and rack of lamb. Appetizers such as bay shrimp cocktail and escargot regularly appear on the menu, while main courses include filet mignon and filet of sole in a lemon and tartar sauce. There are cocktails and wine. Dinner only; Sunday brunch from June through September. Closed Monday and Tuesday. ~ 15405 River Road, Guerneville; 707-869-2615. MODERATE TO DELUXE.

Eight miles southeast of Guerneville in downtown Forestville, **Chez Marie** is a quaint lesbian-owned eatery. The cuisine is always prepared and served by the owners themselves, be it country-French served throughout the year, or Cajun Creole available Tuesday through Thursday during the summer. Duck à l'orange, *poulet des nuits arabes* (chicken marinated in a ginger-honey-sage mixture, then baked in phyllo dough), and *ris de veau supreme* (veal sweetbreads in a nutmeg cream sauce) are among the recommended offerings. Closed Monday and Tuesday; call for winter hours. ~ 6675 Front Street, Forestville; 707-887-7503; www. chezmarie.com, e-mail chezmarie@chezmarie.com. MODERATE.

An excellent bookstore and a true community resource, the **River** **SHOPPING**
Reader, Inc. has a small but strong selection of books, magazines,
cards, games and gifts. Visitors to Guerneville will find plenty of
choices for poolside reading in all categories including fiction,
spirituality and regional topics. There is also a good selection of
gay reading material including books and magazines. ~ 16355
Main Street, Guerneville; 707-869-2240; e-mail rreader@sonic.net.

On the main road between Forestville and Guerneville, you'll
do your sweet tooth a favor by stopping at **Kozlowski Farms**.
They make and sell all-fruit, sugar-free preserves, apple cider
blends, and a variety of baked goods. Other condiments include
mustards, salad dressings, salsas and teriyaki sauces, among others.
A deli serves made-to-order sandwiches. ~ 5566 Gravenstein Highway (Route 116), Forestville; 707-887-1587, 800-473-2767; www.
kozlowskifarms.com, e-mail koz@kozlowskifarms.com.

Fifes, one of the area's first gay resorts, has a beautiful bar area, **NIGHTLIFE**
which spreads through several pine-paneled rooms and extends
out to a poolside deck. They offer disco dancing on Friday and
Saturday nights. ~ 16467 River Road, Guerneville; 707-869-
0656; www.fifes.com, e-mail info@fifes.com.

Like Fifes, the **Russian River Resort** invites nonguests to enjoy
the facilities and mingle with guests at the bar and around the pool.
The bar isn't large but the crowd is friendly and if nothing is jumping in town, there will surely be some people hanging out at the
"Triple R." ~ 16390 4th Street, Guerneville; 707-869-0691; www.
russianriverresort.com, e-mail info@russianriverresort.com.

River Business attracts a mixed crowd of gays and lesbians.
A canoe and oars hang above the bar, and the rainbow flag,
along with posters of nudes and old photos of Guerneville, adorn
the walls. Tuesday is karaoke night while Wednesday is country
and western. A deejay spins tunes on weekends, and occasionally there's live entertainment. ~ 16225 Main Street, Guerneville;
707-869-3400.

Also in the middle of downtown is the **Rainbow Cattle Company**, a gay bar. Offering nothing more than a couple of pool tables, three pinball machines, bar stools, and long benches, this
nightspot doesn't provide much in the way of entertainment, but
it's a congenial place for socializing and drinking. Happy hour is
from 5 to 8 p.m. ~ 16220 Main Street, Guerneville; 707-869-
0206.

Billing itself as a microbrewery with loads of brews, the **Stumptown Brewery** is still finding an identity and a following but is
definitely worth checking out. There's occasional live entertainment. ~ 15045 River Road, Guerneville; 707-869-0705.

PARKS

ARMSTRONG REDWOODS STATE RESERVE AND AUSTIN CREEK STATE RECREATION AREA 🏃 🚲 🐎 🏕 ⛵ ⚓ These two parks, lying side by side, are a study in contrasts. Armstrong features a deep, cool forest of redwood trees measuring over 300 feet high and dating back 1400 years. Rare redwood orchids blossom here in spring and there is a 1200-seat amphitheater that was once used for summer concerts. Austin Creek offers sunny meadows and oak forests. Fox, bobcats, deer, wild pigs, and raccoons inhabit the region, and a nearby shallow bullfrog pond is stocked with sunfish and bass. There are almost two dozen miles of trails threading the park, including a popular trek to a few swimming holes. Facilities include picnic areas, restrooms and a visitors center. Day-use fee, $5. ~ 17000 Armstrong Woods Road, Guerneville; 707-869-2015, fax 707-869-5629.

▲ Austin Creek and Bullfrog Pond Campground has 24 campsites, $12 per night; there are also four hike-in campsites, $10 per night. For restrictions and permit information, call 707-869-2015.

▼▼▼▼▼▼▼▼▼▼▼▼▼▼▼
Outdoor Adventures

This is not an area known for fancy resort courses, but it has cool weather year-round and a couple of courses you could polish off before lunch.

GOLF

The **Sebastopol Golf Course** offers peaceful, countryside golfing. This public nine-hole course rents clubs. ~ 2881 Scott's Right of Way, Sebastopol; 707-823-9852.

Around the Russian River, the Alister MacKenzie–designed **Northwood Golf Course** has nine holes. Clubs and carts are available for rent. ~ 19400 Route 116, Monte Rio; 707-865-1116.

WATER SPORTS

The Russian River is *the* place to explore in a canoe or kayak. The river is a Class I from April to October, and during that time canoe and kayak rentals are plentiful. Several outfits offer everything from one-day excursions to five-day expeditions. Most folks rent for the day, canoe one way, and are picked up by the outfitter and shuttled back. The scenery, ranging from rolling ranch land to dense redwood groves, is stunning. The experience of floating timelessly along this magnificent river will long be remembered.

If you're ready for the adventure, contact **Burke's Canoe Trips**. They offer a ten-mile day trip to Guerneville and outfit you with a canoe, lifejacket, and paddles before sending you on a self-guided ride through the redwoods. Reservations required. ~ At the north end of Mirabel Road at River Road, Forestville; 707-887-1222.

The Russian River is also good for a swim. Favorite spots in the area are **Johnson's Beach** in the town of Guerneville and **Monte Rio Beach** in Monte Rio.

River Road, between Windsor and Guerneville, meanders past
rolling hills and rural scenery, but carries a moderate amount of
traffic.

BIKING

Bike Rentals For mountain bike rentals, repairs or purchases,
try **The Bicycle Factory**. Helmets and locks can be included; the
friendly staff can also provide you with advice and maps. ~ 195
North Main Street, Sebastopol; 707-829-1880.

In **Armstrong Redwoods State Reserve**, there are 22 miles of
trails threading the park. A four-mile hike here takes you to a few
swimming holes that offer relief from the sun.

HIKING

SEVEN

Mendocino County

The image of Mendocino has long been dominated by the vision of windswept cliffs, crashing surf and whirling seabirds. Yet there is another Mendocino, the inland portion that is defined by gently rolling hills, avenues of redwoods and acres of vineyards. If you travel along Route 101, however, you will see a lot of development, especially around Ukiah. Here, motels, shopping malls and fast-food outlets are only an exit away.

As opposed to the latter-day hippie lifestyle associated with the coastal area, the Ukiah neighborhood is all business. As the county seat, the city is home to the courthouse and lawyers' offices and most of the major services, from auto shops to appliance stores, you won't see once you get out into the country. Up in Redwood Valley and out in the larger Alexander Valley, things are more laid-back. These are the kind of places people go to get away from it all, and there's something about this part of the world that attracts rugged individualists, even if they're wearing suits and driving minivans.

The still-rugged landscape probably has a lot to do with that attraction. Whereas Sonoma and Napa counties are well-developed and overpopulated, you can still find many places in Mendocino that must look as they did 100 years ago—thousands of acres of unspoiled wilderness (give or take a telephone line or two) and the occasional two-lane road.

You can get a glimpse into regional history at any of three museums in Mendocino County: the Grace Hudson Museum and the Held-Poage House in Ukiah and the Anderson Valley Historical Museum in Boonville. All three look at the county from different perspectives, from the native Pomo Indians to the farmers who settled the Anderson Valley.

For the most part, however, this area's attractions fall into two categories: scenic and agricultural, including the burgeoning winery scene. Once you get off Route 101 and onto one of the smaller roads that link the interior with the coast, you'll gain an appreciation of the challenges faced by the pioneers who arrived in this rugged region.

Mendocino County's relatively late entry into the California wine business seems to have been dictated by history more than by geography or climate. The area is remote—by early-19th-century standards; the last mission was built far south of here, the early European settlers and even gold diggers flocked to San Francisco and the Sonoma and Napa valleys, giving Mendocino not only a late start, but a slow one, in terms of development. Its distance from San Francisco Bay and the benefits of mass shipping didn't help, either.

However, as the merits of its grapegrowing climate became known, the region has begun attracting dozens of wineries. The price of vineyard land in Napa and Sonoma is another factor since those southern neighbors are running out of room.

The people who live in Mendocino prize the abundance of open space in their part of the world. Manmade Lake Mendocino beckons year-round, but particularly in summer when everyone around Ukiah craves relief from the fierce summer heat. Closer to the coast, hiking trails and campsites along the Navarro River serve the same purpose.

Numerous microclimates add to the mix. While it may be 95 degrees on the streets of Ukiah, you can drive ten miles north to the Redwood Valley and head up to the hills to catch one of the westerly breezes that blow in through one of several gaps. Morning fog is common in the Anderson Valley, particularly during the summer months. The so-called fog line is around Philo; east of that town, the fog burns off by mid-morning, but to the west the fog may linger all day, its tendrils adding a romantic fillip to the sight of seemingly endless redwood groves that line the roads close to the ocean.

These microclimates also greatly affect the taste of wines produced in various vineyards. Historically, white grapes such as gewurztraminer and chardonnay do well in the Alexander Valley, while zinfandel and petit sirah thrive on the warm, rocky hillsides of the interior. But so many factors, from soil to temperature to wind, come into play in winemaking that you will find all kinds of grapes planted in all sorts of places.

Other crops, particularly apples and pears, also thrive in Anderson Valley. In summer and fall, these and other fruits and vegetables are plentiful at roadside stands on or near Route 128. In many cases, these roadside produce outlets are run by the same families who started them. The Gowan family, for one, has been in the business since the 1930s. But urban escape artists as well are discovering the beauty of living off the beaten path. Some newcomers are retirees from the Bay Area who, fed up with gridlock in San Jose or the East Bay, have taken over bed-and-breakfast inns or opened guest ranches. Safe and far from the madding crowd, they may not be all that rugged, but they share the traditional streak of individuality that makes the Mendocino County experience so appealing.

▼ ▼ ▼ ▼ ▼ ▼ ▼ ▼ ▼ ▼
Hopland–Ukiah Inland Area

There may not be a lot to see in Hopland and Ukiah, but the attractions there are tend to be rather extraordinary. There's an Indian casino, a Buddhist center of learning, a museum dedicated to art and Pomo Indian basketry, and a plaque honoring ladies of the night. Beyond these quirky points of interest are some 38 wineries, most of which have tasting rooms open daily to the public. Mendocino will never catch up to Napa's 240 wineries or Sonoma's 165, but the wineries are gaining in popularity and recognition with every passing year. Most of the ones in this part of the county are located near Route 101.

SIGHTS

It's not hard to guess how the town of **Hopland** got its name. While there are brewpubs in both Hopland and Ukiah, the hops have long been supplanted by grapes. The town was founded in 1859 when three local men opened a saloon. In those days it was known as Sanel (Hopland is still in Sanel Valley); it was renamed in the early 1890s. Surrounded by hills and intersected by Route 101, it's still a quiet town.

HIDDEN ►

The Indians are getting even with the White Man, quarter by quarter, at the **Sho-Ka-Wah Casino & Bingo** complex, located just over three miles east of Hopland via Route 175. Hundreds of machines are kept busy, even on weekday mornings, in the cool, dark recesses of the large game room here. If you've been to Las Vegas or other gambling meccas, however, two things will strike you as odd: one, there are no arms on the one-armed bandits; you wager by pressing buttons; two, if you hit a jackpot, you won't be gratified by the sound of all those quarters crashing out—payouts are by a printed slip of paper that winners then present to the cashier. And one other thing, you bet with paper money, not coins (although you can wager as little as 25 cents). There are also table games and a bingo room. ~ 13101 Nokomis Road, Hopland; 707-744-1395, fax 707-744-1698; www.shokawah.com, e-mail shokawah@pacific.net.

When you return to Hopland, you will be facing an impressive facility just across Route 101. Turn left and then right to reach the parking lot. The Brutocao family has been raising grapes in Mendocino for more than half a century, and you may sample the fruits of their labor at the **Brutocao Vineyards**. Their winemaking facilities also harbor a tasting room in addition to a gift shop, a bar and a restaurant. A smaller tasting room is also located on Route 128 north of Philo. ~ 13500 South Route 101, Hopland; 707-744-1066, 800-433-3689, fax 707-744-1046; www. brutocaocellars.com, email info@brutocaocellars.com

Fetzer Vineyards can be found on a well-endowed complex east of Route 101. The Fetzer family began producing wine commercially in 1968 and have expanded the winery to a world leader, known especially for its reasonably priced chardonnays. Visitors can take tours of the gardens and vineyards. The tasting room, visitors center and deli are open to the public daily, as are the spacious picnic grounds. Tasting fee. ~ 13601 East Side Road, Hopland; 707-744-1250, 800-846-8637, fax 707-744-2151; www.fetzer.com.

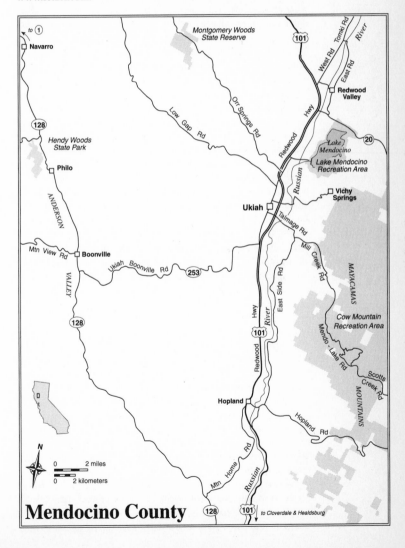

Mendocino County

McDowell Wine and Mercantile gives McDowell Valley Vineyards excellent exposure right on the highway in an 1897 building rigged to resemble a country store. The tasting room showcases McDowell's viognier, syrah and other Rhone varietals. ~ 13380 South Route 101, Hopland; 707-744-8911, fax 707-744-1826; www.mcdowellsyrah.com.

Between Hopland and Ukiah are several wineries, one of the most interesting of which is **Jepson Vineyards**. Its product line includes sauvignon blanc, chardonnay, viognier, pinot noir, sparkling wine and brandy. The sparkler is made with 100-percent chardonnay, using the French *methode champenoise*. The brandy comes from colombard grapes, which thrive in this part of the Sanel Valley. Because of state laws regarding distilled spirits, you can't sample the brandy in the tasting room, and you will need to make an appointment to see the exotic machinery and intricate techniques used to create it. ~ 10400 Route 101, Ukiah; 707-468-8936, fax 707-468-0362; e-mail jepson@jepsonwine.com.

HIDDEN ►

Approaching Ukiah from the south, you can take the Talmage Road exit and follow it east to where it ends at the most unusual attraction in Mendocino County. A magnificent gilded gateway announces the entrance to the **City of 10,000 Buddhas**. Here, amid some 437 acres, the buildings of what used to be a mental hospital are being put to use as classrooms and temples. Arranged along the walls of the temples are some 10,000 small statues of Buddha, as well as impressive larger statues displayed outdoors. As unusual as this place is, it's not a curiosity and should be visited only by people interested in praying, studying or learning about Buddhism. That said, there is a vegetarian restaurant on the premises (see "Dining," below) well worth a detour. There is a bookstore but it has few tomes in English; the best bet is to pick up some postcards depicting the site. Sign in and ask for directions at the guest services desk. ~ 2001 Talmage Road, Ukiah; 707-462-0939.

Ukiah, the county seat, is a real working town with activity centered downtown near the civic buildings. Some old Victorians can be found if you drive along the pretty back streets.

If you're eager to pick up maps and brochures, you can head straight to the **Greater Ukiah Chamber of Commerce** by taking the Perkins Street exit off Route 101 and heading west to School Street. There's an information desk and a wall full of information to the left as you approach the desk. ~ 200 South School Street, Ukiah; 707-462-4705, fax 707-462-2088; www.ukiahchamber.com, e-mail info@ukiahchamber.com.

Otherwise, continue north on Route 101 and exit at East Gobbi Street; turn west and then north onto Main Street, which leads to the heart of Ukiah. The best things about the **Grace Hudson Museum** and **Sun House** are the baskets made by the indigenous

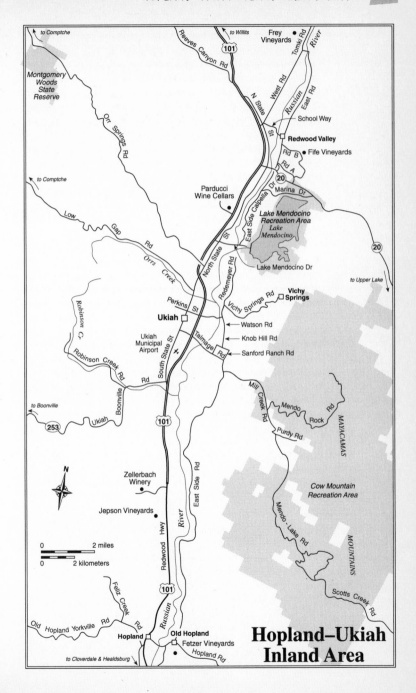

to Comptche

Montgomery
Woods
State
Reserve

Orr Springs Rd

to Comptche

Low Gap Rd

Orrs Creek

Robinson Cr

Robinson Creek Rd

Boonville Rd

to Boonville

253

Ukiah

Reeves Canyon Rd

to Willits

101

Frey Vineyards

Tomki Rd

West Rd

East Rd

Russian River

N State St

School Way

Redwood Valley

Rd B

Fife Vineyards

Rd A

20

Marina Dr

Parducci Wine Cellars

East Side Calpella Dr

Lake Mendocino
Recreation Area
Lake
Mendocino

North State St

Redemeyer Rd

Lake Mendocino Dr

20

to Upper Lake

Perkins St

Vichy Springs Rd

Vichy Springs

Ukiah

Watson Rd

Talmage Rd

Knob Hill Rd

Ukiah
Municipal
Airport

South State St

Sanford Ranch Rd

Mill Creek Rd

Mendo

Rock Rd

MAYACAMAS

Purdy Rd

101

Ukiah Rd

N

Zellerbach
Winery

Jepson Vineyards

East Side Rd

Cow Mountain
Recreation Area

Mendo - Lake Rd

MOUNTAINS

0   2 miles
0   2 kilometers

Redwood Hwy

Russian River

Scotts Creek Rd

Feliz Creek Rd

Old Hopland Yorkville Rd

Hopland

101

Old Hopland

Fetzer Vineyards

Hopland Rd

to Cloverdale & Healdsburg

**Hopland–Ukiah
Inland Area**

Pomo Indians; the next best things are the paintings and photographs of these native Americans that adorn the museum walls. Grace Hudson and her husband (a scholar of basketry) lived in Sun House; she is the artist behind the paintings of Pomo life. The museum, which also exhibits works by local artists on a rotating basis, is open to the public; Sun House is open for half-hour guided tours. Closed Monday and Tuesday. ~ 431 South Main Street, Ukiah; 707-457-2836, fax 707-467-0468; www.gracehudson museum.org, e-mail ghmuseum@jps.net.

The only other place in town to learn about regional history is the nearby **Held-Poage Memorial Home and Research Library**, where archival materials including photographs and maps are available to the public; the library alone has some 5000 volumes. The house is a Queen Anne Victorian that was the home of Mendocino County Superior Court Judge William D. L. Held and Ethel Poage Held. The library has limited hours but the Mendocino County Historical Society will make an effort to open by appointment. Closed mornings and Sunday and Monday. ~ 603 West Perkins Street, Ukiah; 707-462-6969.

After meandering around downtown Ukiah, it's time to go winetasting. Scoot right up Route 101 to **Parducci Wine Cellars**, the first and largest in the area. Founded in 1932 by Adolph Parducci, it was run by family members until the late 1990s. You can taste and tour here, though the winery itself is up on a hill and the tasting room is in a white stucco California Mission–style building. Parducci's moderately priced sauvignon blanc and chardonnay, in particular, have been well-received. ~ 501 Parducci Road, Ukiah; 707-462-3828, 800-362-9463; www.parducci.com.

HIDDEN ► Up the road in the Redwood Valley, **Fife Vineyards** makes so many excellent wines that the tasting room can't offer them all, every day. If you're lucky they'll be pouring estate-grown zinfandel. You can see these vines as well as petite sirah growing on the hillside in front of the winery. For all its quality, the winery

NATURAL GOODS

Just inside the Hopland city limits, **Real Goods Solar Living Center** showcases products utilizing renewable energy sources as well as items manufactured from natural fibers and alternative materials. Merchandise includes natural bed and bath products, cotton clothing, and gourmet kitchenware. More than just a retail store, the center also presents water-conservation and solar-panel demonstrations and offers guided tours of the facilities. ~ 13771 South Route 101, Hopland; 707-744-2100, fax 707-744-1342; www.realgoods.com, e-mail tqueen@real goods.com.

is quite modest, except for the knock-out view of Lake Mendo-cino, way below to the south. Tours by appointment only. ~ 3620 Road B (off Route 20), Redwood Valley; 707-485-0323, fax 707-485-0832.

Frey Vineyards (pronounced "fry") is a godsend for winelovers concerned about sulfites. None are used in making gewurztraminer, chardonnay, sauvignon blanc, cabernet sauvignon, syrah, petite sirah and other reds and whites, all of which are organically farmed. If you plan to visit this small winery set on a 145-acre ranch, you need to call ahead, especially if it's on a weekend. ~ 14000 Tomki Road, Redwood Valley; 707-485-5177, 800-760-3739; www.freywine.com, info@freywine.com.

LODGING

Motels outnumber hotels and inns around inland Mendocino County, though there are some interesting choices—one in Hop-land and another on the outskirts of Ukiah. Straddling the high-way, the bigger city makes a convenient overnight stop for trav-elers heading elsewhere. The old Palace Hotel downtown was renovated in the 1970s but lack of patronage caused it to close soon thereafter. Now the old hotel sits empty while ivy vines climb all over its brick facade.

The most enviable accommodations in Hopland can be found at the **Fetzer Vineyards Bed & Breakfast**. All six rooms and suites are located in the Carriage House, still clad in the clear redwood siding that ranch owner A. W. Foster used to protect the prized draft horses he kept inside. Today only the outer shell gives any hint of the building's original use; the rooms are sparkling fresh and decorated in understated country style. Each room has a pri-vate entry and a vineyard view. The ground-floor accommoda-tions boast private patios, while the upstairs suites feature kitch-enettes and whirlpool baths. All guests have use of the seasonal pool. In addition, guests may rent the entire nearby Haas House, an old residence that has three suites and full kitchen facilities. ~ 12625 East Side Road, Hopland; 707-744-1250, fax 707-744-7605; www.fetzer.com. DELUXE TO ULTRA-DELUXE.

In downtown Hopland, the **Thatcher Inn** is an eye-catching Victorian that opened in 1890 as a rest stop for stage and train travelers between San Francisco and Oregon. All 21 rooms are decorated in a mix of original and reproduction antiques. If you stay here, you won't have far to go if you sample the two local brandies or any of a long list of single-malt scotches in the bar. Full breakfast is included. ~ 13401 South Route 101, Hopland; 707-744-1890, fax 707-744-1219; www.thatcherinn.com.

The only bed and breakfast in Ukiah is the **Sanford House**, one of the prettiest homes in an older neighborhood where every-one seems to have a green thumb. Topped with a turret in one corner, the Queen Anne–style Victorian has five upstairs rooms adorned with family antiques, dark carpeting and pastel wallpaper in various designs. One corner room has a bathtub facing the treetops, encouraging reveries and really long soaks. The house was built in 1904 by longtime state legislator John Bunyon Sanford, and is greatly enhanced by reading chairs on the front porch and a garden with a koi pond in the back. Full breakfast is included. ~ 306 South Pine Street, Ukiah; 707-462-1653, fax 707-462-8987; www.sanfordhouse.com, e-mail dorsey@sanford house.com. MODERATE.

The aqua-and-coral exterior of the **Voll Motel** would look better in Miami, but it's the only pretty feature of this 21-room roadside rest stop. A couple of accommodations are on an upper floor, but most are right on the parking lot and, while clean, truly borderline. At these prices, however, you can't expect a beauty queen. ~ 628 North State Street, Ukiah; 707-463-1610. BUDGET.

HIDDEN ►

Off to the east, the **Vichy Springs Resort** dates to 1854 and has long attracted visitors with its special springs, which are not only warm but as bubbly as a glass of good champagne. Mark Twain, Robert Louis Stevenson and Jack London all paid visits here, one of California's oldest warm-springs retreats. The prettiest accommodations at this 700-acre property are in the cottages arranged in a horseshoe pattern on a slight rise, but there are also rooms in the inn. The resort is open to day visitors as well, who, like guests, can avail themselves of the waters and various spa treatments at this peaceful hideaway. ~ 2605 Vichy Springs Road, Ukiah; 707-462-9515, fax 707-461-9516. MODERATE.

DINING

The concept of five-star dining has not arrived in Hopland or Ukiah, but there are some nice places to dine. In addition to loads of fast-food places, you can find good, inexpensive meals at a number of spots.

The main reason to recommend **Hopland Sho-Ka-Wah Casino & Bingo** as a restaurant is that it is open 24/7. No matter what time you arrive, you will be able to stop your stomach's cries. The menu includes burgers and cheap prime rib as well as a breakfast that doesn't cost much more than a dollar or two. ~ 13101 Nokomis Road, Hopland; 707-744-1395, 877-546-7526. BUDGET TO MODERATE.

For a casual lunch, a good bet is the **Valley Oaks Deli** at Fetzer. It stocks a wide array of very fresh salads and sandwiches made with vegetables, fruits and herbs organically raised on the premises. Visitors are welcome to add a bottle of Fetzer wine (a great choice would be the Bonterra chardonnay, also organic) to their shopping basket and enjoy lunch at one of the patio tables or pack it in the car for picnicking elsewhere. ~ Fetzer Vineyards, 13601 East Side Road, Hopland; 707-744-1737. BUDGET.

Author Picks

CHAPTER FAVORITES

I feel as if I'm back in the Old West whenever I ride a horse deep into the forest and then blast clay pigeons with a shotgun at the **Highland Ranch**. *page 152*

I love pretending I'm in Italy at **Brutocao Vineyards** in Hopland, where I toss small balls across the winery's bocce ball courts, working up an appetite for lunch at The Crushed Grape. *page 136*

Sleeping upstairs with a view of the treetops beside the **Sanford House** takes me—and just about every other guest—back to Grandma's house. *page 141*

When I need to relax, I like taking the 26-mile drive along **Route 253** from Ukiah to the Anderson Valley, a hilly road that has better views and fewer twists and turns than the more-traveled Route 128. *page 149*

Inside the stunning Brutocao winery complex in downtown Hopland, **The Crushed Grape** has an unusual menu ranging from hearty salads and elegant pastas to excellent barbecued ribs and chicken (available with the appropriate side dishes, including a tasteless slaw that incorporates pineapple). The 'cue is the legacy of the old Boneyard Barbecue, which existed across the road before moving over here. The shaded patio seats overlook the formal bocce ball courts, which are open to the public. ~ 1400 Route 175 (at Route 101), Hopland; 707-744-1066, fax 707-744-1046. BUDGET TO MODERATE.

The **Mendocino Brewing Company** is better known for its beer than for its grub, but burgers, sandwiches and salads are quite acceptable, especially on the patio in warm weather. ~ 13351 South Route 101, Hopland; 707-744-1361, fax 707-744-1910. BUDGET.

Deep inside the City of 10,000 Buddhas, the **Jun Kang Vegetarian Restaurant** is comfortable, despite fluorescent lighting and bare floors; framed pictures and other wallhangings warm the place up. Before you order you can look at 20 pages of pictures of the dishes, which incorporate lots of fresh vegetables and a goodly amount of tofu. Everything is available for take-out, and locals in-the-know make a habit of dropping in. ~ 2001 Talmage Road, Ukiah; 707-462-0939. BUDGET TO MODERATE.

◄ HIDDEN

In a turreted building on a downtown corner, the **Ukiah Brewing Co. & Restaurant** has a big bar, bare floors and soar-

Text continued on page 146.

New England—California Style

Mendocino, which sits on a headland above the sea, is New England incarnate. Settled in 1852, the town was built largely by Yankees who decorated their village with wooden towers, Victorian homes, and a Gothic Revival Presbyterian church. The town, originally a vital lumber port, has become an artists' colony. With a shoreline honeycombed by beaches and a villagescape capped with a white church steeple, Mendocino is a mighty pretty corner of the continent.

The best way to experience this antique town is by stopping at the **Kelly House Museum**. Set in a vintage home dating from 1861, the museum serves as an historical research center (open Tuesday through Friday from 9 a.m. to 4 p.m.) and unofficial chamber of commerce. The museum is open daily from 1 to 4 p.m. from June 1 through November 1, and Friday through Monday from December through May. Admission. ~ 45007 Albion Street; 707-937-5791, fax 707-937-2156; e-mail kellyhs@mcn.org.

Among Mendocino's intriguing locales are the **Chinese Temple**, a 19th-century religious shrine located on Albion Street (open by appointment only); the **Presbyterian Church**, a national historic landmark on Main Street; and the **MacCallum House**, a Gingerbread Victorian on Albion Street, which has been reborn as an inn and restaurant. Another building of note is the **Masonic Hall**, an 1865 structure adorned with a hand-carved redwood statue on the roof. ~ Ukiah Street.

Then after meandering the side streets, stop at the **Mendocino Art Center**. Here exhibits by painters, potters, photographers, textile workers, and others will give an idea of the tremendous talent contained in tiny Mendocino. It's also a great place to shop. ~ 45200 Little Lake Street; 707-937-5818, fax 707-937-1764; e-mail mendoart@mcn.org.

Mendocino Headlands State Park, located atop a sea cliff, offers unmatched views of the town's tumultuous shoreline. From the bluffs you can gaze down at placid tidepools and wave-carved grottoes.

Adjacent to the park is the historic **Ford House**, an 1854 home with a small museum, which also serves as a visitors center for the park. ~ Main Street; 707-937-5397, fax 707-937-3845.

WHERE TO STAY   Set in a falsefront building which dates to 1878, the 51-room **Mendocino Hotel** is a wonderful place, larger than other nearby country inns, with a wood-paneled lobby, full dining room, and living quarters adorned with antiques. There are rooms in the hotel with both private and shared baths as well as quarters in the garden cottages out back. ~ 45080 Main Street; 707-937-0511, 800-548-0513, fax 707-937-0513. MODERATE TO ULTRA-DELUXE.

The queen of Mendocino is the **MacCallum House Inn**, a Gingerbread Victorian built in 1882. The place is a treasure trove of antique furnishings, knickknacks, and other memorabilia. Many of the rooms are individually decorated with rocking chairs, quilts, and wood stoves. Positively everything—the carriage house, barn, greenhouse, gazebo, even the water tower—has been converted into a guest room. Except for the dining rooms, which are still...dining rooms. ~ 45020 Albion Street; 707-937-0289, 800-609-0492, fax 707-937-2243; e-mail machouse@mcn.org. DELUXE TO ULTRA-DELUXE.

FINE DINING   Mendocino's best-known dining room is well deserving of its renown. **Café Beaujolais**, situated in a small antique house on the edge of town, serves designer dishes. Dinner, served seven nights a week, is ever changing. Perhaps they'll be serving warm duck salad and Thai rock shrimp salad with entrées like *poulet verjus*, chicken braised with Navarro vineyards Verjus, leg of lamb stuffed with garlic, and steamed salmon with chervil *sabayon* sauce. Excellent cuisine. Closed from the day after Thanksgiving until December 26. ~ 961 Ukiah Street; 707-937-5614, fax 707-937-3656; e-mail cafebeau@mcn.org. DELUXE.

BREAKFAST   A morning ritual for locals and visitors alike is to climb the rough-hewn stairs to the loft-like **Bay View Café** for coffee, French toast, or fluffy omelettes. On sunny afternoons, the deck overlooking Main Street and the coastal headlands makes an ideal lunch spot, especially for fish and chips or a jalapeño chile burger. ~ 45040 Main Street; 707-937-4197, fax 707-937-5300. BUDGET.

SHOPPING   Housed in the town's old Victorians and Cape Cod cottages is a plethora of shops. Most are located along woodframe Main Street, but also search out the side streets and passageways. One particularly note-worthy gallery is the **William Zimmer Gallery**, which houses an eclectic collection of contemporary and traditional arts and crafts. ~ Kasten and Ukiah streets; 707-937-5121; e-mail wzg@mcn.org. Be sure to also check out **Highlight Gallery**, featuring displays of handmade furniture, contemporary art, jewelry, and woodwork. ~ 45052 Main Street; 707-937-3132. The **Mendocino Art Center** houses numerous crafts studios as well as two art galleries. ~ 45200 Little Lake Street; 707-937-5818; e-mail mendoart@mcn.org.

ing ceilings. Everything is organic here, from the food to the beer (house label as well as others) to even the local wine (best bet: Bonterra chardonnay). The menu varies but typical are pasta primavera, Thai red-curry vegetables, fish-and-chips, and a Flemish pot roast, in addition to burgers and lots of side orders. Closed Sunday. ~ 102 South State Street, Ukiah; phone/fax 707-468-5898. BUDGET TO MODERATE.

A simple one-room lunch spot by day, **dish** will also provide dinner on weekday evenings—but only on a take-out basis. Too bad, since some locals swear it dishes up the best food in town. Roast turkey breast, Black Forest ham, vegetarian and other sandwiches dominate the menu, but the side pastas and salads could be meals in themselves. Dinners change daily and may include a vegetable gratin, curried sea bass or chicken sausage dish. Closed Sunday. ~ 109 South School Street, Ukiah; 707-462-5700. BUDGET.

There's one near every courthouse: a lunch spot where, sooner or later, you'll probably encounter every lawyer and judge in town. In Ukiah, that spot is **Schat's Courthouse Bakery and Café**. Sandwiches have delightful names like Subpoena, Legal Eagle, Melvin Belli, and Not Guilty (the vegetarian option) and are available with roast beef, turkey, ham, Louisiana hot sausage, roast chicken or turkey. Or all of the above. Salads, quiches, pizzas, soups, burritos and build-your-own-baked-potato also appear on the docket. And remember, if you are up early, you can get espresso and baked things here as early as 6 a.m. No dinner. ~ 113 West Perkins Street, Ukiah; 707-462-1670. BUDGET.

Ruen Tong serves patrons excellent Thai food, using ultrafresh ingredients and a light hand. Somehow it suits the little bungalow it occupies, where the open floor plan adds a sense of space; there's also patio seating. Thai silks and crafts and ubiquitous photographs of the royal family make the restaurant festive. Daily specials are recommended here; Ruen Tong comes up with some winners featuring unexpected ingredients such as

✦✦

FOR THE LADIES

Despite no evidence of the world's oldest occupation on the streets of Ukiah nowadays, you can find a memorial honoring it. Just south of Hayes Music (200 South State Street at West Church Street) on the righthand side of the street, look for a granite boulder in front of an office building. A **bronze plaque** reads: "To the ladies of the night who plied their trade upon this site." The plaque marks the location of what was a ladies' "boarding house" in the 1930s.

pumpkin. ~ 801 North State Street, Ukiah; 707-462-0238.
BUDGET TO MODERATE.

Offbeat merchandise is the name of the game when it comes to   **SHOPPING**
retail choices in inland Mendocino. Don't expect the kinds of
boutiques that proliferate the cute coastal towns. At the other
end of the spectrum are the "big-box" stores next to the highway in Ukiah just east of the airport.

Real Goods Solar Living Center stocks a variety of appliances
using renewable energy sources, including flashlights, refrigerators and heaters. In addition, it carries a dizzying array of house-
wares, bed and bath products and clothing made of natural fibers
and recycled materials. ~ 13771 South Route 101, Hopland;
707-744-2100, fax 707-744-1342; www.realgoods.com, e-mail
tqueen@realgoods.com.

The gift shop in the **Brutocao Vineyards Tasting Room**, which
faces Route 101, is a cut above the usual, featuring an excellent
array of food- and wine-related books as well as the usual bottle
tags and tableware. ~ 13500 South Route 101 175, Hopland;
707-744-1664.

The best stores in Ukiah are strung along Church Street between
Perkins and Clay streets, where the parking is generally free and
plentiful. The **Mendocino Book Company** is a spacious and gracious store with a helpful staff and a wide selection of regional
guidebooks along with fiction, nonfiction and children's books.
~ 102 South School Street, Ukiah; 707-468-5940.

Candles, home accessories, potpourri and the like are beautifully displayed at the aptly named **Habitat**. ~ 100 South School
Street, Ukiah; 707-462-3920.

Mendocino Bounty, accessible from the lobby of the Mendocino Conference Center, has a quirky collection of food-related
gifts and other knicknacks (not to mention one of the few espresso
machines in the neighborhood). ~ 200 South School Street, Ukiah;
707-463-6711.

Sho-Ka-Wah Casino & Bingo is open 24/7 for gaming, including   **NIGHTLIFE**
slot machines, roulette and a bingo room. ~ 13101 Nokomis Road,
Hopland; 707-744-1395.

The **Mendocino Brewing Company** isn't quite the entertainment palace it used to be, but it is still the best game in town when
it comes to live music. The tunes may include blues or country
or whatever, depending on which Saturday night you're asking.
Cover. ~ 13351 South Route 101, Hopland; 707-744-1361.

The **Emerald Café** dishes up reggae, rhythm-and-blues, rock-
and-roll and other live music on Saturday night. The last Thursday of each month is poetry night. Closed Sunday. Cover. ~ 205
South State Street, Ukiah; 707-463-3336.

The **Mendocino Ballet** presents an annual *Nutcracker* each holiday season and other ballets, featuring local dancers and professional guest artists, throughout the year at various locations in Ukiah and around the county. ~ 707-463-2290; www.wildiris design.com/ballet.

The **Ukiah Civic Light Orchestra** was founded in 1989 and showcases a wide variety of productions from mid-summer through spring. As the resident theater company of Mendocino College, the group produces a major musical on campus in the spring and other performances there in July and/or August. In November and January, they do dinner theater productions. The best way to learn what's going on is to call their offices. ~ 1000 Hensley Creek Road, Ukiah; 707-462-9155.

Just across the border in Lake County via Routes 175 or 20, **Konocti Harbor Resort** features the only big-name entertainment in the area. Major rock, soul, blues and country bands appear regularly. Cover. ~ 8727 Soda Bay Road, Kelseyville; 707-279-4281, 800-660-5253; www.konoctiharbor.com.

PARKS

LAKE MENDOCINO RECREATION AREA An easy 20-minute drive from downtown Ukiah, this manmade lake was created in 1958 by the Army Corps of Engineers, which dammed the Russian River at Coyote Valley. Now 1822 acres of water provide recreational opportunities and much-needed relief from hot summer days. Fishing, swimming (off protected beaches), boating, waterskiing and windsurfing are major sports, and jet skis can be rented at one of the marinas. The lake is flanked by foothills that encompass nearly 700 acres of protected wildlife habitat. The **Visitors Center**, which is .2 mile south of Route 20 at the Marina Drive entrance, has exhibits on natural history and American Indian culture. ~ Entrances are at Marina Drive (east of East Side Calpella Road) and at Lake Mendocino Drive (east of North State Street). The recreation area office is at 1160 Lake Mendocino Drive; 707-462-7581; www.anglernet.com/web/maps/mendo1.htm.

▲ There are 300 tent/RV sites with water and electricity available on a first-come, first-served basis; $8 to $35 per night.

MONTGOMERY WOODS STATE RESERVE Located 15 miles west of Ukiah via Comptche–Orr Springs–Ukiah Road, this reserve has expanded from the original nine acres donated by Robert Orr in 1945 to its present size of 1132 acres. A two-mile hiking trail leads along Montgomery Creek, connects five of the reserve's memorial redwood groves and leads to a stand of Douglas fir. Walking this route is the only way to get a close look at the salamander and newt habitats that provide sustenance for snakes, frogs and large toads. ~ Off Orr Springs Road, about 15 miles northwest of Ukiah; 707-937-5804.

For visitors northbound from San Francisco or Sonoma, the standard route through the Anderson Valley
is via Route 128, which cuts northwest from Route
Anderson Valley

101 around Cloverdale in northern Sonoma and links the inland
part of the county with the coast. The road is a corkscrew for the
first few miles, featuring a few hairpin turns that make drivers
glad that they are driving in hills, not mountains. Eventually,
those kinks are loosened as the road reaches the halfway point
between Yorkville and Boonville. By the time the road straightens
out, drivers are likely to feel they've been delivered into a secret
valley, tucked away from the hustle and bustle of civilization and
protected by all those twists and turns.

And in a way, they have been delivered. Delivered, at least, from
fast-food joints and shopping malls, interstates and traffic lights. It
is peaceful out on Route 128, even more so along the handful of alternative roads that snake through the surrounding hills in a maze
of remote connections that only locals ever fully comprehend.

SIGHTS

With a handful of intriguing exceptions, the attractions in this
scenic Mendocino valley are all wineries. It's a dream of an itinerary, a gorgeous drive that's rarely crowded, leading along a neck-
lace of wineries that seem perfectly spaced for slow-paced exploring. If you're driving out to the valley from Ukiah, you'll get
there faster if you take **Route 253**, the scenic two-lane road through
the hills, to the intersection with Route 128.

Just west of downtown Boonville, the **Anderson Valley Historical Museum** is headquartered in a little red schoolhouse, with
auxiliary space in a glorified shed at the end of a grassy field.
Exhibits tell the story of Anderson Valley pioneer life in photographs and household and farm tools, and there is a small display
of Pomo basketry. Out back are old pieces of equipment from
the valley's logging and early agriculture days. Closed Monday
through Thursday. ~ Located one mile north of Boonville at Anderson Valley Way off Route 128; 707-895-3207.

THE FOG LINE

The Anderson Valley is relatively small, but it has its own invisible dividing
line, the so-called fog line. The closer you get to the ocean, the greater the
likelihood that a day that starts foggy will stay socked in all day. As a result,
the cooler, western end of the valley is well suited to growing pinot noir,
chardonnay and gewurztraminer. Planted up above the fog, zinfandel can
also do quite well closer to the ocean. Chardonnay also grows well in
the sunnier and warmer interior surrounding Boonville, as does some
sauvignon blanc.

The cool weather in the Philo area is considered excellent for raising grapes like pinot noir and chardonnay, premium champagne varietals. One of the best producers of California sparkling wines, **Pacific Echo Cellars** has a tasting room in a 1916 Craftsman bungalow just off the highway (the main winery is behind it). Tours by appointment only. ~ 8501 Route 128, Philo; 800-824-7754, fax 707-895-2758; www.pacific-echo.com, e-mail avfizz@pacific.net.

Navarro Vineyards, best known for gewurztztraminer, also makes other premium whites as well as pinot noir. This is a relaxed place, even by Anderson Valley standards, and the lovely landscape of rolling hills cries out for a picnic under an arbor of grape vines. It's best to call ahead to find out about the tour schedule, if any. ~ 5601 Route 128, Philo; 707-895-3686, 800-537-9463; www.navarrowine.com

Husch Vineyards, on everyone's list of favorite family wineries, uses only grapes grown on the family-owned vineyards. The winery makes more than a dozen wines, including some under the La Ribera label (more affordable than the Husch label); don't miss the chardonnay, sauvignon blanc or pinot noir. ~ 4400 Route 128, Philo; 707-895-2216, 800-554-8724, fax 707-895-2068; www.huschvineyards.com.

The tasting room at **Handley Cellars** would make a nice stop whether you sample wine or not. The views are delightful and the space doubles as a gallery for African, Indonesian, Asian, Indian and Latin American art. But you should try the wines, especially the chardonnay estate, Anderson Valley. An exception to the whites is a 1997 pinot noir that gets excellent ratings. ~ 3151 Route 128, Philo; 800-733-3151, fax 707-895-2603; e-mail info@handleycellars.com.

LODGING

The Anderson Valley is not the kind of place where you'll find a traditional motel, much less any chain lodging. The handful of accommodations in this bucolic valley are all highly individual, and all but a couple are located far enough off the highway to guarantee a quiet night's sleep.

The two-story, red-frame **Boonville Hotel** provides the most sophisticated lodgings in the valley. Not that they're fancy—in fact, they're pared-down. Furnishings have been handcrafted by regional artisans to give each of the six rooms and two suites a crisp, distinctive look. All the accommodations are on the second floor, opening onto a central hallway. ~ Route 128 at Lambert Lane, Boonville; 707-895-2210, fax 707-895-2243; www.theboonvillehotel.com. MODERATE TO ULTRA-DELUXE.

HIDDEN ►

Keep an eye out for the llamas if you're looking for the **Anderson Creek Inn**. At the end of a lane off a road that runs parallel to Route 128 on the south side, this contemporary bed and breakfast has five spacious rooms, three of which have fireplaces and most of which open onto a courtyard near the pool. The ranch-style house is surrounded by rolling hills dotted with old oaks and redwoods. When it's nap time, opt for the hammock—you'll find it up in the treehouse. Full breakfast is included. ~ 12050 Anderson Valley Way, Boonville; 800-552-6202; www.anderson valleyinn.com. DELUXE TO ULTRA-DELUXE.

Facing Route 128 is a a two-story bed and breakfast called the **Philo Pottery Inn**. It sits in an 1888 farmhouse (once an old stage-coach stop) built entirely of redwood. The five bedrooms are

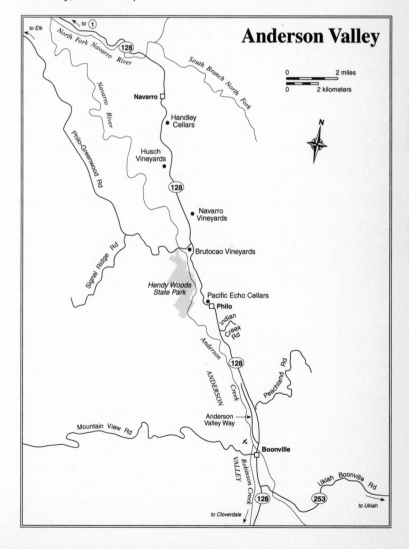

Anderson Valley

high-ceilinged, wood-paneled affairs with such decorative flourishes as oak dressers, patchwork quilts, and brass beds; some rooms share a bath. The garden cottage features a queen bed and a woodburning stove. Relax by the fire in the living room, lounge on the porches or stroll through the gardens. It's a great place for a few days of easy living. Full breakfast is included. ~ 8550 Route 128, Philo; phone/fax 707-895-3069; www.innaccess.com/phi, e-mail philoinn@pacific.net. MODERATE TO DELUXE.

On the north side of Philo, the **Apple Farm** has been a fixture for quite some time. The farm sells apples and related products and offers occasional cooking classes. In part to accommodate those weekend chefs, the owners constructed three cottages, right in the middle of the orchards. Each has its own decor but all are done in the same style, with a large bedroom and bath (one has an outdoor shower) and countrified colors like apple red, butter yellow and sky blue. The gardens alone are worth a visit; some 2000 trees include more than 60 varieties of apples. The Farm prints a brochure with dates of their Farm Weekend Classes; if you plan to visit at any of those times you will have to make reservations far in advance for the classes, the rooms or both. ~ 18501 Greenwood Road, Philo; 707-895-2461. ULTRA-DELUXE.

Off the road linking Philo and the coast and just a stone's throw from the entrance to Hendy Woods State Park is a private road leading up—way up—to the wonderful **Highland Ranch**. The setting is glorious, a highlands vale surrounded by forests intersected with hiking and horseback riding trails for the lucky guests of this hideaway. Highly popular for small conferences and family reunions, the ranch has eight cottages sparingly but attractively furnished, each with a fireplace and a small front porch. At breakfast and dinner everyone gathers in the century-old farmhouse; lunch can also be arranged. Amenities include horseback riding, clay pigeon shooting, swimming, fishing in a big (stocked) pond, hiking, mountain biking and wall-to-wall peace and quiet. Everything's included at this casual but extremely well-run retreat. ~ On a private road off Philo-Greenwood Road just west of Hendy Woods State Park, Philo; 707-895-3600; www.highlandranch.com. ULTRA-DELUXE.

The cheapest—in fact, the only inexpensive—lodging in the Anderson Valley can be found in **Hendy Woods State Park**. Four extremely basic cabins, with little more than bunk beds and no indoor plumbing, are available for a song. It's cheaper to camp, but on cold nights the security of these primitive accommodations may seem mighty appealing. ~ Philo-Greenwood Road, Philo; 707-895-3141, district office 707-937-5804. BUDGET.

DINING

The restaurant scene here is sparse but eclectic, from a relentlessly authentic coffeehouse to a Mexican café to a hotel dining room where most of the food could be classified as gourmet. You can also find a hamburger joint as well as take-out food in delis and small markets and, in season, a couple of top-notch roadside stands. All are friendly and none is really expensive. Call ahead, especially in off-season, if you plan to dine out mid-week, as most places rely heavily on tourists for their clientele.

Particularly recommended for dinner is the **Boonville Hotel**, an outstanding California cuisine restaurant with a gourmet menu. Entrées run along the lines of mussels steamed with red Thai curry, crusted Alaskan halibut, and grilled rib-eye steak. Lunch served Wednesday through Sunday; no dinner Tuesday. Closed January. ~ Route 128, Boonville; 707-895-2210, fax 707-895-2243; www.boonvillehotel.com. MODERATE.

Right in town, the **Buckhorse Saloon** serves well-known beers from Anderson Valley Brewing Company; the food is a cross between light pub fare and American roadside cuisine. ~ 14081 Route 128, Boonville; 707-895-3369, fax 707-895-3581; www. avbc.com. BUDGET.

If you've heard about the local dialect known as Boontling, you can get a taste of it along with your coffee, eggs, burgers and sandwiches at the **Horn of Zeese Café** (the name itself translates to cup of coffee). If you ate at this coffee shop every day, and learned the Boontling word-of-the-day written on the blackboard, you might become bilingual yourself. ~ 14025 Route 128, Boonville; 707-895-3525. BUDGET.

Libby's is owned by a former cook at the Boonville Hotel, a plain diner enlivened by colorful Mexican tablecloths. Ambience is irrelevant here, though, because the food is so wonderfully fresh and beautifully prepared. A simple cheese quesadilla, for example, with a requested addition of shrimp, arrives as a plump

---

"BOONTLING"

As Route 128 rolls down into Anderson Valley, it passes **Boonville**, a farming community of 1000 folks. Back in the 1880s, this town invented a kind of local pig Latin, "boontling," known only to residents. With a vocabulary of over 1000 words, it neatly reflected Anderson Valley life. A photo became a "Charlie Walker" after the Mendocino fellow who took portraits. Because of his handlebar whiskers, "Tom Bacon" lent his name to the moustache. Rail fences were "relfs," heavy storms became "trashmovers," and pastors (those heavenly skypilots) were "skipes." Vestiges of the old lingo remain—restaurants, for instance, still boast of their "bahl gorms," or good food. They also produce good wine in these parts, and several award-winning wineries dot the Anderson Valley.

and flaky meal in itself, adorned with a lively salsa and sour cream to balance things out. Specialties include enchiladas and several dishes incorporating flavorful mole sauce. On weekends, breakfast is also served. Closed Monday. ~ 8651 Route 128, Philo; 707-895-2646. BUDGET TO MODERATE.

The Mendocino coast (see "New England—California Style"), less than 18 miles from Philo, is worth a drive for travelers looking for more upscale fare than is available in the Anderson Valley. In Albion and up and down the coast highway are half a dozen fine dining establishments within ten miles of one another.

SHOPPING Besides the obvious wine purchases to be considered, chances to shop in this rural area are few and far between. From late spring into fall, however, you may find roadside stands open. Travelers bound for the coast will find boutiques galore in the nearby town of Mendocino.

For the freshest of seasonal fruit, look under **Gowan's Oak Tree**, which has been providing homegrown produce here since the 1930s. With a swing for the kids, shaded picnic groves and a public restroom, this white clapboard roadside stand is an ideal pit stop. The bounty is best in mid- to late-summer. ~ 6600 Route 128, Philo; 707-895-3353.

Apples and all manner of apple and other fruit products such as chutney are available at **The Apple Farm**, where purchases are made on the honor system. ~ 18501 Greenwood Road, Philo; 707-895-2461.

NIGHTLIFE Out here in farming country, people get up with the sun—or the fog—and so visitors can't expect much action after dark. But Ukiah or Mendocino is less than an hour away.

ELK COVE INN

Out on the coast, south of Route 128, you'll find the **Elk Cove Inn**. A message in a guest room diary here reads: "A view, with a room." The view is of knobby coast and simmering surf of ice blue and shaggy dunes falling away. The room is perfect for watching it all: a comfortable cabin with dramatic beamed ceiling, gas fireplace at the foot of your featherbed, carafe of port waiting on the nightstand. In the morning, there's an elaborate buffet— baked pears stuffed with almonds and cream cheese, egg and cheese soufflés—in the main 1883 Victorian house, a short walk from the four blufftop cabins. There are six guest rooms in the main house, some with dormer windows overlooking ocean, others with doors opening onto riotous gardens. ~ 6300 South Route 1, Elk; 707-877-3321, 800-275-2967, fax 707-877-1808; www.elkcoveinn.com, e-mail elkcove@mcn.org. DELUXE TO ULTRA-DELUXE.

The **Buckhorse Saloon** is by far the liveliest place in the Anderson Valley, especially after dark. The saloon has an erratic schedule of live music (usually without a cover charge), so it's best to call ahead. ~ 14081 Route 128, Boonville; 707-895-3369.

HENDY WOODS STATE PARK 🚶 🚴 🏊 ⛵ One of the most beautiful parcels in the Anderson Valley is that occupied by this 850-acre state park, an enclave of pristine old- and second-growth redwood forest on and near the banks of the Navarro River. (Another reason it's popular is that leashed dogs are welcome, though not allowed on trails.) The site was originally purchased in the 19th century by Joshua Hendy, a San Francisco foundry owner who exhibited little if any interest in logging or otherwise developing the property. After World War II, title was transferred to the Masonite Corporation, which set aside the best part of the old-growth forest to be preserved as the Joshua Hendy Grove. (Now two pieces survive: the 80-acre Big Hendy Grove and the 20-acre Little Hendy Grove.) In the late 1950s the site was deeded to the state by the Save-the-Redwoods League; the state park was developed and dedicated in 1963. Most of the campsites are deep in shade; the ones set in sunlight are indicated on the map available from rangers at the park's entrance, which is located half a mile off Route 128 three miles west of Philo. Restrooms, showers, telephones and handicap sites are among the amenities at this popular but low-key park. Day-use fee, $2. ~ Philo-Greenwood Road, Philo; 707-895-3141; district office 707-937-5804.

PARKS

▲ There are 92 campsites (no water or electricity), $16 a night; and four cabins, $40 a night (for up to six people; $5 surcharge for second vehicle).

While the Mendocino coast is famous for fishing and boating, the interior Wine Country is more geared to hiking and swimming.

Outdoor Adventures

This is not the golfing paradise that Napa and Sonoma counties are, but there is one place to play in Ukiah.

GOLF

The major links are at the **Ukiah Municipal Golf Course**, an 18-hole par-70, 5859-yard course that won't discourage novices. Carts are available. ~ 599 Park Boulevard, Ukiah; 707-467-2832.

Summers get really toasty in inland Mendocino, and the only way to cool off—aside from driving all the way out to the coast—is to find the nearest swimming hole.

SWIMMING

Protected beaches make **Lake Mendocino** a wonderful place to cool off during hot summer days. ~ 1160 Lake Mendocino Drive; 707-462-7581.

The **Ukiah Municipal Swimming Pool** is the largest public facility for water lovers in town. ~ 511 Park Boulevard, Ukiah; 707-467-2831.

The **Navarro River** starts drying up in mid-summer, but spring and early summer are good times to take a dip. There are several access points, including Hendy Woods State Park; the best swimming is near the town of Navarro.

FISHING

Out on the coast, you can fish for salmon and other deep swimmers, but all the fish are not in the sea. No fishing is allowed within Hendy Woods State Park because it fronts the part of the Navarro River upstream from the Philo-Greenwood bridge protected as spawning habitat.

In **Lake Mendocino**, anglers go for large- and smallmouth bass, striper, crappie, blue gill and catfish. A full-service marina, 1.3 miles east of Calpella on Marina Drive, has fishing-boat rentals and a snack bar, but no bait and tackle. Bring your own fishing supplies or try the bait and tackle shop on Lake Mendocino Drive. ~ 1160 Lake Mendocino Drive, Ukiah; 707-462-7581, 707-485-8644 (marina).

HIKING

You'll find some easy and moderate trails in Mendocino County. Spring is the best time to hike, when the trails lead past blooming wildflowers and the weather, which can be blistering hot in the summer, is mild. All distances listed for hiking trails are one way unless otherwise noted.

Low Gap Park Loop (1.5 miles roundtrip) can be easily hiked in one or two hours. To reach the trailhead, take the North Ukiah/North State Street exit from Route 101 and go .6 mile south to Low Gap Road, then west for a mile to the park entrance, which will be on your left. The trail parallels a creek through oak, bay laurel and California buckeye trees. Like many hikes, this moderate one is highly recommended for a spring morning, when wildflowers are abundant. The area gets quite hot in summer, and poison oak is always a threat in decent hiking weather.

There is a two-mile nature trail in **Montgomery Woods State Reserve** north of Ukiah. It takes you through tall trees, with steps carved into fallen redwoods. Watch out for poison oak, which is plentiful here. Pick up a printed guide at the trailhead. ~ Montgomery Wood State Reserve, off Orr Springs Road, about 15 miles northwest of Ukiah; 707-937-5804.

A series of trails loop through the forests at **Hendy Woods State Park**. Most are level or have an easy grade. The **Gentle Giants trail** in the 80-acre Big Hendy Grove is a short handicapped-accessible route. **Eagle Trail** (3 miles), the longest, runs from the visitors center to the day-use area, about half of it tracing the Navarro

River. On the far side of the park, **Azalea Creek Trail** (.5 mile) meanders along with various loops like **Hermit Hut** (.6 mile) and **Water Tank Loop** (.6 mile) offering alternatives. The hillier outer perimeter trails at Big Hendy provide another 1.6 miles of hiking.

Index

A. Rafanelli Winery, 108–109
Air travel, 26–27
Alexander Valley, 110
Anderson Valley, 149–55; camping, 155; dining, 152–54; lodging, 150–52; map, 151; nightlife, 154–55; parks, 155; shopping, 154; sights, 149–50
Anderson Valley Historical Museum, 149
Animals, 10
Annadel State Park, 107
Armstrong Redwoods State Reserve, 125, 132
Artesa (winery), 34–35
Austin Creek State Recreation Area, 132

Bale Grist Mill State Historic Park, 58
Balloon rides, 52, 114
Benziger Family Winery, 89–90
Beringer Vineyards, 56
Biking, 52–53, 75–76, 96, 114–15, 133
Birds and birdwatching, 10
Blackstone/Martin Ray Winery, 120
Bodega: lodging, 121
"Boontling," 153
Boonville: dining, 153; lodging, 150–51; nightlife, 155; sights, 149
Bothe-Napa Valley State Park, 64–65
Boyes Hot Springs (town): dining, 93; lodging, 90–91; sights, 89
Brannan Cottage, 66
Brutocao Vineyards, 136; shopping, 147
Buena Vista Historical Winery, 83
Burbank (Luther) Gold Ridge Experiment Farm, 120
Burbank (Luther) Home & Gardens, 98, 100
Bus travel, 27. See also Public transit

Calendar of events, 14–16
California Wine Country Cruises, 23
Calistoga, 65–75; camping, 75; dining, 72–74; lodging, 68–69; map, 67; nightlife, 74; parks, 74–75; shopping, 74; sights, 65–68; spas, 70–71
Calistoga Ranch Club, 75
Camping, 25. See also Camping in area and town entries
Canoeing, 114
Car rentals, 27
Car travel, 26
Carneros Creek (winery), 34
Carneros District, 41

Caymus Vineyares, 46
Cazadero: lodging, 129
Chateau Potelle (winery), 36–37
Chateau Souverain (winery), 110
Château Montelena (winery), 66
Château St. Jean Winery, 90
Children, traveling with, 21
Chinese Temple, 144
City of 10,000 Buddhas, 138; dining, 143
Cline Cellars, 80
Clos Pegase (winery), 66
Clothing, 18
Cruises, 23

Depot Park Museum, 83
Di Rosa Preserve, 33–34
Dining, 19–20. See also Dining in area and town entries; see also Dining Index
Disabled travelers, 23–24
Domaine Carneros (winery), 34
Domaine Chandon (winery), 44; dining, 48–49
Dry Creek Valley, 108
Dry Creek Vineyard, 108

El Verano: nightlife, 88
Elk: lodging, 154
Events, 14–16

Fauna, 10
Ferrari-Carano Vineyards & Winery, 109–10
Fetzer Vineyards, 137
Fife Vineyards, 140–41
Fisher Vineyards, 102
Fishing, 114, 156; permits, 25
Flora, 8–9
Foreign travelers, 24–25
Forestville: dining, 130; shopping, 131; sights, 125
Freestone: sights, 120
Frey Vineyards, 141
Fulton Community Park, 107

Gay travelers, 22; lodging, 60. See also Russian River area
Geology, 6
Geyserville: dining, 113; lodging, 111–12; sights, 110
Glen Ellen: dining, 92, 93; lodging, 91–92; nightlife, 94; shopping, 94; sights, 89–90

Gloria Ferrer Champagne Caves, 80–81
Golf, 52, 75, 95, 114, 132, 155
Grace Hudson Museum, 138, 140
Graton: dining, 122; shopping, 123–24; sights, 120
Guerneville area, 124–32; camping, 132; dining, 129–30; lodging, 126–29; map, 127; nightlife, 131; parks, 132; shopping, 131; sights, 124–26; visitor information, 124–25
Gundlach Bundschu (winery), 83

Hakusan Sake Gardens, 32–33
Handley Cellars, 150
Healdsburg and points north, 108–14; camping, 114; dining, 112–13; lodging, 110–12; map, 109; nightlife, 113; parks, 113–14; shopping, 113; sights, 108–10; visitor information, 108
Healdsburg Museum, 108
Healdsburg Plaza, 108
Held-Poage Memorial Home and Research Library, 140
Hendy Woods State Park, 152, 155
Hess Collection (winery), 36
Hiking, 53, 76, 96, 115, 133, 156–57
Historic Railroad Square, 100
History, 6–8
Hopland–Ukiah inland area, 136–43, 146–48; camping, 148; dining, 142–43, 146–47; lodging, 141–42; map, 139; nightlife, 147–48; parks, 148; shopping, 147; sights, 136–41; visitor information, 138
Horseback riding, 75, 95
Hubcap Ranch, 58
Hudson Museum, 138, 140
Husch Vineyards, 150

Ice skating. See Skating
International travelers, 24–25
Iron Horse Vineyards, 126

Jack London State Historic Park, 89, 94
Jepson Vineyards, 138
Jesse Peter Museum 100
John F. Kennedy Park, 42
Johnson's Alexander Valley Winery, 110
Johnson's Beach, 125
Jordan Vineyard & Winery, 110

Kelly House Museum, 144
Kelseyville: nightlife, 148
Kenwood: dining, 93–94; lodging, 92; sights, 90
Kenwood Vineyards, 90
Korbel Champagne Cellars ,125

La Casa Grande, 82
Lachryma Montis, 83
"Ladies of the night" plaque, 146
Lake Hennessey Recreation Area, 51
Lake Mendocino Recreation Area, 148
Lake Sonoma, 113–14
Larson Park, 94
Lesbian travelers, 22; lodging, 60. See also Russian River area
Liquor laws, 20
Litto Damonte's Hubcap Ranch, 58
Lodging, 18–19. See also Lodging in area and town entries; see also Lodging Index
Luther Burbank Gold Ridge Experiment Farm, 120
Luther Burbank Home & Gardens, 98, 100

MacCallum House, 144
Marriage licenses, 20
Martini & Prati (winery), 126
Maxwell Farms Regional Park, 88
Mayacamas Vineyards, 36
McDowell Wine and Mercantile, 138
Mendocino, 144–45; dining, 145; lodging, 144–45; shopping, 145; sights, 144
Mendocino Art Center, 144
Mendocino County, 12, 134–57; events, 14–16; map, 137; outdoor adventures, 155–57; transportation, 26–28; visitor information, 138. See also specific areas and towns
Mendocino Headlands State Park, 144
Mendocino Masonic Hall, 144
Mendocino Presbyterian Church, 144
Monte Rio: lodging, 128–29
Montgomery Woods State Reserve, 148
Monticello (winery), 35
Mount St. Helena, 47
Mumm Napa Valley (winery), 45

Napa area, 32–42; camping, 42; dining, 38–40; lodging, 37–38; map, 33; nightlife, 40, 42; parks, 42; shopping, 40; sights, 32–37; visitor information, 35
Napa Firefighters Museum, 35
Napa Valley Museum, 44
Napa Valley Wine Train, 36
Napa Valley. See Northern Napa Valley; Southern Napa Valley
Navarro Vineyards, 150
Niebaum–Coppola Estate Winery, 45
Northern Napa Valley, 11, 54–76; events, 14–16; map, 57; outdoor adventures, 75–76; transportation, 26–28. See also specific areas and towns

Northern Sonoma County, 11, 97–115; events, 14–16; map, 99; outdoor adventures, 114–15; transportation, 26–28. *See also specific areas and towns*

Northern Sonoma Valley, 89–95; camping, 95; dining, 92–94; lodging, 90–92; map, 91; nightlife, 94; parks, 94–95; shopping, 94; sights, 89–90

Oakland International Airport, 26, 27
Oakville: dining, 48, 50; sights, 44
Occidental: lodging, 121–22
Old Faithful Geyser, 68
Older travelers, 22–23
Opus One (winery), 44
Osmosis Enzyme Bath & Massage, 120

Pacific Coast Air Museum, 100–19
Pacific Echo Cellars, 150
Packing, 18
Paradise Ridge Winery, 100
Parducci Wine Cellars, 140
Permits, 25
Petrified Forest, 68
Petrified Forest Loop trail, 73
Philo: dining, 153–54; lodging, 151–52; shopping, 154; sights, 150
Phones, 20
Plants, 8–9
Prager Winery and Port Works, 56
Price ranges: dining, 19; lodging, 18–19
Public transit, 27–28

Ragle Ranch Regional Park, 124
Real Goods Solar Living Center, 140
Redwood Empire Ice Arena, 107
Redwood Valley: lodging, 140–41
Riding stables, 75, 95
Ritchie Block, 56
RMS Brandy Distillery, 35
Robert Louis Stevenson Silverado Museum, 56
Robert Louis Stevenson State Park, 47, 74–75
Robert Mondavi Winery, 44
Robert Pecota Winery, 66, 68
Rollerblading. *See* Skating
Route 128 drive, 110
Russian River area, 11, 116–33; events, 14–16; map, 119; outdoor adventures, 132–33; transportation, 26–28; visitor information, 119, 124–25. *See also specific areas and towns*
Russian River Vineyards Topolos, 125
Rutherford. *See* Yountville to Rutherford route

St. Helena, 55–56, 58–65; camping, 65; dining, 61–63; lodging, 58–61; map, 59; nightlife, 64; parks, 64–65; shopping, 63–64; sights, 55–56, 58
St. Helena IOOF Building, 55
St. Supéry Winery, 44–45
Safari West, 101–102
Sam Brannan Cottage, 66
San Francisco International Airport, 26, 27
Santa Rosa, 98, 100–107; camping, 107; dining, 103–105; lodging, 102–103; map, 101; nightlife, 106–107; parks, 107; shopping, 105–106; sights, 98, 100–102, 126; visitor information, 100
Santa Rosa Junior College, 100
Santa Rosa Rural Cemetery, 100
Schramsberg Vineyards, 66
Seasons, 12
Sebastopol area, 118–24; dining, 122; lodging, 120–22; map, 121; nightlife, 124; parks, 124; shopping, 122–24; sights, 118–20, 126; visitor information, 119
Senior travelers, 22–23
Shafer Vineyards, 46
Sharpsteen Museum, 66
Sho-Ka-Wah Casino & Bingo, 136; nightlife, 147
Silverado Trail scenic drive, 46–47
Skating, 107, 114
Skyline Wilderness Park, 42
Smoking laws, 20
Sonoma (town): dining, 85–87; lodging, 83–85; nightlife, 88; shopping, 87–88; sights, 80–83; visitor information, 80, 82
Sonoma Barracks, 82
Sonoma County. *See* Northern Sonoma County
Sonoma County Farm Trails, 118–19
Sonoma County Museum, 100
Sonoma Mission, 82
Sonoma Plaza, 82
Sonoma State Historic Park, 82
Sonoma Valley, 11, 77–96; events, 14–16; map, 79; outdoor adventures, 95–96; transportation, 26–28. *See also specific areas and towns*
Sonoma Valley Regional Park, 94
Southern Napa Valley, 10, 29–53; events, 14–16; map, 31; outdoor adventures, 52–53; transportation, 26–28; visitor information, 35. *See also specific areas and towns*
Southern Sonoma Valley, 78, 80–88; dining, 85–87; lodging, 83–85; map, 81; nightlife, 88; parks, 88; shopping,

87–88; sights, 80–83; visitor information, 80, 82
Spas, in Calistoga, 70–71
Spring Lake Park, 107
Stags' Leap Wine Cellars, 37
Steltzner Winery, 37
Sterling Vineyards, 47
Stevenson (Robert Louis) Museum, 56
Sugarloaf Ridge State Park, 94–95
Sun House, 138, 140
Sutter Home Winery, 56
Swimming, 155–56

Taxis, 28
Telephones, 20
Tennis, 52, 95
Topolos (winery), 125
Toscano Hotel, 82
Train Town, 82
Transportation, 26–28
Trefethen Vineyards, 35–36
Tudal Winery, 58

Ukiah. *See* Hopland-Ukiah inland area

V. Sattui Winery, 58
Valley of the Moon Winery, 90
Viansa Wetlands, 80
Viansa Winery & Italian Marketplace, 80

Vintage 1870 (shopping area), 44; shopping, 50–51
Visitor information, 18. *See also* Visitor information *in area and town entries*

Water sports, 114, 132. *See also* Fishing; Swimming; *etc.*
Weather, 12
Wermuth Winery, 66
West County Museum, 118
Westwood Hills Wilderness Park ,42
Wine Country (overview), 1–28; animals, 10; areas, 10–12; events, 14–16; dining, 19–20; geology, 6; history, 6–8; lodging, 18–19; map, 3; outdoor adventures, 25–26; plants, 8–9; telephones, 20; three-day weekend, 4–5; transportation, 26–28; visitor information, 18; weather, 12. *See also specific areas and towns*
Winery visits and winetasting, 13, 15, 34, 41, 51. *See also specific wineries*
Women travelers, 21–22

Yountville to Rutherford route, 42–51; dining, 48–50; lodging, 45–48; map, 43; nightlife, 51; parks, 51; scenic drive, 46–47; shopping, 50–51; sights, 43–45, 46–47

Lodging Index

Anderson Creek Inn, 150–51
Apple Farm, 152
Applewood Inn, 128
Auberge du Soleil, 48

Beltane Ranch, 92
Boonville Hotel, 150

Calistoga Inn & Brewery, 68–69
Calistoga Spa Hot Springs, 69
Camellia Inn, 111
Chablis Lodge, 38
Chateau Hotel, 38
Churchill Manor, 37–38
Cottage Grove Inn, 69

El Bonita, 58
El Dorado Hotel, 85
Elk Cove Inn, 154

Fern Falls, 129
Fern Grove Inn, 128
Fetzer Vineyards Bed & Breakfast, 141
Fifes Resort, 126
Flamingo Resort Hotel, 102
Fountaingrove Inn, 102–103

Gaige House Inn, 92
Glenelly Inn, 91–92

Harbin Hot Springs, 72
Harvest Inn, 59–60
Haydon Street Inn, 110–11
Healdsburg Inn on the Plaza, 111
Hendy Woods State Park, 152
Highland Ranch, 152
Highlands Resort, 127–28
Hilltop House, 61
Holiday Inn Express Hotel & Suites
  (Sebastopol), 120
Hope-Merrill House, 111
Hotel La Rose, 102
Hotel St. Helena, 60
Huckleberry Springs Country Inn,
  128–29

Indian Springs Hotel Resort, 69
Ink House Bed & Breakfast, 60
Inn at Occidental, 121–22
Inn at Southbridge, 58–59
Isis Oasis, 112

La Belle Epoque, 37

MacArthur Place, 84
MacCallum House Inn, 145
Madrona Manor Country Inn, 111
Maison Fleurie, 46–47
Meadowlark Country House, 72
Meadowood, 60–61
Mendocino Hotel, 144–45
Mount View Hotel, 69
Mountain Home Ranch, 69, 72
Muir Manor, 92

Napa Valley Railway Inn, 45

Old World Inn, 38

Petit Logis, 45–46
Philo Pottery Inn, 151–52

Rancho Caymus Inn, 48
Russian River Resort, 126–27

Sandman Motel, 102
Sanford House, 141–42
Sebastopol Inn, 120
Sonoma Coast Villa, 121
Sonoma Hotel, 84
Sonoma Mission Inn and Spa, 90–91
Swiss Hotel, 84

Thatcher Inn, 141
Thistle Dew Inn, 84

Vichy Springs Resort, 142
Village Inn, 128
Vineyard Inn, 84
Vintage Inn Napa Valley, 48
Vintners Inn, 103
Voll Motel, 142

White Sulphur Springs, 60
The Willows, 128

Yountville Inn, 45

LODGING SERVICES
Accommodations Referral, 68
Bed & Breakfast California, 19
Wine Country Rentals, 19

Dining Index

Acre Café & Lounge, 112–13
All Seasons Café, 73
Auberge du Soleil, 50

Bay View Café, 145
Big 3 Diner, 93
The Bistro, 93
Bistro Don Giovanni, 39–40
Bistro Jeanty, 49
Bistro Ralph, 112
Boonville Hotel, 153
Bosko's, 73
Bouchon, 49
Brannan's Grill, 72–73
Brava Terrace, 62
Brix, 50
Buckhorse Saloon, 153
Burdon's, 130

Café at the Winery, 113
Café Beaujolais, 145
Cafe Citti, 93–94
Café La Haye, 87
Cantinetta, 61
Catahoula Restaurant and Saloon, 72
Celadon, 38–39
Chez Marie, 130
Coffee Bazaar, 129
Compadres, 49
Crushed Grape, 143
Cucina Viansa, 86–87

Della Santina, 87
Deuce, 87
The Diner, 49
dish, 146
Domaine Chandon, 48–49

El Capitan, 104
El Farolito Mexican Restaurant, 113
Emile's Creekside Bistro, 104

Felix & Louie's, 112
Fifes, 130
Foothill Café, 38
French Laundry, 49–50

Gail's Café, 62
Gary Chu's, 104
General's Daughter, 86
The Girl & The Fig, 93

Hank's Creekside Café, 103–104
Heirloom, 86
Hopland Sho-Ka-Wah Casino & Bingo, 142
Horn of Zeese Café, 153

Jhanthong Banbua, 104
John Ash & Co., 105
Juanita Juanita, 85
Jun Kang Vegetarian Restaurant, 143

Kenwood Restaurant and Grill, 93

La Casa, 86
La Salette, 92–93
Libby's, 153–54
Livefire, 49
Ludy's BBQ Grill and Catering, 104

Marioni's Restaurant, 86
Mendocino Brewing Company, 143
Mistral, 105
Mixx, 104
Mustards Grill, 50

Oakville Grocery, 48
Old Adobe Bar and Grille, 39
101 Main Bistro & Wine Bar, 122

Pine Cone, 122
Pometta's, 50

Restaurant at Sonoma Mission Inn, 93
Ruen Tong, 146–47

Saketini Asian Diner and Lounge, 39
Schat's Courthouse Bakery and Café, 146
Smokehouse Cafe, 73–74
Sonoma Cheese Factory, 85–86
Spring Street, 62
Stella's Café, 122
Sweet's River Grill, 130

Taylor's Refresher, 62
Terra Restaurant, 62
Tomatina, 62
Tra Vigne, 61
Triple S Ranch, 74

Ukiah Brewing Co. & Restaurant, 143, 146

Valley Oaks Deli, 142

Wappo Bar Bistro, 73
Willow Wood Market Café, 122

Willowside Café, 105
Wine Spectator Greystone Restaurant,
   62–63

Travel With Someone You Trust®

Wherever you go, it's good to have a guide. Someone who knows the territory. Someone who can help you find those hidden spots and great deals. For generations of travelers, AAA has been that guide.

When you join AAA, you gain access to a world of information: AAA TourBooks, TripTiks, and maps help you find exciting things to do and wonderful places to stay. As a member of one of the world's largest consumer organizations, you receive the best deals from the world's best travel providers as well as valuable discounts from a wide range of Show Your Card & Save® partners. In addition, AAA financial and insurance services provide the freedom to help you pay for your travels and enjoy peace of mind on the ride.

As a AAA member, you join a community that numbers over 42 million members and that provides partnerships with the biggest names in travel. We invite you to explore the world. Let AAA be your guide. With over 4000 offices nationwide, you can find us in many local communities or on the Web at www.aaa.com.

HIDDEN GUIDES

Adventure travel or a relaxing vacation?—"Hidden" guidebooks are the only travel books in the business to provide detailed information on both. Aimed at environmentally aware travelers, our motto is "Adventure Travel Plus." These books combine details on unique hotels, restaurants and sightseeing with information on camping, sports and hiking for the outdoor enthusiast.

THE NEW KEY GUIDES

Based on the concept of ecotourism, The New Key Guides are dedicated to the preservation of Central America's rare and endangered species, architecture and archaeology. Filled with helpful tips, they give travelers everything they need to know about these exotic destinations.

Order Form

HIDDEN GUIDEBOOKS

____ Hidden Arizona, $14.95
____ Hidden Bahamas, $14.95
____ Hidden Baja, $14.95
____ Hidden Belize, $15.95
____ Hidden Boston and Cape Cod, $13.95
____ Hidden British Columbia, $17.95
____ Hidden Cancún & the Yucatán, $16.95
____ Hidden Carolinas, $17.95
____ Hidden Coast of California, $17.95
____ Hidden Colorado, $14.95
____ Hidden Disneyland, $13.95
____ Hidden Florida, $17.95
____ Hidden Florida Keys & Everglades, $12.95
____ Hidden Georgia, $16.95
____ Hidden Guatemala, $16.95
____ Hidden Hawaii, $17.95
____ Hidden Idaho, $14.95

____ Hidden Maui, $13.95
____ Hidden Montana, $14.95
____ Hidden New England, $18.95
____ Hidden New Mexico, $14.95
____ Hidden Oahu, $13.95
____ Hidden Oregon, $14.95
____ Hidden Pacific Northwest, $18.95
____ Hidden San Francisco & Northern California, $18.95
____ Hidden Southern California, $17.95
____ Hidden Southwest, $18.95
____ Hidden Tahiti, $17.95
____ Hidden Tennessee, $15.95
____ Hidden Utah, $16.95
____ Hidden Walt Disney World, $13.95
____ Hidden Washington, $14.95
____ Hidden Wine Country, $13.95
____ Hidden Wyoming, $14.95

THE NEW KEY GUIDEBOOKS

____ The New Key to Costa Rica, $17.95
____ The New Key to Ecuador and the Galápagos, $17.95

Mark the book(s) you're ordering and enter the total cost here ➡ [   ]

California residents add 8% sales tax here ➡ [   ]

Shipping, check box for your preferred method and enter cost here ➡ [   ]

❑ BOOK RATE   **FREE! FREE! FREE!**

❑ PRIORITY MAIL $3.20 First book, $1.00/each additional book

❑ UPS 2-DAY AIR $7.00 First book, $1.00/each additional book   [   ]

Billing, enter total amount due here and check method of payment ➡ [   ]

❑ CHECK   ❑ MONEY ORDER

❑ VISA/MASTERCARD _____ EXP. DATE _____

NAME _____ PHONE _____

ADDRESS _____

CITY _____ STATE _____ ZIP _____

MONEY-BACK GUARANTEE ON DIRECT ORDERS PLACED THROUGH ULYSSES PRESS.

ABOUT THE AUTHORS

RAY RIEGERT is the author of seven travel books, including *Hidden San Francisco and Northern California*. His most popular work, *Hidden Hawaii*, won the coveted Lowell Thomas Travel Journalism Award for Best Guidebook. In addition to his role as publisher of Ulysses Press, he has written for the *Chicago Tribune*, *Saturday Evening Post*, *San Francisco Examiner and Chronicle*, and *Travel & Leisure*. A member of the Society of American Travel Writers, he lives in the San Francisco Bay area with his wife, co-publisher Leslie Henriques, and their son Keith and daughter Alice.

MARTY OLMSTEAD is a freelance writer based in Sonoma, California. She is author of *Hidden Tennessee* and *Hidden Georgia* (Ulysses Press) and co-author of *San Francisco & the Bay Area* (Windsor Publications, Inc.). Her articles have appeared in numerous national and regional publications, including *Travel & Leisure*, *Appellation*, the *Los Angeles Times*, TWA *Ambassador*, *Odyssey* and the *San Francisco Chronicle*.

ABOUT THE ILLUSTRATOR

DOUG MCCARTHY, a native New Yorker, lives in the San Francisco Bay area with his family. His illustrations appear in a number of Ulysses Press guides, including *Hidden Tennessee*, *Hidden Bahamas* and *The New Key to Ecuador and the Galápagos*.